The Political Economy of Trade Policy

Jagdish Bhagwati. Photograph taken in 1995.

The Political Economy of Trade Policy
Papers in Honor of Jagdish Bhagwati

edited by
Robert C. Feenstra
Gene M. Grossman
Douglas A. Irwin

The MIT Press
Cambridge, Massachusetts
London, England

This book was set in Times Roman by Asco Trade Typesetting Ltd., Hong Kong.
Printed on recycled paper and bound in the United States of America.

Library of Congress Cataloging-in-Publication Data

The political economy of trade policy : papers in honor of Jagdish
 Bhagwati / edited by Robert C. Feenstra, Gene M. Grossman, Douglas
 A. Irwin.
    p. cm.
 Includes bibliographical references and index.
 ISBN 0-262-06186-4 (alk. paper)
 1. Commerical policy—Congresses. 2. International trade—Congresses.
 I. Feenstra, Robert C. II. Grossman, Gene M.
 III. Irwin, Douglas A., 1962–
 HF1411.P59116 1996
 382'.3—dc20   96-2479
                                                             CIP

Contents

Contributors

Robert E. Baldwin
Department of Economics
University of Wisconsin

Richard A. Brecher
Department of Economics
Carleton University

Ehsan U. Choudhri
Department of Economics
Carleton University

Peter Diamond
Department of Economics
Massachusetts Institute of
Technology

Robert C. Feenstra
Department of Economics
University of California, Davis

Ronald Findlay
Department of Economics
Columbia University

Earl L. Grinols
Department of Economics
University of Illinois

Gene M. Grossman
Woodrow Wilson School
Princeton University

Gordon H. Hanson
Department of Economics
University of Texas, Austin

Elhanan Helpman
Eitan Berglas School of Economics
Tel-Aviv University

Douglas A. Irwin
Graduate School of Business
University of Chicago

Paul Krugman
Department of Economics
Stanford University

Arvind Panagariya
Department of Economics
University of Maryland

B. Peter Rosendorff
Department of Economics
University of Southern California

Paul A. Samuelson
Department of Economics
Massachusetts Institute of
Technology

T. N. Srinivasan
Department of Economics
Yale University

John Douglas Wilson
Department of Economics
Indiana University

Acknowledgments

We wish to record our deep appreciation to Dean John Ruggie of the School of International and Public Affairs (SIPA) at Columbia University for providing financial support for the November 1994 conference in honor of Jagdish Bhagwati. We are also indebted to Kay Achar (of the SIPA) and Sherri Ellington (formerly of Princeton University) for administrative assistance. Finally, we thank Terry Vaughn of The MIT Press for his assistance and his support of this volume.

Introduction

In 1994 Jagdish Bhagwati marked his sixtieth birthday. Although he continues to be a highly energetic and productive scholar, a group of his former students arranged a conference in his honor to celebrate not just the occasion but also his career as one of the most important scholars and teachers of international economics in the world. More than forty international economists from North American and elsewhere, as well as numerous colleagues and students, attended the conference held at Columbia University in November 1994. The theme of the conference was the political economy of trade policy, the most recent of the many areas to which Bhagwati has made important intellectual contributions. This volume contains the papers delivered at the conference by his former students and colleagues.

This introduction is divided into two parts. First, we present a brief overview of Jagdish Bhagwati's academic career, including his main contributions to the theory of international trade and commercial policy. Second, we provide a brief description of the papers in this volume, noting how each relates to Bhagwati's various contributions to the political economy of trade policy.

The Contributions of Jagdish Bhagwati to International Economics

Jagdish Bhagwati was born on July 26, 1934, in Bombay, India, to a family with abundant intellectual achievement.[1] Bhagwati attended St. John's College, Cambridge University, as an undergraduate where he studied for the Economics Tripos in 1954–56. He proved to be a gifted and precocious student, and it was there that his talents came to the attention of Harry Johnson.[2] During his second year at Cambridge, in reaction to Johnson's work on international trade and economic expansion presented in his Cambridge lectures, Bhagwati wrote a paper on what he called "immiserizing" growth, economic growth that so deteriorates the terms of

1. For example, Bhagwati's brother became a chief justice of India, and another brother became a distinguished physician.

2. Harry Johnson dominated the field of international economics in the 1950s and 1960s, as much through his personal influence in encouraging younger scholars and in speaking before conferences around the world as through his publications, which numbered over 500 in roughly thirty years. He and Bhagwati coauthored two papers. See Bhagwati and Johnson (1960) and (1961), and also Bhagwati (1977) for a personal tribute to Johnson.

trade that it actually reduces economic welfare. This paper, the first of many brilliant ones to come, eventually turned into his first academic publication, "Immiserizing Growth: A Geometrical Note," published in June 1958 by the *Review of Economic Studies*. The concept immediately gained a niche in economic theory and spawned numerous extensions and developments by Bhagwati and others.

On Harry Johnson's advice and to Joan Robinson's dismay, Bhagwati spent the 1956–57 year studying in the Economics Department of the Massachusetts Institute of Technology. At MIT, Bhagwati attended courses offered by his future colleagues Charles Kindleberger, Paul Samuelson, and Robert Solow, while also becoming acquainted with a wide array of young talent in international economics, including Ronald Findlay, Carlos Diáz-Alejandro, Egon Sohmen, and Jaroslav Vanek. He then returned to Britain on fellowship and studied at Nuffield College, Oxford University, from 1957–59. There his supervisors were John R. Hicks and Donald MacDougall, and he attended Roy Harrod and MacDougall's seminar on international economics.

Bhagwati then returned to India to work at the Indian Statistical Institute in Delhi.[3] There he wrote one of his most influential papers, "Domestic Distortions, Tariffs, and the Theory of Optimum Subsidy," with V. K. Ramaswami, which was published in the *Journal of Political Economy* in 1963. This paper analyzed the long-standing argument for the use of trade protection to correct for inefficient wage distortions (divergences between the wage and the marginal value product of labor) between sectors. Bhagwati and Ramaswami provided a specific ranking of the various policies to address the assumed market failure, concluding that trade policies were less efficient in improving economic welfare than a factor-employment subsidy or a production subsidy. As such, the paper made a key contribution to the emerging theory of "domestic divergences" pioneered by Gottfried Haberler and James Meade.[4] In 1963 Bhagwati joined the faculty of the Delhi School of Economics where, among many other projects, he completed his famous "Survey of the Theory of International Trade" for the *Economic Journal* in 1964.

---

3. He also worked with the Indian Planning Commission, and his experience there helped shape the views in his book *The Economics of the Underdeveloped Countries*, published as a Cambridge Economic Handbook in 1965.

4. Bhagwati (1971), one of his most frequently cited papers, summarizes and synthesizes many developments in this important branch of the theory of economic policy.

Bhagwati's string of notable publications and other accomplishments gained for him a vast international reputation, and he soon returned to the United States. He visited Columbia University in 1966–67 and joined the faculty of MIT in 1968, where he was Ford International Professor of Economics. During this period Bhagwati continued his incredibly productive publishing record. In 1968 he delivered the Frank Graham Memorial Lecture on "The Theory and Practice of Commercial Policy" at Princeton University. In 1970 he published *India: Planning for Industrialization* (OECD Development Center and Oxford University Press) with his wife, Padma Desai, also a distinguished economist. In 1971 he founded the *Journal of International Economics*, which remains the premier scientific journal devoted exclusively to international economic research. With Anne Krueger, he directed a National Bureau of Economic Research Study on Foreign Trade Regimes and Economic Development in the early 1970s, authoring the volume on *India* (with T. N. Srinivasan) and the summary volume *Anatomy and Consequences of Exchange Control Regimes* (Cambridge: Ballinger, 1978). Bhagwati also edited or coedited several other volumes on such topics as international migration and taxation, illegal trade (smuggling and underinvoicing), and other international economic issues.

All of these accomplishments were in addition to the dozens of important published articles on various aspects of commercial policy that he produced in the late 1960s and through the 1970s, which included many fruitful collaborations with T. N. Srinivasan. These wide-ranging contributions covered distortions and welfare, the nonequivalence of tariffs and quotas, illegal trade and smuggling, effective protection in general equilibrium, cost-benefit analysis in an open economy, international migration and transfers, to name but a few. Many of these contributions have been collected in Bhagwati (1983), the first two volumes of his collected works. His extensive writings on economic development have been collected in Bhagwati (1985).

Toward the end of the 1970s, Bhagwati's interest in the political economy of trade policy began to grow, an interest that deepened after his move to Columbia University in 1980. Bhagwati (1982) developed the term "directly unproductive profit-seeking activities" to refer to lobbying and other activities that use real resources to capture economic rents. This research spurred his interests in international economic policy, a theme analyzed in the book *Protectionism* (1988) based on his Ohlin Lectures at the Stockholm School of Economics. Bhagwati's extensive writings during the 1980s, in this and in other areas, were collected in another volume, Bhagwati (1991). Bhagwati also authored such books as *Lectures on International Trade* (MIT Press, 1983, with T. N. Srinivasan), the leading graduate text in the field; *The World Trading System at Risk* (Princeton University Press, 1991), which forcefully presents his views on regional trade arrangements and global trade negotiations; and *India in Transition* (Oxford University Press, 1993), reflecting his ongoing interest in Indian economic affairs. He also served as Economic Policy Advisor to the Director-General of the General Agreement on Tariffs and Trade from 1991 to 1993.

Jagdish Bhagwati has been not only one of the premier international economists of his generation but also one of the premier teachers of international economics. Bhagwati is known for his rapid, breathless style of lecturing, and his courses are an exhilerating combination of deep economic insights and intuition, punctuated by amusing illustrations and anecdotes. Perhaps most important, he taught his courses in a way that emphasized that there was more to be learned through further research and study by his students, and he was always bubbling over with new ideas for research topics. Starting with Stephen Magee's dissertation on wage distortions at MIT in 1971, Bhagwati has supervised numerous doctoral students at both MIT and Columbia, many of whom became established as top international or development economists. In this vein Bhagwati has been unique in the time he has devoted to his students, in his willingness to listen to their ideas and give encouragement, and in the support he has given to his students throughout their careers.

Bhagwati continues to teach and write on a diverse set of topics at Columbia University, where he is the Arthur Lehman Professor of Economics and Professor of Political Science. As this exceedingly brief overview suggests, Bhagwati's contributions and influence in the field of international economics have been manifold but can perhaps be summarized in three respects. First, there is not one but several seminal contributions to the theory of international trade and commercial policy, including immiserizing growth, domestic distortions, economic development, and political economy. Each of these important contributions reflects a concern for making theory relevant to real economic issues. Second, he has achieved success and influence as a teacher and mentor of numerous students at both MIT and Columbia, many of whom have gone on to have successful careers in academe, international economic institutions, and elsewhere. Third, he has acted as a leader of his discipline, by founding the *Journal of International Economics*, spearheading the efforts of international economists to influence policymakers who determine trade policy, and by communicating cogently and wittily the ideas of international economists to a broader audience in an impressive array of popular writings. All of these make Jagdish Bhagwati a unique mentor in international economics.

Contents of the Volume

Even though Jagdish Bhagwati's research has ranged so broadly, the editors of this volume felt that a conference on a single theme would provide the most fitting tribute to him, as it would generate a book that could stand alone as a contribution to scholarship. We chose the political economy of trade policy as the theme for the conference, because we saw this as Bhagwati's most recent area of keen interest and because the questions addressed in this area remain so salient and topical.

This volume is organized into four parts. Part I consists of papers on market distortions and thus provides a link to the earliest literature on trade-policy setting. In this literature, much of which grew out of Bhagwati's pioneering work with V. Ramaswami in the 1960s and with T. N. Srinivasan in the 1960s and 1970s, the government is seen as seeking to identify market failures and tailor appropriate first-best palliatives. This literature sharpened our understanding of which policies would be most efficacious in various circumstances. However, economists such as Bhagwati, Robert Baldwin, Anne Krueger, and Stephen Magee soon came to realize that governments often fail to enact the policies identified in the theory. A positive theory of government would need to recognize that policy affects income distribution as well as economic efficiency and that individuals often take political actions to maximize their share of national income even if that means compromising its overall size. Part II consists of papers on the effects of trade and policy on income distribution, an inevitable input into any positive theory of trade policy.

The latter half of the book focuses on the positive theory more directly. Part III consists of two reflective pieces by pioneering theorists in the fields of international trade and public finance who have taken an interest in the political processes that give rise to economic policy. The authors of these pieces share their insights on how formal modeling of political actions ought to be approached. Finally, the last part contains papers that provide explicit models of the political process, much as Bhagwati himself has done in his work on directly unproductive profit seeking, quid pro quo foreign investment, regional trade agreements, and the like.

The volume begins with an evaluative survey by T. N. Srinivasan of the literature on domestic distortions and policy rankings that has evolved in the nearly three decades since the beginning of his own invaluable collaboration with Bhagwati and since Bhagwati's publication of his well-known 1971 synthesis paper. In chapter 1, "The Generalized Theory of Distortions and Policy Rankings Two Decades Later." Srinivasan observes that the general theory has proved remarkably flexible in its applications to various theoretical issues in economic policy. He concludes that "the general theory of distortions and welfare is alive and well after twenty-five years!"

In chapter 2, "What Trade Theory Was Like in the Age of Bhagwati," Paul Samuelson reflects upon the increase in the wage gap between skilled and unskilled workers in the United States during the 1980s, and on whether this increased gap can be explained by international trade. Bhagwati's long-standing interest in this issue dates from his early article on "Protection, Real Wages and Real Incomes" in the *Economic Journal* in 1959 to his recent contribution (with Vivek Dehejia) "Freer Trade and Wages of the Unskilled—Is Marx Striking Again?" in the volume he coedited (with Marvin Kosters) *Trade and Wages: Leveling Wages Down?* (AEI Press, 1994).

In chapter 3, "Domestic Distortions and the Deindustrialization Hypothesis," Paul Krugman addresses current concerns about the role of import competition in the loss of high-wage manufacturing jobs to the expanding service sector. Krugman develops a two-sector Ricardian model (manufacturing and services) with a wage distortion in manufacturing and then considers the impact of "globalization," the ability to export services in exchange for manufactures. The wage distortion ensures that this trade will lower welfare, but Krugman aims to discover the size of the loss, which he finds to be extremely small even on assumptions strongly favorable to those fearing the consequences of deindustrialization.

Douglas Irwin leads off the section of trade and income distribution with a study of voting patterns in an election that hinged on the issue of free trade and protection. His aim in chapter 4, "Industry or Class Cleavages over Trade Policy? Evidence from the British General Election of

1923," is to ascertain whether trade-related political behavior is more consistent with the Heckscher-Ohlin model (wherein economic interests are organized around different factors of production) or the specific factors model (wherein economic interests are determined by industry of employment). Irwin finds evidence that cross-county variations in employment by industry better explain the election outcome than variations in factor groupings.

In chapter 5, "Liberalizing Multinational Investment: The Stolper-Samuelson Question Revisited," Richard Brecher and Ehsan Choudri address whether direct investments by multinationals in low-wage countries reduce the incomes of low-wage workers in the developed countries. In a monopolistic competition model with multinational investment, Brecher and Choudri show that the Stolper-Samuelson effect is operative, with an additional response of real wages to tax-induced changes in the number of product varieties.

In chapter 6, "Foreign Investment, Outsourcing, and Relative Wages," Robert Feenstra and Gordon Hanson reexamine the link between trade and the relative wages of skilled and unskilled workers in a model where various stages of production occur in different countries. Increases in the extent of outsourcing by firms in the industrial countries can lead to the changes in relative wages that have occurred in the United States and other countries. Feenstra and Hanson provide empirical evidence on the outsourcing of components by multinationals investing in Mexico through the maquiiladora plants.

In chapter 7, "Pure and Mixed Price and Income Compensation Schemes: Breaking Political Roadblocks to Trade Reform," Earl Grinols concludes the part of the book on income distribution. Grinols considers whether various proposed compensation schemes, which could be used to ensure the Pareto-superiority of free trade, would be practical to implement. His conclusions about the practicality of these schemes are largely negative: The informational requirements needed to formulate compensation are daunting, and private agents have an incentive to misrepresent the information they possess.

The two reflective pieces mentioned above are by Robert Baldwin and Peter Diamond. In chapter 8, "The Political Economy of Trade Policy: Integrating the Perspectives of Economists and Political Scientists," Baldwin discusses the similarities and the differences between the treatment of trade policy by economists and political scientists.

Baldwin argues that practitioners in both fields have discovered important insights. But both fields also have notable shortcomings and blindspots in their approach and therefore each group stands to learn much from the other. Baldwin proposed several areas in which economists and political scientists should modify their approach to accommodate the discoveries of the other field.

In chapter 9, "On the Political Economy of Trade: Notes of a Social Insurance Analyst," Peter Diamond draws on his deep knowledge of the politics of social insurance to reflect on how institutions might matter for trade policy outcomes. He also discusses the incompleteness of legislation, which does not cover all possible contingencies, and of economic markets, which similarly fail to distinguish all states of the world. Diamond discusses his personal views on how such incompleteness ought to be treated by theorical modelers.

The chapters by Baldwin and Diamond lead the way to more formal modeling of political processes. The remainder of the volume illustrates some of the many alternative approaches. In chapter 10, "Foreign Investment with Endogenous Protection," Gene Grossman and Elhanan Helpman propose an alternative model of the quid pro quo foreign investment to that developed by Bhagwati and his coauthors in their pioneering work. Grossman and Helpman consider a set of decentralized foreign producers who must decide whether to open subsidiaries in a country to which they export before they know what trade barriers they would face if they failed to do so. After the investment decisions are made, the host country's trade policy is set according to an explicit political process. The authors characterize the fulfilled-expectations equilibria and examine its comparative static and normative properties.

In chapter 11, "The Tax Treatment of Imperfectly Mobile Firms: Rent-Seeking, Rent-Protection, and Rent-Destruction," John Wilson considers a government's optimal tax policy vis-à-vis an imperfectly mobile firm in a nonpolitical and then in a political equilibrium. A government might seek to induce new firms to locate in a country through subsidies but then tax them once they have located there. However, potential entrants anticipate this policy and become unwilling to pay high wages. If existing firms are allowed to lobby for reduced taxes in the future, potential new firms anticipate an outcome of lower taxes and become willing to pay higher wages. Thus Wilson finds that residents may benefit from lobbying activities.

In chapter 12, "Endogenous Trade Restrictions and Domestic Political Processes," Peter Rosendorff examines whether voluntary export restraints (VERs) can result from the lobbying process by firms, despite their inefficacy relative to import tariffs. He finds that the VER is preferred to the optimal tariff by the local government and foreign firm if the weight on the profits of the protected industry in the government's objective function is large enough.

In chapter 13, "A Political Economy Analysis of Free Trade Areas and Customs Unions," Arvind Panagariya and Ronald Findlay analyze the welfare effects of regional integration in a model of endogenous protection. Their model suggests that a customs union more effectively dilutes the power of interest groups than a free trade area because the free-rider problem is more pronounced in a customs union with a common external tariff among member countries than in a free trade area where each country chooses its tariff. In addition the greater the number of participants in a customs union, the more likely it will improve the welfare of member countries by reducing external tariffs.

References

Bhagwati, Jagdish. 1971. The generalized theory of distortions and welfare. In Jagdish Bhagwati, Ronald Jones, Robert Mundell, and Jaroslav Vanek, eds., *Trade, Balance of Payments, and Growth: Papers in International Economics in Honor of Charles P. Kindleberger*. Amsterdam: North Holland.

Bhagwati, Jagdish. 1977. Harry G. Johnson, 1923–1977. *Journal of International Economics* 7:221–29.

Bhagwati, Jagdish. 1983. *Essays in International Economic Theory*, ed. by Robert Feenstra. Vol. 1: *The Theory of Commercial Policy*; Vol. 2: *International Factor Mobility*. Cambridge: MIT Press.

Bhagwati, Jagdish. 1985. *Essays in Development Economics*, ed. by Gene M. Grossman. Vol. 1: *Wealth and Poverty*. Vol. 2: *Dependence and Interdependence*. Cambridge: Basil Blackwell.

Bhagwati, Jagdish. 1991. *Political Economy and International Economics*, ed. by Douglas A. Irwin. Cambridge: MIT Press.

Bhagwati, Jagdish, and Vivek Dehejia. 1994. Freer trade and wages of the unskilled—Is Max striking again? In Jagdish Bhagwati and Marvin H. Kosters, eds., *Trade and Wages: Leveling Wages Down?* Washington: AEI Press.

Bhagwati, Jagdish, and Harry G. Johnson. 1960. Notes on some controversies in the theory of international trade. *Economic Journal* 70:74–93.

Bhagwati, Jagdish, and Harry G. Johnson. 1961. A generalized theory of the effects of tariffs on the terms of trade. *Oxford Economic Papers* 13:225–53.

Bhagwati, Jagdish, and John Ruggie, eds. 1984. *Power, Passions, and Purpose: Prospects for North–South Negotiations*. Cambridge: MIT Press.

I MARKET DISTORTIONS

1 The Generalized Theory of Distortions and Welfare Two Decades Later

T. N. Srinivasan

1.1 Introduction

Three decades ago Bhagwati and Ramaswami (1963) wrote their classic paper on "Domestic Distortions, Tariffs and the Theory of Optimum Subsidy." It spawned a voluminous theoretical literature on the theory of optimal policy intervention in open economies in the presence of different market failures. Harry Johnson (1965) recognized its importance early. He characterized his own argument and the two central propositions of his paper as "derived from discussion with Jagdish Bhagwati, and particularly from an early reading of his brilliant joint article with V. K. Ramaswami," and to this he added that "To these two authors belongs the credit for reducing a mass of *ad hoc* arguments concerning tariffs to a simple application of second-best welfare theory."

A decade later Bhagwati (1971) turned to the vast theoretical literature that had been triggered by this article throughout the 1960s, and to other contributions such as the theory of policy intervention to achieve noneconomic objectives that had been pioneered by Max Corden (1957), to produce a creative synthesis entitled "The Generalized Theory of Distortions and Welfare" (hereafter, the Generalized Theory) in his paper for the Charles P. Kindleberger *festschrift*. With his characteristic enthusiasm he described the results of his efforts in the following words:

> We have thus succeeded in unifying a considerable body of literature on the welfare economics of trade into a series of major propositions that constitute a generalized theory of distortions and welfare. Aside from the intrinsic elegance of such unification, this has resulted in a number of insights into, and extensions of, the theorems to date in this significant area of economic policy. (p. 281)[1]

This paper has proved to be influential and has defined for trade theorists the analytical framework and insights of the modern theory of commercial policy (see Srinivasan 1987). I propose in this chapter to examine whether, and in what way, the latest developments in the theory of commercial policy, especially during the 1980s and later, fit into Bhagwati's framework. As I will show, they indeed fit well and the insights of Bhagwati (1971) continue to be relevant even as the problems have changed.

Bhagwati distinguished four *principal* types of distortions, starting from the first-order conditions (FOC) characterizing a competitive equilibrium under free trade of a small open economy. As is well-known, such an economy will be *productively efficient* and also *Pareto optimal*. This follows from the properties of a competitive equilibrium in the absence of nonpecuniary externalities. These FOC (ignoring possible "corner" equilibria) are that the domestic marginal rate of substitution (DRS) between *any two goods* in *consumption* (which must be the same for all consumers consuming the two goods in positive amounts) must equal the domestic marginal rate of transformation (DRT) between the *same two goods* along the economy's efficient production possibility frontier and that this common value of DRS and DRT must equal the ratio of their world prices (i.e., the foreign rate of transformation, FRT, between the same two commodities if they are traded in world markets). A departure from productive efficiency (the production vector not being on the efficient production possibility frontier) and violation of any *two* of the three equalities (DRS = DRT, DRS = FRT, FRT = DRT) while the third held were the four types of distortions. He distinguished three *causes* of such distortions. A distortion is deemed to be *endogenous* if it arises from a cause that makes a laissez-faire competitive market equilibrium no longer Pareto optimal, a cause that is usually viewed as a market imperfection or failure.[2] A distortion is *policy imposed* if the inequality characterizing it, for example, DRT ≠ DRS = FRT, is created by policy (i.e., a production tax cum subsidy as in this example). A policy-imposed distortion could be *autonomous* in the sense that the policy creating it was not imposed as an instrument to achieve some well-specified policy objective. Then, by definition, a *nonautonomous policy-imposed* distortion has to be instrumental.

Bhagwati found that "a logical coherence and unity around these (four) alternative classes and (three) causes of distortions" could be given to the diverse literature on (1) suboptimality laissez-faire under market imperfection, (2) immiserizing growth, (3) welfare ranking of alternative policies that could be used to address market imperfections, (4) welfare ranking of equilibria under alternative *levels* of tariffs, (5) welfare ranking of *free trade* and autarky competitive equilibria, (6) welfare ranking of *restricted trade* and autarky equilibria, and, finally, (7) welfare ranking of alternative policies that could be used to achieve a noneconomic objective.

Of the seven "central propositions" developed by Bhagwati as analytically unifying this literature, the first simply described the four classes and three causes of distortions. The remaining six could be divided into two groups of three, the first group covers the case of a *single* distortion to be addressed or a *single* endogenous variable to be constrained, and the second covers the cases of the change of an exogenous variable or in the level of a distortion in the presence of another unaddressed or partially addressed distortion (or its instrumental equivalent).

In the first group, the major and oft-cited proposition is that (1) the first-best policy to address a *single endogenous or autonomous, policy-imposed* distortion is to set an appropriate tax cum subsidy to offset the distortion at its *source,* and (2) the first-best *instrumental distortion* created by policy for constraining the equilibrium value of an endogenous variable is the one that affects that variable directly. The second proposition relates to the welfare ranking, starting from the first best, of *alternative policies* that could be used to address the single distortion (endogenous or autonomous, policy imposed) or alternative instrumental distortion creating policies that could be used to constrain the *single endogenous* variable of interest. The third proposition establishes the monotonicity of welfare with respect to the *level* of the policy instrument specified by the first proposition, starting from a level of zero (laissez-faire) to its first-best optimal level. Monotonicity holds, whether the policy is used to address a single distortion that is endogenous or policy imposed or used instrumentally to constrain a single endogenous variable.

The three propositions of the second group are illustrations of the theory of the second best, or put more colloquially, of the proposition that with a distortion present and unaddressed, all hell *could* (not necessarily *would*) break lose if there is a change in a policy or an exogenous variable. Thus growth (due to exogenous factors) *could* be immiserizing, the social (i.e., shadow) price of a factor *could* be negative, and so on, if some unaddressed endogenous or policy-imposed autonomous distortion is present. A *reduction* in the level of *one* distortion need not be *welfare improving* (which it would be if it is the *only* distortion) if another is present. Finally, distortions cannot be uniquely ranked vis-à-vis one another. An implication of these propositions is the celebrated theorem of Tinbergen (1956) that for achieving several policy goals optimally one would need as many policy instruments as goals.[3] Thus one would need as many policies as there are distortions to achieve the first-best optimum.

In what follows I briefly and selectively survey some recent developments in five important areas in the literature on distortions inspired by Bhagwati (1971). These are DUP activities and endogenous distortions, the transfer problem, strategic trade policy, piecemeal policy reform, and intertemporal distortions, credibility, and time consistency.

1.2 Some Recent Developments since the General Theory of Distortions

Directly Unproductive Profit-Seeking Activities and Endogenous Distortions

In another celebrated paper, Bhagwati (1982) christened as directly unproductive productive profit-seeking (DUP) activities all ways of making a profit or earning an income by undertaking activities that are directly unproductive in the sense of *producing* neither producer intermediates nor goods and services that enter the utility function of some consumer.

In several papers (e.g., Bhagwati 1980 and Bhagwati, Brecher, and Srinivasan 1984), he has distinguished between two classes of DUP activities: first, where the policy distortion (e.g., the tariff) is itself exogenous while it triggers in different ways an added distortion (e.g., revenue-seeking), and second, where the policy distortion is itself endogenously determined as in several tariff-seeking models such as the Madisonian single-government model in Findlay and Wellisz (1982), the two-government branches model of the efficient tariff in Feenstra and Bhagwati (1982), and the numerous subsequent models of Hillman (1989), Magee, Brock, and Young (1989), Mayer (1989), and many others.

In the former class of DUP-activity cases, it is evident that we transit from the first class of Bhagwati's single-distortion propositions to the second class where there is more than one distortion. In the latter class of DUP-activity cases, however, the problem is deeper. When DUP activity makes the primary distortion itself endogenous, the consequence in this class of models is that the degree of freedom to vary policy is lost; the policy itself becomes part of the solution to the political-economy model that endogenizes the (distortionary) policy. Since the propositions of the Generalized Theory are based on the view that policies can be exogenously set by governments, and hence rank-ordered from the viewpoint of their suitability as welfare-improving and welfare-maximizing effects, they do not extend directly to accommodate the endogenous-policy variety of DUP activities. But the reasoning underlying some of the propositions can nonetheless be shown to apply.

Exogenous-Policy DUP Activities   It turns out, as the following illustrations from Anam (1982) and Bhagwati, Brecher, and Srinivasan (1984) show, that if a distortion triggers DUP activities, then some of the six propositions described above need not hold. Thus, for example, from the first proposition in the first group, it follows that the first-best instrumental distortion creating policy to constrain the equilibrium *consumption* of the importable is a tax on consumption of that commodity. But a consumption tax need not be the first best if the revenue generated by the tax is not rebated to consumers in a nondistortionary lump-sum fashion but its availability triggers resource-using activities seeking it, and the entire revenue is dissipated by such activities. In such a case a tariff would be superior, even though all the tariff revenues are also dissipated by seeking activities as well.

To take another example, for a small open economy with a positive tariff on the capital-intensive importable, growth from domestic capital accumulation could be immiserizing given that tariff revenues are rebated to consumers in a lump-sum fashion. But once the tariff triggers revenue-seeking activities that dissipate the entire tariff revenue, such growth can never be immiserizing. By the same token, growth from foreign capital inflow, which was shown by Brecher-Alejandro (1977) to be necessarily immiserizing in the absence of revenue seeking, leaves welfare unchanged once DUP activities dissipate the entire revenue.

What the above examples in fact show is not that the Generalized Theory is invalid, but that once DUP activities are viewed as an unaddressed distortion, then a problem that was in the domain of its first group of propositions moves into the domain of its second group. Thus the instrumental policy-imposed distortion in the form of a consumption tax that is optimal for constraining consumption in the absence of any other distortion need not be so in the presence of another unaddressed distortion, namely in the form of DUP activity. Growth, which could be immiserizing in the presence of one unaddressed distortion, namely a tariff, need not be so in the presence of an *additional* unaddressed distortion, namely the DUP activity. Thus taken together the two groups of propositions are valid.

Endogenous-Policy DUP Activities   When DUP activities endogenously determine the level at which some policy instrument is set, the question of such a policy triggering yet other DUP activities does not arise: They would have been already accounted for in arriving at the endogenously set level of policy. Consequently the question of the welfare ranking of equilibria under several such endogenous policies being altered by DUP activities triggered by them does not arise either. Yet one could raise a different and interesting question.

Suppose that the DUP activities associated with one of several endogenously determined policies cease, thereby releasing resources they used but leaving us still with the same policy (exogenously set in effect). Is it possible to rank the new equilibrium relative to the old equilibrium in welfare terms? This is the analogue of the question whether removing one among many *exogenous* distortions raise welfare. The answer to the latter question according to the Generalized Theory is, in general, "not necessarily." It is therefore reasonable to expect the same answer to the former question. Equally it should cause no surprise that the welfare ranking of an exogenously determined set of policy instruments is altered if the same set is endogenously determined.

The reason underlying both conclusions is the same as that in the Generalized Theory in the case of exogenous distortions. Thus, in the first case, the distortionary effect of the remaining set of endogenous policies could be attenuated or augmented when the DUP activities associated with one of them ceases and the resources thereby released are reallocated in equilibrium between productive and remaining DUP activities. In the second case, the resources (e.g., capital, labor) used in determining a policy endogenously need not be the same in levels or composition as the resources used up by DUP activities triggered when the same policy is exogenously set, possibly at the same level. The following examples illustrate each of these two cases.

Bhagwati (1980) illustrates the first case when comparing a distorting tariff in a small country, at rate x percent, arrived at endogenously, with an identical tariff set exogenously. He argues that the former would not necessarily be welfare ranked with the latter. While the latter equilibrium is using no resources (unproductively) to arrive at the tariff, those resources may have a negative shadow price: The comparison is at tariff-distorted equilibria.[4] Thus the resources used in lobbying may end up attenuating the tariff distortion.

On the other hand, Rodrik (1986) illustrates the second case when he argues that "paradoxical welfare rankings can be obtained not only in the presence of *additional* distortions of revenue-seeking type but more generally when the original distortion itself is endogenously generated" (pp. 285–86). Two policies, tariffs, and production subsidies are compared. If they are set exogenously to achieve a production objective, the former yields lower welfare than the latter. In Rodrik's model the level of the policy is *endogenously* determined by private sector lobbying. However, a tariff has a public good aspect in that all firms in an industry face the same tariff whether or not some of them lobbied for it. A subsidy, on the other hand, could in principle be firm-specific, and hence involve no public good feature. As such, tariff-seeking behavior will normally be underprovided from the perspective of the industry as a whole. The asymmetry between tariffs and subsidies in resources used in lobbying leads then to the result that tariff and subsidy equilibria cannot be ranked unambiguously in welfare terms.

Another example considered by Rodrik illustrates the subtlety and power of the Generalized Theory in yet another direction. He starts with an *exogenous* (possibility policy-imposed) distortionary wage-differential between two sectors. In accordance with the Generalized Theory, the first-best policy is to offset the distortion at its *source* through an appropriate wage subsidy to the employers in the sector with the higher wage. He then considers the case where the same intersectoral wage-differential emerges *endogenously* from the rent-maximizing employment choice of a labor union monopoly in the high-wage sector. A wage subsidy to this sector no longer eliminates the distortion. This is because, with the union reoptimizing its employment choice given the subsidy (to the employers), a wage-differential still remains. At first this might seem to contradict the Generalized Theory. The endogenous wage-differential could, after all, be viewed as the distortionary outcome of market failure (i.e., the absence of perfect competition in the labor market in that sector), and as such, by the Generalized Theory, an appropriate policy should eliminate it. Yet, as Bhagwati has argued, the first-best wage subsidy that offsets a distortionary, but exogenous, wage-differential fails to do so when the differential arises from the endogenous behavior of the union. However, this failure, far from invalidating the Generalized Theory, affirms it! The reason is subtle: The source of the distortion in the case of exogenous wage differential is the differential itself. On the other hand, in the case of *endogenous* differential the source of the distortion is the monopoly power of the union: The differential is a consequence and not the cause of the distortion. It is not surprising that the wage subsidy policy that seeks to address the consequence while leaving the cause unaddressed fails. The first-best policy, by the Generalized Theory, will address the cause, namely the monopoly power of the union. Such a policy by eliminating the union's monopoly power will at the same time eliminate the wage differential as well.

Transfer Problem

The effect of a resource transfer by one country (donor) to another (recipient) on the terms of trade, and on the welfare of recipient and donor, attracted the attention of a number of illustrious economists including Keynes, Leontief, and Ohlin in the pre–Second World War era. Samuelson (1952, 1954) addressed the issue in the 1950s. The presumption was, and it was shown to be valid in a two-country, two-commodity, two-factor model, that a transfer cannot immiserize the recipient and enrich the donor if all markets are Walrasian stable.

In a number of recent papers on the problem, many of which he wrote with various coauthors, Bhagwati shows that transfers can be immiserizing despite market stability, if, for example, the transfer takes place between two countries that are part of a many-country trading world. Alternatively, in analogy with immiserizing growth, transfer can be immiserizing in the presence of an unaddressed domestic distortion. Bhagwati, Brecher, and Hatta (1983) unified the transfer and the distortions literatures by identifying the analytical core of the myriad examples of recipient-immiserizing or donor-enriching transfer despite market stability as the presence of an unaddressed distortion. Even the three-country example, in which seemingly there is no market distortion, can be viewed as involving a *foreign* distortion. The reason is that in this case the failure of the recipient to impose an optimal tariff is the cause of welfare deterioration. Indeed it is the adverse shift in terms of trade following a transfer that turns a necessarily welfare-improving transfer under unchanging terms of trade into an immiserizing one.

Kemp and Wan (1976) showed that a common external tariff structure for a customs union among any number of trading partners in a many-country world can always be found that ensures that no consumer outside the union is hurt and that at least one consumer within the union is better off by the formation of the union. Their elegant proof was based on keeping the net trade of the nonmembers unchanged at preunion equilibrium levels through the use of an appropriate set of common tariffs by the union.

Using this methodology, Grinols (1986) shows the existence of a "family of always feasible corrective tax policies which guarantees normal welfare response" to transfers. Grinols interprets growth more broadly than merely that associated with factor accumulation or with technical progress by viewing, for example, the formation of a customs union as growth from removal of trade barriers. In his way of defining growth, "a move from a customs union to a common market, the receipt of a transfer, and even the removal of impediments to internal resource allocation (for example, an externality or distorting tax) are other forms of growth" (p. 488). Of course, it follows that each of these forms of growth could be immiserizing.

Grinols's main proposition is: "For each type of growth, there exists a set of policies available to the participants in the growth process to guarantee welfare gains to the growth country or countries." The basic intuition behind this is the same as that of the Kemp-Wan proposition: Prices and income in the nonparticipant countries could be kept fixed by an appropriate set of trade taxes (*and* profit taxes if foreign factor ownership is allowed) by the participants. In *any* resulting postgrowth equilibrium, welfare is unchanged by construction in nonparticipant countries, while it can be made to be welfare improving to growth participants. Once the existence of a *feasible* set of tariffs and profit taxes and of an associated postgrowth equilibrium with the desired properties are shown, it is easy to see that an *optimal* set, in the sense of maximizing the gains from growth, will also exist.

One way of interpreting the analysis of Grinols in terms of Bhagwati's propositions relating to immiserizing growth, and to the immiserizing consequences of reducing the level of one distortion while another is present, is to note, as Bhagwati did, that the "paradoxical" outcomes arise when the change (growth or reduction in the level of a distortion) accentuates the *welfare-reducing* distortionary effect of the remaining distortions to an extent that offsets the primary *welfare-enhancing* effect of the change. In effect, what Grinols does is to show the existence of policies that *prevent* any change in the possible adverse effect of the remaining distortions as growth occurs so that the primary welfare-enhancing effect is not offset. Since such policies need not be *fully* "optimal," it follows that Bhagwati's statement that "...immiserizing growth would be impossible if *fully*

optimal policies were followed in each situation, i.e. if the distortion resulting from the endogenous policy-imposed cause were offset by optimal
policy intervention..." (p. 276, emphasis added) describes a set of *sufficient*,
though not *necessary*, conditions for the impossibility of immiserization.

Oligopolistic Competition and Strategic Trade Policy

Bhagwati formulated his Generalized Theory for economies in which each
individual producer and consumer is atomistic (has no actual or perceived
market power). For such an economy, market power in international
competition can arise only at the national level. As Dixit and Grossman
(1986) have stressed, any terms-of-trade advantage that a country could
reap would be best pursued by restricting trade through tariffs (on imports
or exports). Subsidizing domestic firms in their competition with foreign
rivals would be an inferior, though welfare-improving, policy. These
results are consistent with the first two propositions of the Generalized
Theory.

If firms are not atomistic, so that competition is oligopolistic and oligopoly rents arise, a policy that shifts some of these rents to home firms
could be welfare augmenting. However, as Eaton and Grossman (1986)
have shown, whether or not a rent-shifting policy exists, and if it does,
whether it takes the form of a subsidy or a tax, depends sensitively on the
specification of the form of oligopolistic competition. In particular, in a
model of a domestic firm competing with a foreign firm in a third market,
with neither selling at home, if each harbors a consistent conjecture about
the reaction of the other firm to its action in equilibrium, it is not feasible
to transfer rents to the home firm through policy intervention, and hence
free trade is optimal. Dixit and Grossman (1986) examine the rent-shifting
argument in a context where industries compete for the services of a
specific factor that is essential to production. As in the consistent conjectures case of Eaton and Grossman, it turns out free trade is optimal if the
ratio of rents earned to the requirement of the specific factor at the margin
are the same across industries. These results are consistent with the Generalized Theory in that, in the absence of consistent conjectures or diversity
among firms in rent/specific factor ratio, a distortion requiring policy
intervention exists.

Krishna and Thursby (1991) analyze the jointly optimal levels of a
variety of policy instruments when markets are imperfectly competitive,
focusing on a simple model in which firms are monopolists in their home

market but are duopolists in a third market. The policy instruments are taxes or subsidies on exports, domestic production and consumption, although, for this model, instead of three separate policies affecting exports, production, and consumption, only two, namely the sum of the consumption and export subsidies and the sum of production and export subsidies, are relevant. The reason is that each firm is a monopoly in its home market.

There are two distortions in the Krishna-Thursby model. The first is a *domestic distortion* arising from the firm being a monopoly in the home market, and the second is a *foreign or strategic distortion* arising from the home firm's conjecture of the change in foreign firm's sale in the third market in response to a change in its own sale not being the same as the slope of the foreign firm's best-response function; that is, its conjecture is not consistent. Thus in conformity with the Generalized Theory, it is optimal to use one instrument, namely *a consumption tax/subsidy*, for addressing the domestic distortion, and *a second instrument*, namely an export tax/subsidy, to address the strategic distortion. Of course, if there are more than one domestic firm, each domestic firm imposes a not fully internalized externality on other domestic firms through the effect of its sales on the price realized by *all* firms in the third market. This is the standard terms-of-trade distortion, and in setting the trade policy instrument optimally, this effect would have to be taken into account as well.

The above conclusions are based on the home and external markets being segmented. If the government uses domestic price regulation to address the monopoly distortion, that is, it requires that the net consumer price equal marginal cost, then clearly the firm is not free to choose its domestic sales. As such, as long as marginal cost of production is not constant, this lack of freedom links foreign and domestic sales so that market segmentation no longer holds. Thus the trade policy instrument has to be set at a level to address the strategic distortion as well as the regulation-induced spillover effect. Krishna and Thursby indeed use the Bhagwati terminology of "policy-imposed instrumental distortion" to describe this effect.

Krishna and Thursby also consider integration of the home and foreign markets so that price arbitrage ensures that the same price rules in the both markets. Unlike in the cases of domestic price regulation, the home firm could choose *both* home *and* foreign sales, though not independently of each other. Although the general theory of distortions holds, in the sense of *targeting*—in that a *consumption tax subsidy* is used to address the monopoly distortion and a *production tax subsidy* is used to address the strategic distortion—the latter subsidy as well has to address the linkage between domestic and foreign markets caused by arbitrage. As such, the determination of the *level* each instrument addressing a specific distortion independently of the levels of other distortions is impossible.

Rodrik (1989) considers a setup in which, in contrast to the conventional case of firms being atomistic, the domestic industry consists of a continuum of traders differentiated both by size and behavior. Optimal policy, when the country has market power in foreign markets, then involves a *structure* of trade taxes rather than a uniform tariff, with larger firms taxed at lower rates than smaller firms. In his empirical example of nutmeg exports from Indonesia, for the parameter values considered, the tax on the dominant export firm is less than half of what would be predicted by using the conventional inverse demand elasticity rule. Viewed from the perspective of the Generalized Theory, the optimal tariff structure across firms is the sum of two terms, a conventional term equaling the reciprocal of foreign demand elasticity that will apply if all domestic firms were atomistic, and a term that captures the variation across firms in size (market share) and behavior. The first term addresses the external market power or *foreign distortion*, and the second addresses the *domestic* distortion caused by nonatomistic firm behavior. However, the second term involves also the reciprocal of foreign demand elasticity, as it should, since the consequence of departure of atomistic behavior of a firm depends on foreign demand function because all firms are competing in that market. Thus in this case, as in the case of arbitrage considered by Krishna and Thursby, while it is possible to *target* each policy instrument to a specific distortion, it is not possible to choose the *level* of each instrument based only on the level of the distortion it addresses independently of the levels of other distortions.

Piecemeal Policy Reform

There is a considerable literature on the effect of *piecemeal* trade policy reform (e.g., Bertrand and Vanek 1971; Dixit 1985; Fukushima 1979, 1981; Hatta 1977), representing a *partial* movement toward first-best trade policy. From the Generalized Theory we know that such a partial move need not be welfare improving. I now turn to theoretical and empirical studies that seek welfare-enhancing piecemeal reforms.

Beghin and Karp (1992b) point out that there are two approaches in the theoretical literature. The first seeks sufficient conditions to ensure that a particular type of reform (on equiproportionate reductions in all tariffs, a decrease in the largest tariff, etc.) is welfare improving. The other seeks to determine the optimal levels of policy instruments in the presence of fixed distortions.

Examples of the first approach are Beghin and Karp (1992a), Diewert et al. (1991), Hatta (1977), Fukushima (1979), and Falvey (1988). Hatta (1977) and Fukushima (1979) establish that an equiproportionate reduction in all tariffs is welfare improving in a model with nontraded goods if such goods are net substitutes for all other goods. Falvey (1988) considers a model in which imports of some traded goods are restricted by unremovable quotas and shows that the same result holds under the same assumption of net substitutability.

Given that an unremovable quota turns a traded good into a nontraded good at the margin as long as the quota binds, Falvey notes that this result is not surprising. Falvey also considers piecemeal quota reform and finds that although the entire quota structure is important in determining the structure of implicit tariffs, in the absence of any explicit tariffs the direction in which a particular quota should be adjusted, if any, is independent of the implicit distortions in the other quota-restricted markets. This again is a consequence of the facts that, in the absence of explicit tariffs, there is no distortion in trade with respect to non-quota-restricted goods and that, as long as the quotas continue to bind, a change in the quota of one good does not affect the trade in other quota-restricted goods. Falvey also proves that if all commodities are net substitutes, then a loosening (resp. tightening) of any quota whose implicit tariff is higher (resp. lower) than the highest (resp. lowest) explicit tariff will increase welfare.

Diewert, Turunen-Red, and Woodland (1991) is perhaps the most general of the papers adopting the first approach. Their focus is establishing necessary and sufficient conditions for the existence of strict Pareto-improving changes in tariffs and accompanying household transfers in a model of a small open economy with many households and in the presence of tariff as well as domestic distortions and nontraded goods. They find that a piecemeal reform consisting in an equiproportional reduction in *all* distortions, including domestic distortions, is Pareto improving but not necessarily a reform involving a reduction in tariffs only. This is of course in conformity with the Generalized Theory.

Beghin and Karp (1992b), taking the second analytical approach, first derive the necessary conditions characterizing the optimality of the tariff and subsidy applicable to a part of the economy in the presence of unchanging distortions in other parts. They explain how the optimal levels of the two instruments respond differently to the levels of unchanging distortions. Theirs is a simple model in which there are two tradable sectors, each protected by tariffs and subsidies. By keeping fixed the tariffs and subsidies in sector 2, they derive the optimum (second-best) tariffs and subsidies for sector 1 and how they (under strong substitution assumptions) turn out to be more sensitive to the tariffs kept fixed than to the subsidies. They then apply their theory to an empirical model of the U.S. economy. Their main conclusion is that the high protection for agricultural sectors cannot be justified on the second-best ground of offsetting the effects of unchanged tariffs and subsidies in other sectors. This conclusion is shown to be very robust to substantial changes in elasticity of factor substitution or by different assumption-regarding consumer taxes.

Harrison, Rutherford, and Tarr (1993) study trade reform in Turkey in the context of that country's plan to harmonize its external tariff structure to that of the European community in anticipation of admission to EC. They consider the effects of alternative trade reform packages using a forty-sector computable general equilibrium model. Turkey had already completed a major liberalization of its trade policies in the 1980s by abolishing import quotas, reducing tariffs, and making the lira convertible. Given these substantial liberalizations, further piecemeal across-the-board tariff reductions are not always beneficial and must be coordinated with export subsidy reductions to achieve welfare gains. Thus the reduction of tariffs alone causes welfare gains initially, but further reductions (beyond 40 percent of the initial value) produce welfare losses. The reasons are that the average initial level of tariffs is just above average export-subsidy and that, on the average, there is only a slight anti-export bias. Small reductions in tariff reduce this bias and improve welfare. But further reductions turn anti-export bias to a pro-export bias, which is again distortionary. On the other hand, benefits from export subsidy reductions increase up to a 70 percent reduction primarily because an across-the-board reduction simultaneously reduces the dispersion in subsidies. They find that

Because of the offsetting effects of tariffs and export subsidies, reducing export subsidies and tariffs jointly leads to even greater welfare gains than just reducing export subsidies does. Similarly, because of the presence of domestic distortions, reductions in foreign distortions fail to generate welfare gains at the margin when they reach the 80 percent level. Only when all distortions are removed is the optimal policy to reduce export subsidies and tariffs jointly by 100 percent. This is the first-best policy. (p. 199)

Harmonization with EC external tariff structure has little beneficial effect.

These authors confirm the analytical findings of the Generalized Theory with their most important policy conclusion about

... the fragility of first-best rules of thumb as to the welfare benefits of piecemeal trade policy reforms for countries that have reduced trade barriers as much as Turkey has but that have retained export subsidies. The results of trade policy reforms then depend crucially on both the level and the dispersion of import tariffs and especially of export subsidies. In other words, it is not the case that any partial movement toward the first-best trade policy for Turkey will result in some fraction of the welfare gains from that first-best package. (p. 207)

Intertemporal Distortions, Credibility, and Time Consistency

It is well-known that superiority of free trade over autarky can be shown to hold for a small dynamic open economy *even if the autarkic steady state is welfare superior to the free trade steady state* (Smith 1977; Srinivasan and Bhagwati 1980; Bhagwati and Srinivasan 1984, ch. 31). In such a case the present value of welfare along the *transition path* from the autarky to the free trade steady state exceeds the present value of welfare along the autarkic steady state. Bark (1987) extends the static result, that free trade could be inferior to autarky if some unremovable distortion is present, to a dynamic small open economy. He shows that

if either a distortion or an increase in the degree of an already existing distortion moves the economy's new steady-state capital stock away from the socially optimal level, trade intervention is superior to free trade. By contrast, if either a removal of or a reduction in its degree of an already existing distortion moves the economy's new steady-state capital stock closer to the socially optimal level, exactly the opposite is true. In the course of the above demonstration, we have also seen that the fundamental conclusions drawn in the traditional static model remain intact even if intertemporal considerations are introduced. (p. 165)

Consider next the related issues of credibility and time consistency of announced reform packages and that of the inability of governments to precommit. These two issues have attracted the increasing attention of scholars, particularly in the 1980s, because a number of developing countries undertook market-oriented reform during that period. Rodrik (1992, 89), for example, points to a credibility problem—that is, the inability of governments to "convince business, labor or consumers that trade reform will be lasting"—as a major reason for the unsustainability of reform. These are also problems that can be put into the framework of the generalized theory of distortions.

A policy can be optimal or first best if the government's commitment to the policy is credible, but not so otherwise: The lack of credibility, in effect, constitutes a distortion that, if unaddressed, makes free trade no longer a first-best or even a welfare-improving policy. Engel and Kletzer (1991) illustrate this for a small open economy in which, in the absence of credibility problems, free trade is the optimal policy. In their two-period model

> ... there is a single imported consumption good which is not produced at home, and an export good which is not used domestically and is available in an exogenously fixed supply each period. The private sector is represented by a single household which maximizes the expectation of a discounted sum of utility of current consumption. The discount rate is constant and equal to the world rate of interest. The government's only role is to set trade policy and redistribute any tariff revenue in a lump sum fashion. The government seeks to maximize the welfare of the representative household. However, the government lacks credibility with the private sector: the household believes that the government is the true welfare maximizing one with positive probability less than unity ... the only alternative possibility is a government which adopts the rule: impose a tariff in the next period with probability q $(0 < q < 1)$ or choose free trade with probability $1 - q$. The public believes that the probability this government is in power is $1 - \lambda$. (p. 215)

In this model with $\pi \equiv q(1 - \lambda)$ as the subjective probability that the tariff will be imposed in period 2, if the government chooses free trade in the first period, as long as $\pi > 0$ (i.e., there is a positive probability that there will be a tariff in the second period), households borrow in the first period, and the effective market rate of interest faced by the household is less than the world interest rate.

The outcome thus involves an intertemporal distortion. However, if π is zero or one, there is no distortion. In the first case, free trade will be first-best optimal in the first period, and in the second, a tariff will be first-best optimal, since in either case intertemporal distortion is eliminated. When π is between zero and one, there is lack of credibility, resulting in an intertemporal distortion that creates a welfare loss under either free trade or the tariff. Engel and Kletzer identify the lack of perfect information about the government's motives as a *distortion*, addressing which might require a *tariff* as an optimal response by the government. By introducing Bayesian learning by consumers in more than two periods, they show that the prior probability that the government is of the false type is reduced as long as the government optimally chooses free trade or tariff imposition in every period and the private sector believes with positive probability that the government could be of either type. In a finite amount of time, free trade becomes optimal. In a similar setup Calvo (1987) suggests that capital inflow controls in the first period instead of a tariff could also be used as an optimal response by a government lacking credibility.

Rodrik (1989) considers credibility issues in a two-period model of a small open economy similar to that of Engel and Kletzer. The economy produces a single good that is not consumed at home, and all consumption and investment goods are imported. No foreign capital flows are allowed in the model. The government reduces the tariff to zero in the first period and announces it will be zero in the second period as well. While this clears the way for foreign aid, the public does not believe the reform will be maintained and believes that the tariffs in the second period will be a specified positive level. This lack of credibility, as in the Engel-Kletzer model, induces greater consumption, lower savings and investment in the first period, and welfare is reduced because of the suboptimal level of investment. Rodrik partially endogenizes the credibility problem by considering two types of governments, a liberalizing government and a redistributive government that uses tariff revenues (the only source of revenue for this purpose) to redistribute income to a favored group efficiently, by maximizing the welfare of the favored group subject to a constraint that the welfare of others does not fall below some specified level. The public maximizes its expected utility given its prior beliefs regarding the likelihood that the reform will be aborted. In the absence of any foreign aid contingent on trade reform (i.e., reducing the tariff to zero in the first period and promising to keep it at zero in the second), each type of government will reveal itself by its choice of trade policies in the initial period. However, with a sufficiently high level of contingent foreign aid, a redistributing government may pretend to be a liberalizing government, reduce the tariff to zero in the first period, and reimpose it in the second.

Rodrik distinguishes between a "pooling" equilibrium, in which both types of governments set first-period tariffs equal to zero and hence become indistinguishable, and a "separating" equilibrium, in which the liberalizing government either does not face a credibility problem or can successfully signal its type so as to achieve separation from its redistributive rival. In the model it turns out that the most direct such signal is a *negative* tariff, that is, the import subsidy in the first period. Since this signal imposes an efficiency cost, it is not always the case that a liberalizing government would wish to signal its type. As long as the rate of subsidy that generates the same level of intertemporal distortion as in the pooling equilibrium exceeds the smallest level of subsidy that achieves separation, the liberalizing government will signal and achieve separation. Thus credible reform involves "overshooting" in the sense of reducing tariffs not to zero but to a negative level. This illustrates the distortionary effect of lack of credibility: The level of tariffs has to be set below its otherwise optimal level of zero to achieve credibility!

Froot (1988) considers a two-period model of a small open economy in which both exportables and importables are produced and consumed. A representative consumer maximizes expected welfare. The government liberalizes in the first period by eliminating import tariffs. The issue is whether the government will reimpose a tariff (at some known level) in the second period. It is assumed that the government will do so if at the end of the first period its foreign exchange reserves fall below some minimum level. The level of reserves is the sum of the current account deficit and a random shock. The minimum level is set equal to the deficit that private sector would incur in the first period were it to believe that tariffs would be reimposed in the second period with probability one. Froot first derives the rationally expected level of credibility (i.e., the probability that tariffs will be reimposed), the current account, and the level of welfare under *complete liberalization*. He then investigates the justification for positive first-period tariffs as a second-best tool for reducing the *distortion* introduced by lack of credibility. He concludes that this distortion due to lack of perfect credibility of liberalization becomes rationally *intensified* under the typical first-best policy of immediate liberalization. A more gradual lowering of trade barriers leads to higher welfare and greater probability that the program will succeed.

A similar result in favor of gradual liberalization of trade over abrupt liberalization is obtained by Edwards and van Wijnbergen (1986) in an intertemporal (once again, a two-period) model in which the two policy options considered are liberalizing capital accounts first while trade restrictions remain, and the other is liberalization of trade in the presence of capital accounts restriction. The reason for the possible superiority of the latter, as could be expected from the general theory, is that in the former case, if capital inflows from abroad are used to increase investment, the preexisting trade distortion will be amplified.

An overshooting result analogous to that of Rodrik (1989) is also obtained by Aizenman (1992), once again in a two-period model of a small open economy with an exportable (outward-oriented) and an importable (inward-oriented) sector. Capital stock is specific to each sector, being the outcome of past investment by public and private sectors. As in the models discussed above, in the first period the economy is liberalized, but the public expects the possibility of policy reversal in the second period. He characterizes

...the equilibrium deriving the optimal investment and the private investment tax-cum-subsidy policies. Policy uncertainty is shown to depress saving and growth, and to operate as a subsidy on inward investment, and as a tax on outward investment. The signaling and the commitment effect of public investment generates a positive externality for public investment in the outward sector, and a negative externality for public investment in the inward-oriented activity. Using the investment path with full credibility as the benchmark, he shows that the signaling externality increases the optimal share of public relative to the private investment in the outward-oriented activity, and lowers that share in the inward-oriented activity. Thus, to overcome the lack of credibility the government biases the public/private capital share in favor of the outward sector, and against the inward sector. (pp. 165–66)

Thus public investment in the outward-oriented sector overshoots.

Finally, Staiger and Tabellini (1989) bring out clearly the time consistency issue in trade policy. Theirs is a model in which all goods are traded and individuals act as producers or consumers, but with a crucial timing assumption that producers choose first from a possibly distorted production possibility frontier. Simultaneously with the producers or after them, the government chooses its tariff policy. Finally consumers make their decisions. Since a tariff is a production subsidy/tax and a consumption tax/subsidy at the same rate, the timing assumption forces the government to take producers' decisions as bygones and hence to ignore any production distortions introduced by production tax/subsidy aspect of the tariff. Thus the tariff is set as if the distortions were only those associated with consumption. But the expectation of a tariff policy exerts an influence on production even if in equilibrium the government ignores it.

Staiger and Tabellini recall that the Generalized Theory shows that the first-best intervention typically calls for targeting each distortion with a separate tax/subsidy. They point out that a tariff will be a more effective policy tool if its consumption tax aspect can be separated from its production subsidy dimension. Consequently, if production decisions are made prior to consumption decisions, a government with sufficient policy flexibility will be tempted to surprise producers with policies other than those announced in an effort to make this separation. This leads optimal trade policy intervention to be time inconsistent in a wide range of environments. They derive three main implications from their analysis.

First, because trade policy distorts the decisions of both producers and consumers and because the decisions of the former typically precede those of the latter, sufficient government flexibility is likely to undermine the optimal use of trade policy as a remedy for the existence of distortions. That is, optimal trade policy in this broad class of problems will in general be time-inconsistent. Whenever this is the case, rules may be better than discretion in the conduct of trade policy. Second, given that optimal trade policy is generally time-inconsistent in this environment, policy rankings that acknowledge this time-inconsistency will generally differ from the analogous rankings based on the optimal (time-inconsistent) tariff. Finally, with the existence of domestic consumption distortions considered to be empirically unimportant as a trade policy rationale, these results suggest that a government with policy discretion will use tariffs primarily in two cases: either as redistributive tools, or whether it has world market power. (pp. 1269–70)

1.3   Conclusion

I can be very brief: The generalized theory of distortions is alive and well after its birth nearly twenty-five years ago. Its robust insights continue to apply in all the numerous recent analyses of exogenous policy models for which it was devised. Even though it was not devised for the endogenous policy models of the 1980s to which Bhagwati has himself made several important contributions, the reasoning underlying its central propositions can be extended to these models as well.

Notes

I thank Max Corden and Douglas Irwin for their comments and Wolfgang Keller for research assistance. Jagdish Bhagwati's extensive comments on several drafts were extremely valuable. Had this chapter not been for his festschrift, I would have insisted on his being a coauthor!

1. This page refers to the version reprinted in Bhagwati (1987).

2. In the recent literature on lobbying, rent seeking, and directly unproductive profit-seeking activities, the term "endogenous policy" has been used to describe policies emerging as equilibrium outcomes in frameworks in which agents devote resources to influence the policy-making process (see section 1.2 below for a discussion). It would avoid confusion now to rename Bhagwati's "endogenous distortions" as "market failures."

3. Strictly speaking, Tinbergen's proposition is valid only for linear models.

4. Bhagwati used this argument to show that the optimal way to decompose the cost of endogenous protection into the lobbying cost and the conventional cost of protection was to measure the former at the distortion-free free-trade foreign prices between the two production possibility curves, with and without the resources spent on lobbying for and against the tariff, and the latter along the production possibility curve without the resources used up in lobbying. In that way both effects would be signed negative and hence would be intuitive.

References

Aizenman, Josua. 1992. Trade reforms, credibility, and development. *Journal of Development Economics* 39:163–87.

Anam, Mahmudul. 1982. Distortion-triggered lobbying and welfare: A contribution to the theory of directly-unproductive profit-seeking activities. *Journal of International Economics* 13:15–32.

Bark, Taeho. 1987. Distortions and intertemporal welfare in a small open economy. *Journal of International Economics* 23:151–66.

Beghin, John, and Larry Karp. 1992a. Piecemeal trade reform in presence of producer-specific domestic subsidies. *Economics Letters* 39:65–71.

Beghin, John, and Larry Karp. 1992b. Tariff reform in the presence of sector-specific distortions. *Canadian Journal of Economics* 25:294–309.

Bertrand, T. J., and J. Vanek. 1971. The theory of tariffs, taxes and subsidies: Some aspects of the second best. *American Economic Review* 61:925–31.

Bhagwati, Jagdish, ed. 1987. *International Trade: Selected Readings.* Cambridge: MIT Press.

Bhagwati, Jagdish. 1982. Directly-unproductive, profit-seeking (DUP) activities. *Journal of Political Economy* 90:988–1002.

Bhagwati, Jagdish. 1980. Lobbying and welfare. *Journal of Public Economics* 14:355–63.

Bhagwati, Jagdish. 1971. The generalized theory of distortions and welfare. In Jagdish Bhagwati, Ronald Jones, Robert Mundell, and Jaroslav Vanek, eds., *Trade, Balance of Payments, and Growth: Papers in International Economics in Honor of Charles P. Kindleberger.* Amsterdam: North Holland.

Bhagwati, Jagdish, Richard Brecher, and Tatsuo Hatta. 1983. The generalized theory of transfers and welfare: Bilateral transfers in a multilateral world. *American Economic Review* 73:606–18.

Bhagwati, Jagdish, Richard Brecher, and T. N. Srinivasan. 1984. DUP actvities and economic theory. In Jagdish Bhagwati, ed., *International Trade: Selected Readings*, 2d ed. Cambridge: MIT Press, pp. 311–28.

Bhagwati, Jagdish, and T. N. Srinivasan. 1984. *Lectures on International Trade*. Cambridge: MIT Press.

Bhagwati, Jagdish, and V. K. Ramaswami. 1963. Domestic distortions, tariffs and the theory of optimum subsidy. *Journal of Political Economy* 71:44–50.

Brecher, Richard, and Carlos Diáz-Alejandro. 1977. Tariffs, foreign capital and immiserizing growth. *Journal of International Economics* 7:317–22.

Calvo, G. 1987. On the costs of temporary liberalization/stabilization experiments. *Journal of Development Economics* 27:245–61.

Corden, W. Max. 1957. Tariffs, subsidies and the terms of trade. *Economica*, New Series, 24:235–42.

Diewert, W. E., A. H. Turunen-Red, and A. D. Woodland. 1991. Tariff reform in a small open multi-household economy with domestic distortions and nontraded goods. *International Economic Review* 32:937–57.

Dixit, Avinash, and Gene Grossman. 1986. Targeted export promotion with several oligopolistic industries. *Journal of International Economics* 21:233–50.

Dixit, Avinash. 1985. Tax policy in open economies. In A. J. Auerbach and M. Feldstein, eds., *Handbook of Public Economics*. Amsterdam: North Holland, pp. 313–74.

Eaton, Jonathan, and Gene Grossman. 1986. Optimal trade and industrial policy under oligopoly. *Quarterly Journal of Economics* 101:383–406.

Edwards, Sebastian, and Sweder van Wijnbergen. 1986. The welfare effects of trade and capital market liberalization. *International Economic Review* 27:141–48.

Engel, Charles, and Kenneth Kletzer. 1991. Trade policy under endogenous credibility. *Journal of Development Economics* 36:213–28.

Falvey, Rodney. 1988. Tariffs, quotas and piecemeal policy reform. *Journal of International Economics* 25:177–83.

Feenstra, Ronald, and Jagdish Bhagwati. 1982. Tariff seeking and the efficient tariff. In Jagdish Bhagwati, ed., *Import Competition and Response*. Chicago: University of Chicago Press, pp. 245–58.

Findlay, Ronald, and S. Wellisz. 1982. Endogenous tariffs, the political economy of trade restrictions, and welfare. In Jagdish Bhagwati, ed., *Import Competition and Response*. Chicago: University of Chicago Press, pp. 223–33.

Froot, Kenneth. 1988. Credibility, real interest rates, and the optimal speed of trade liberalization. *Journal of International Economics* 25:71–93.

Fukushima, T. 1981. A dynamic quantity adjustment process in a small open economy, and welfare effects of tariff changes. *Journal of International Economics* 11:513–29.

Fukushima, T. 1979. Tariff structures, nontraded goods, and the theory of piecemeal policy recommendation. *International Economic Review* 20:427–35.

Grinols, Earl. 1986. Transfers and the generalized theory of distortions and welfare. *Economica* 54:477–91.

Harrison, Glenn, Thomas F. Rutherford, and David Tarr. 1993. Trade reform in the partially liberalized economy of Turkey. *World Bank Economic Review* 7:191–217.

Hatta, T. 1977. A recommendation for a better tariff structure. *Econometrica* 45:1859–69.

Hillman, Arye. 1989. *The Political Economy of Protection*. Chur, Switzerland: Harwood Academic Publishers.

Johnson, H. G. 1965. Optimal trade intervention in the presence of domestic distortions. In R. Caves, H. Johnson, and P. Kenen, eds., *Trade, Growth and the Balance of Payments*. Amsterdam: North Holland.

Kemp, M., and H. Wan. 1976. An elementary proposition concerning the formation of trade unions. *Journal of International Economics* 6:95–98.

Krishna, Kala, and Marie Thursby. 1991. Optimal policies with strategic distortions. *Journal of International Economics* 31:291–308.

Magee, Stephen, William Brock, and Leslie Young. 1989. *Black Hole Tariffs and Endogenous Policy Theory: Political Economy in General Equilibrium*. Cambridge: Cambridge University Press.

Mayer, Wolfgang, and Raymond Reizman. 1989. Tariff formation in a multidimensional voting models. *Economics and Politics* 1:61–79.

Rodrik, Dani. 1992. The limits of trade policy reform in developing countries. *Journal of Economic Perspectives* 6:87–105.

Rodrik, Dani. 1989. Optimal trade taxes for a large country with non-atomistic firms. *Journal of International Economics* 26:157–67.

Rodrik, Dani. 1986. Tariffs, subsidies, and welfare with endogenous policy. *Journal of International Economics* 21:285–99.

Samuelson, Paul. 1954. The transfer problem and transport costs. II: Analysis of effects of trade impediments. *Economic Journal* 64:264–89.

Samuelson, Paul. 1952. The transfer problem and transport costs: The terms of trade when impediments are absent. *Economic Journal* 62:278–304.

Staiger, Robert, and Guido Tabellini. 1989. Rules and discretion in trade policy. *European Economic Review* 33:1265–77.

Smith, M. 1977. Capital accumulation in the open two-sector economy. *Economic Journal* 87:273–82.

Srinivasan, T. N., and Jagdish Bhagwati. 1980. Trade and welfare in a steady state. In John S. Chipman and Charles Kindleberger, eds., *Flexible Exchange Rates and the Balance of Payments: Essays in Memory of Egon Sohmen*. Amsterdam: North Holland, pp. 341–53.

Srinivasan, T. N. 1987. Distortions. In J. Eatwell, M. Newgate, and P. Newman, eds., *The New Palgrave*. London: Macmillan, pp. 865–67.

Tinbergen, Jan. 1956. *Economic Policy: Principles and Design*. Amsterdam: North Holland.

2 The Age of Bhagwati et al.

Paul A. Samuelson

Keynes speaks somewhere in his *Essays in Biography* of the wonderful way that a genius like Newton or Ramsey can, while still young, in almost a matter of months learn all that has been ever known about a science, and then proceed from that springboard to make great leaps forward. So it is with what on this occasion we may call the Age of Bhagwati in international trade.

This generation began after the pioneers of Ohlin, Viner, and Haberler had clarified and generalized the great analytical breakthroughs in trade of Ricardo, J. S. Mill, Mangoldt, Pareto, Taussig, and Edgeworth. And after Lerner, Leontief, Meade, and others had similarly perfected the models of *their* teachers.

It is a mistake in science to think that any generation arrives at the banquet table late, *after* the feast has been consumated. Science's work is never done. Science is a movable feast. One solved problem fans out into many new open questions that beg in turn for solutions.

Having lived in the old order and the new, I can call attention to the improved facility with which later generations are equipped to tackle emerging problems. What they take for granted can escape their own explicit recognition. Shucks, any dolt can understand the interactions of geographical specialization with differentials in factor endowments (and in tastes) and their interactions with unequal factor intensities of goods. Well, David Ricardo was no dolt. And neither was Frank Taussig. Somewhere in their writings you will encounter vague perceptions of Heckscher-Ohlin realities, but what remains implicit remains in need of development and articulation.

Indeed a first generation imperfectly explicates its own scientific innovations. Arthur Koestler refers to Kepler as a sleepwalker who stumbled over his elliptical laws of planetary behavior. We used to joke that Hegel didn't understand his own philosophy until he read the French translation. Actually Kepler's system of nature can only be truly understood after you have read its Newton translation.

To illustrate the psychological process of perceiving (irreversibly) a new gestalt, I recall talking to Harvard's learned economic historian, Alexander Gerschenkron, in his terminal years. He was a good—not a great—chess player. Usually he carried a pocket chessboard, and in idle moments on a park bench or subway ride, Gerschenkron told me he would work out solutions to end game problems. Until one day, suddenly and for no explicable reason, he found himself able to perceive the successive steps of play in his mind's eye. And so it is when Jagdish comes to contemplate the Penn puzzle of why poor countries measure poorer than they really are relative to the affluent regions if you follow the World Bank's naive conversion of nominal GNP's by use of varying market exchange rates rather than by the Penn team's corrections of purchasing power parities through use of valid local prices data. With the speed of light a Bhagwati reads Lerner factor-price-equalization diagrams to show that nontradable labor-intensive services are not likely to be cheapened in land-rich places as much as tradables will be. The Ohlin who argued against Keynes's presumption that the payer of reparations would suffer a secondary worsening of its terms of trade thus lacks the understanding of a Bhagwati when it comes to the Heckscher-Ohlin gestalt. (Similarly a sharp-eyed Harry Johnson could spot in an early Samuelson diagram curved lines that revealed less than full comprehension of the "Rybczynski theorem." Touché. Homer nodded.)

Here is another example where a later generation's enhanced sophistication can illuminate older doctrines. Elasticity pessimism, like herpes, lies ever dormant but ready to erupt when exchange rates seem to get out of kilter. "Exchange rate changes will do little to cure our dollar shortage," politicians complain. A Milton Friedman, or in this historical case an Egon Sohmen, writes: "Try depreciation. At some parity, exports and imports will balance." They might even quote some existence theorem of Debreu concerning the existence of an equilibrium in a standard production-exchange model. However, it takes a sophisticate to debunk a sophisticate. Bhagwati and Johnson demonstrated long ago that the necessarily existent equilibrium might well be where the pound sterling sells for *zero* dollars. To the mathematician zero is a real number, to a human consumer it can be starvation!

I can illustrate a more interesting relook at old findings with an up-to-date problem. As a visiting professor at NYU, I participated recently in a panel of American professors and a leading Japanese official from MITI. My intervention was entitled: "Is The 'Krugman Heresy' Heresy?" What was at issue was the thesis of a Paul Krugman article in the 1994 Summer *Harvard Business Review*, reassuring us that catchup progress in the Third

World, although it could help or hurt the First World, was unlikely in plausible effect to be harmful on our *total* real incomes (even though it might well have some minor adverse effects on how much of that total gets distributed to our unskilled and disadvantaged).

I presented a standard Ricardian model involving three goods and two countries. It could have been understood by a clever 1890s reader of Edgeworth or Mangoldt. I have a vague recollection that, when Arthur Lewis got his Nobel Prize for work in economic development, it may have been Jagdish Bhagwati who explicated the Lewis model in terms of such a simple Ricardian paradigm.

In friendly auditing of the Krugman journalism, I ventured the hypothesis that there was some presumption—a rebuttable presumption of course—that when a China enjoys Schumpeterian technological advance in lines of production where an America has long enjoyed comparative advantage (for home and export production), then China is likely to garner some benefit at the expense of America's *total* and *average per capita* real national product.

To be cogent, I had to address Krugman's assertions that the total of world product had to go somewhere, and that Americans as a whole could benefit as *consumers* despite their nominal losses as *producers*. My dramatic ploy was to have a graduate student phrase in some .detail the Krugman syllogisms on a take-home exam. Humpty Dumpty like, I awarded a failing F to that scapegoat, and an $A+$ to another graduate student whose take-home exam proved that our gains *qua* consumers could not quite bulk as large as our losses *qua* producers.

To save time, I posit that *Am* and *Chi* each can produce three tradable goods from labor alone with respective productivities of $(\pi_1\ \pi_2\ \pi_3) = (6\ 3\ \frac{3}{2})$ and $(\pi_1^*\ \pi_2^*\ \pi_3^*) = (\frac{1}{2}\ 1\ 2)$. Folks everywhere spend their incomes in the same *homothetic* fractions. Before (and after) its innovation, *Chi* has triple *Am*'s labor supply to just neutralize *Am*'s tripled real wage, leaving absolute GDPs about the same.

Obviously *Am* is sure to produce all of good 1 and *Chi* all of good 3: by chance razor-edged symmetry, good 2 is initially neither exported nor imported.

If Penn Kravis-Heston-Summers studies of tradables' relative productivities in poor and affluent places suggest to you that the easiest and likeliest future change is for π_2^* to increase, by easier imitation, then we must hypothesize a biased fall in *Am*'s P_1/P_3 (or P_1^*/P_3^*) terms of trade. World "output" grows because *Chi*'s rise in "output" must outweigh *Am*'s fall in "output."

I put the words "output" in quotation marks to make the point that no 1890s virtuoso in trade theory could have understood our post-1939 way of defining the measure of *society's* total output (defining it *unambiguously* under stipulated uniform homothetic demand). Our A + graduate student with a modern toolbox could cogently deflate the journalistic rhetoric about how *Chi*'s induced real-wage rise would negate her competitive capacity to render us harm. Etc.

Models are mercenary soldiers who will work for anybody. The formula

$$\frac{P_1}{P_3} = \frac{\pi_3^*}{\pi_2^*}\frac{\pi_2}{\pi_1}$$

can authenticate the *Harvard Business Review* assertion that a rise in π_3^* (*Chi*'s productivity in goods we ever import from her) *must* be beneficial to *Am*. (Whether that invention *hurts Chi* depends on how elastic tastes and demands are. *Chi*'s higher total productive potential *could* be outweighed by the terms-of-trade drop in her P_3/P_1, or, under elastic demands, the first effect of *Chi*'s enhanced overall productivity *could* outweigh the induced deterioration of her terms of trade.)

Some important qualifications and caveats are in order:

1. First World harm, if it occurs, is a ceteribus paribus harm not a presumable catastrophe or absolute decline in welfare. It might mean that our positive growth is a bit less than it would otherwise have been if China had remained stagnant. (And don't forget that if π_3^* growth exceeds π_1^*, the net impact on us could be favorable.)

2. The $(\pi_3^*/\pi_2^*)(\pi_2/\pi_1)$ formula, remember, holds only so long as good 2 is producible in both places. If *Chi* begins to be competitive in *Am*'s π_1 goods, *Am*'s harm is all the greater.

3. If *Am* is a great continental economy, enjoying *relatively* little consumers' surplus from all its trade, it stands to lose relatively little from dynamic changes in comparative advantage. Paul Krugman has done useful service in reminding us of these quantitative realities.

4. A labor-only model was good enough for 1817 or 1927 but not good enough for post-1930 economists. Heckscher-Ohlin effects, whereby *Chi*'s

enhanced prosperity makes her newly compete to use up renewable and exhaustible natural resources that we previously exploited, would enhance any presumable harm to the First World.

5. To the degree that Young-Chamberlin-Krugman-Helpman-Gomory-Baumol *increasing returns to scale* phenomenon is important, the analysis becomes more complicated. As Adam Smith noticed, all the world could benefit from extension of the market. On the other hand, Japan, we, and any others who have enjoyed a historic jump on the competition in producing on a large scale what might be producible at that scale anywhere—such as these might be hurt by a new formidable rival.

Fulfillment

There was an age before the Age of Bhagwati. And there will be an age after Bhagwati. That is science's way. And it is that way that gives us scholars the only immortality possible. Our brain children live forever. They live on not only in the seminars of our own pupils and their pupils. The house of science is itself a cumulative mansion. We in each generation add our embodied bricks in the corpus that is growing knowledge.

Birthdays serve to punctuate what is a continuous trend. On this happy occasion Jagdish Bhagwati can take pride and pleasure in his lifetime of contributing to the art and science of economics. We, his friends, pupils, and admirers, take pleasure in his pleasure.

3 Domestic Distortions and the Deindustrialization Hypothesis

Paul Krugman

The theory of international trade and trade policy in the presence of distorted markets has had a paradoxical history. Market failures such as wage differentials between sectors and external economies were first emphasized by developing-country economists advocating protectionist policies. But when Jagdish Bhagwati formalized the analysis of distortions and welfare in terms of second-best theory—a formalization that was one of the major achievements not only of his career but of international economics as a whole—his analysis actually ended up serving primarily as an argument *against* protection.

The reason was that as Bhagwati and Ramaswami (1963) showed (and as Johnson 1965 and Bhagwati 1971 were to reemphasize), protectionism is never the first-best policy response to a domestic distortion such as wage differentials. Instead, the appropriate policy is always a surgical strike on the source of the distortion. For example, suppose that manufacturing pays higher wages than agriculture. Then a tariff on manufactured goods may be better than complete laissez-faire, but such a tariff is too blunt a tool to fix the problem without damaging side effects. That is, while a wage differential leads to a less than optimal level of employment in the manufacturing sector, and a tariff on manufactured goods can induce labor to move back into the sector, the tariff will at the same time introduce new distortions, both in the allocation of productive factors other than labor and in consumption. The right policy is therefore to eliminate the wage differential if possible, to adopt a labor market tax-cum-subsidy scheme if not. If, as is usually the case, objections are raised to such a scheme—it is too costly, and it involves subsidizing the wages of the very workers who are already the best paid—the answer is that a protectionist solution is even more expensive and has distributional consequences just as undesirable, with the only difference being that these adverse effects are less visible to the voters.

Today the domestic distortions argument for protection is rarely heard in developing countries, many of which have indeed turned with remarkable enthusiasm to liberal trade policies. Yet the analysis has acquired a new source of relevance: Many of the arguments made by economists who are concerned about the "competitiveness" of advanced nations are (though their proponents rarely are aware of it) domestic distortion arguments very similar to those analyzed by Jagdish Bhagwati and his followers in the 1960s and 1970s.

In this chapter I want to focus on one of these arguments—the claim of many American pundits that the loss of high-paying manufacturing jobs to import competition is a major source of our economic difficulties. I will argue that in this case, as in the case of the domestic distortions arguments confronted by Jagdish Bhagwati and others in the 1960s, a serious analysis of the argument—an analysis that grants that markets are indeed imperfect but that attempts to use economic theory to derive the policy implications of market failure, rather than taking the imperfection of markets as a license to abandon systematic analysis altogether—does not support these pundits' view.[1]

There will be some differences between the approach taken here and that in the classic Bhagwati papers on the subject. In particular, he and his colleagues were largely concerned with *normative* analysis based on *qualitative* arguments. That is, they tried to show that on logical grounds protectionism was the wrong policy. In the current "competitiveness" debate—which takes place in an intellectual environment in which economists are constantly attacked for disregarding reality—I have found it essential to offer a *positive* analysis based on *quantitative* arguments. In other words, it turns out to be very useful to be able to offer calculations that show that the emperor of competitiveness is wearing no clothes, or at least not enough clothes to cover the places that matter.

This chapter, then, is in six sections. Section 3.1 is a brief review of the emergence of the doctrine of "deindustrialization," a doctrine that has largely bypassed the professional economics journals but has had a deep impact on the thinking of policy intellectuals. Section 3.2 offers a simple model that attempts to use a domestic distortions framework to formalize the concerns expressed by those who believe that deindustrialization is a problem. Section 3.3 then shows how that model—a model that in principle justifies the concerns of the "deindustrializers"—can be used to produce an estimate of the actual importance of these concerns and that, as a practical matter, such concerns are of quite small importance. Section 3.4 discusses several objections that have been raised when I and others have offered similar calculations. Section 3.5 reviews some qualifications to the model, which suggest that if anything a more realistic analysis would find that the true importance of deindustrialization is even smaller than this chapter's estimates. Finally, I offer some concluding remarks.

3.1   The Deindustrialization Hypothesis

Those who listened to President-elect Clinton during the "economic summit" he held in Little Rock during December 1992, and who focused on what we might call his implicit model of the U.S. economy rather than on his impressive command of facts, noticed that he consistently returned to one theme: the loss of manufacturing jobs to international competition. Indeed Clinton went so far as to propose a numerical target, suggesting that we should try to find a way to get the share of manufacturing in total employment from its then 17 percent back up to at least 20 percent. The reason Clinton returned again and again to this theme was that he believed it to be a settled fact that the loss of the high-paying jobs that manufacturing used to offer was a major reason for American economic difficulties.

It was not surprising that Clinton should have held such a view. Concern about deindustrialization among liberal (and some conservative) intellectuals dates back to the late 1970s, when a number of observers, especially Bennett Harrison, Barry Bluestone, and Robert Kuttner began warning that America's industrial base was eroding. Bluestone and Harrison's 1982 book *The Deindustrialization of America* struck a responsive chord with many liberals, with its argument that the loss of high-paying manufacturing jobs was eliminating the American middle class.

Let me call this view—more specifically, the view that the loss of high-wage manufacturing jobs *due to foreign trade* (as opposed to purely domestic shifts in demand or technology) has been a major cause of stagnating or declining incomes among American workers—the *deindustrialization hypothesis*.

Few economists with mainstream credentials have taken the deindustrialization hypothesis seriously. Those few who worried about the issue at all before the early 1980s immediately noticed that the U.S. trade balance in manufactures had remained in rough balance from 1970 to 1980, suggesting that while growing import penetration might have eliminated some manufacturing jobs, growing exports must have had a more or less offsetting job creation effect—in other words, the declining share of manufacturing in employment had little to do with international trade. Robert Lawrence (1983) carried out an elaborate input-output analysis and reached the conclusion that there had been essentially no net effect of trade on the level of manufacturing employment during the 1970s. And although the United States began to run large manufacturing trade deficits during the 1980s, most economists associated these deficits with the Reagan-era combination of budget deficits and tight money, rather than viewing them as a structural issue.

The proponents of the deindustrialization hypothesis, however, essentially ignored the professional economists. Instead they continued to propound their views in influential books such as Cohen and Zysman's 1987 *Manufacturing Matters*, articles by Robert Kuttner, Lester Thurow, and others in such magazines as *The Atlantic, The New Republic* and *The New York Review of Books*, and documents such as the 1998 Cuomo Commission report. These views achieved very wide acceptance. Indeed it would be misleading to say that by the time of Clinton's election, liberal intellectuals had come to discount the objections of economists to the deindustrialization hypothesis. Rather, for the most part they were unaware that there *were* any objections. The image of former steelworkers earning minimum wage flipping hamburgers had become part of what everyone knew to be true. Of course the loss of high-wage jobs in manufacturing was one of the biggest problems facing the American economy; the only question was what to do about it.

It is interesting to ask how an intellectual consensus could emerge about an economic issue with essentially no support from professional economic research; it is also interesting to ask why only a handful of economists made any effort to argue in public forums with this consensus, and were ineffective when they did. But in this chapter I want to focus on the substantive economics of the deindustrialization hypothesis.

The key point to notice is that while its proponents did not and do not put it this way, the deindustrialization hypothesis is essentially a second-best argument based on domestic distortions. Manufacturing, the proponents of this hypothesis believe, is where the high-wage jobs are—that is, for some reason there is a wage differential between manufacturing and other sectors. And growing international trade leads to the loss of many of these jobs—that is, something that would be a good thing in an undistorted economy (increased opportunities for trade) turns out to be a bad thing because of that preexisting domestic distortion. This is a classic second-best argument, the same in logical structure as the arguments that customs unions can cause harmful trade diversion or that growth can be immiserizing.

The standard answer to this argument, the one that Bhagwati taught us, is that even if you believe this story the appropriate response does not involve trade policy. That is, we should not follow Kuttner's advice to impose MFA-type managed trade on all manufactured goods. Instead we should attack the domestic distortion at its source: Eliminate the wage differential between manufacturing and other sectors, or subsidize high-wage employment.

This answer is certainly correct. It is also a complete non-starter in real-world discussions, where the general belief is that economists know nothing about reality and that their a priori arguments are of no practical importance. Thus it is important to supplement Bhagwati's answer with a different kind of answer: one that puts the shoe on the other foot and shows that, on the contrary, it is the deindustrialization hypothesis that is of hardly any practical importance.

3.2 Modeling the Deindustrialization Hypothesis

To be useful, a model of trade in the presence of domestic distortions (or of anything else) must involve strategic simplifications. Even if one is willing to specify the nature of the distortion, there are other crucial aspects of the model that must be decided on the basis of some mixture of evidence, intuition, and analytical convenience. In particular, the literature on domestic distortions suggests three important dimensions along which modeling choices must be made.

First, what is the production structure of the model? Should it be Ricardian, Heckscher-Ohlin, specific factors, or something more elaborate?

Second, how should trade be modeled? Should we think of the model economy as a small country facing world prices, or should it be regarded as a large country whose "rest-of-world" presents it with a nonlinear offer curve?

Third, how should we model the shock that the economy faces? In the context of the deindustrialization hypothesis, this amounts to the question of what we think of as the driving force behind the emergence of a U.S. trade deficit in manufactures.

In this chapter I will make a particular set of strategic simplifications that seems to me to offer the clearest way to make sense of the

deindustrialization hypothesis, and that has the major additional virtue of
allowing easy quantification. I will try to examine how different assumptions would affect the conclusions in sections 3.4 and 3.5, but meanwhile
here is the assumed structure of the model.

First, the production structure is the simplest possible: a Ricardian
framework in which one factor, labor, can be used to produce two goods,
Manufactures and Services.

How can such a radical simplification be justified? For one thing, nothing about the deindustrialization hypothesis as described seems to involve
capital or other factors in any essential way—the important thing is
high-wage versus low-wage jobs for workers of equivalent skill. It is of
course nonetheless possible for a one-factor model to give misleading
estimates about the effects of trade on the sectoral composition of employment because the model rules out, by assumption, changes in relative
goods and factor prices that might be important in practice. As a numerical matter, however, the production possibility frontiers implied by two-
or three-factor models with any reasonable elasticity of substitution are
quite flat, so trade flows of the magnitude discussed below would have
only minor impacts on relative factor and good prices; some preliminary
experiments I have conducted with semirealistic CGE models suggest that
the Ricardian model is a pretty good approximation for these purposes.
By using a one-factor model, of course, we miss the possibility of changes
in the distribution of income between factors, and by using a two-good
model, we exclude the possibility of saying anything useful about the fact
that the United States exports as well as imports manufactures. I will
return to both issues in sections 3.4 and 3.5.

With regard to the modeling of trade, I will not assume that the model
economy is a price-taker. Instead it faces a rest-of-world offer curve. This
assumption may be justified simply by noting that the United States is
indeed a large economy. There is also, however, a crucial issue of modeling
convenience. If one wants to avoid corner solutions—and as we will see,
the reality of U.S. trade experience is very much *not* a corner solution—
then one must either build decreasing returns into the production structure or get the necessary decreasing returns out of the foreign offer curve.
(On this, see Brecher 1974). So, if the technology is Ricardian, it is a great
help to adopt a large-country approach to trade.

Finally, how should we model the shock that is supposed to cause
deindustrialization? Most people, including professional economists, would

grant that over the past generation there has been a process of "globalization" of the U.S. economy, whose measurable impact is a sharp rise in the share of both exports and imports in GDP. Surprisingly, however, it is quite hard to be explicit about the sources of this increased trade share. A country might be induced to engage in more international trade if given an incentive to do so—that is, if its terms of trade improve—but U.S. terms of trade, at least as measured, have if anything deteriorated slightly over the past generation. Or there could be a fall in transport costs, which would raise the ratio of f.o.b. to c.i.f. prices—but while there has indeed been a decline in transport costs for goods, even a generation ago these costs were so low that their continuing decline could not explain the rapid growth in trade. The same is true of trade liberalization, which has reduced tariffs, but from an initial level that was fairly low by historical standards.

What, then, is the nature of globalization? The best available answer would be that it involves the reduction of invisible transaction costs in international trade, a reduction that is presumably due to improvements in communication and information processing—that is, we invoke the magic of silicon to explain trade trends. And how should this be modeled? The easiest way is simply to imagine that some goods and services that were previously nontradable become tradable.

In the context of a two-sector model, this boils down to starting with a situation in which the United States is in autarky, and then opening up the possibility of trading services for manufactures; the result is then a trade deficit in manufactures, which implies a contraction of manufacturing employment.

The objections to this description are obvious. First of all the United States is an exporter as well as an importer of manufactured goods—and manufactures exports have grown almost as rapidly as imports. Second, for the most part the emerging deficit in manufactures has not had service exports as a counterpart but rather has been reflected in a current account deficit.

The first of these objections is essentially an objection to a two-sector model; I will try to discuss the ways in which the results might change if manufactures were disaggregated in sections 3.4 and 3.5. The second objection amounts to saying that we cannot deal with the issue of deindustrialization except in terms of an intertemporal model. Indeed, the advocates of the deindustrialization hypothesis are notably unconcerned about the implications of intertemporal budget constraints, and they sometimes seem to imagine that the United States can run trade deficits forever. It is therefore a charitable gesture to represent their views by imagining that the country exports *something* to pay for its imports of manufactures. As an empirical matter, we may play somewhat dirty and argue that there are substantial unrecorded U.S. service exports, or we may claim that "services" are a proxy for export of IOUs, to be repaid at a later date with a future trade surplus in manufactures. This raises some obvious questions about the interpretation of what must then be a transitory deindustrialization, but let us postpone that discussion until later sections of the chapter as well.

Finally, then, we are prepared to lay out the model, which after all that will be very simple. We imagine a two-sector economy in which one factor, labor, may produce either Manufactures or Services under constant returns to scale. For some reason, say, the existence of unions, workers in Manufactures must be paid a higher wage than those in Services; let the ratio of the Manufactures to the Services wage be $w > 1$. We consider an initial equilibrium in which no trade is allowed, and a subsequent equilibrium in which Services may be traded for Manufactures, with the rest of the world represented by an offer curve.

Figure 3.1 shows the pre- and post-trade equilibria. The line *PF* shows the economy's production possibility frontier. In a one-factor model the wage differential will not put the economy inside that frontier, but it will distort the prices consumers face: The autarky relative price of Manufactures will be w times the opportunity cost of Manufactures in terms of Services. Thus the autarky equilibrium will be at a point such as A, with *BB* the perceived budget line.

Now we allow trade with a rest of world, whose import demand/export supply is represented by the offer curve *QR*. As long as the country remains nonspecialized, the relative price of Manufactures must be the same after as before trade (which also implies, incidentally, that even an undistorted economy would not gain from trade—in other words, this model is biased toward producing losses). But the possibility of Manufactures imports leads to a decline in Manufactures production; the production point shifts to Q. Consumption C must be on the new budget line $B'B'$, and the implied trade vector QC must be a point on the rest-of-world

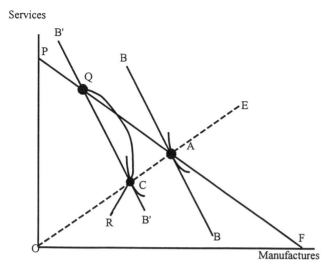

Figure 3.1
Pre- and post-trade equilibrium

offer curve. (One can think of finding the new equilibrium by sliding Q *northwest along PF* until C lies on the consumption expansion path OE that passes through A.)

It is immediately apparent that welfare is reduced. The opening of trade, which should make the country better off or at least no worse off, instead leads to a decline in income because it pushes workers out of the high-wage manufacturing sector into the low-wage service sector. The interaction of trade with the preexisting domestic distortion leads to losses.

Figure 3.1, then, offers what appears to be a rationale for the deindustrialization hypothesis. But it is one thing to show that something can happen in principle; it is something quite different to show that it is an important effect in practice. *How large* is the negative impact of trade implied in figure 3.1?

3.3   The (Un)Importance of Deindustrialization

To assess the welfare loss from deindustrialization, it is useful to define two functions that are implied by the utility function. First, let us define the indirect utility function,

$$U = N(y, p), \tag{3.1}$$

where y is income in terms of Services and p is the relative price of Manufactures. Second, let us write an expression for expenditure on Manufactures (measured in terms of Services),

$$E_M = E(y, p). \tag{3.2}$$

We may also note that income y arises entirely from wage earnings. Let L be total employment, L_M and L_S employment in the two sectors, and choose units so that one unit of labor produces one unit of Services. Then we have

$$y = L_S + wL_M$$
$$= L + (w - 1)L_M. \tag{3.3}$$

Finally, note that income earned in Manfactures is total expenditure on Manufactures, less spending on Manufactures imports:

$$wL_M = E(y, p) - E_{IM}. \tag{3.4}$$

In the situation depicted in Figure 3.1, what happens when we move from A to C? Given the assumptions, there is no change in the relative price p; all that happens is that the budget line shifts in, a reduction in y. The driving force behind this change in y is the diversion of some demand for Manufactures to imports, that is, a rise in E_{IM}. So all we need to do is analyze the effects of a rise in E_{IM}.

It is easiest (though not essential) to do this by considering a small change, so we can use calculus. From (3.2), (3.3), and (3.4), we easily find that

$$\frac{dy}{dE_{IM}} = -\frac{w - 1}{w - \mu(w - 1)}, \tag{3.5}$$

where μ is the marginal propensity to spend on manufactures. The welfare effect is then

$$\frac{dU}{dE_{IM}} = -\frac{\partial N}{\partial y}\left(\frac{w - 1}{w - \mu(w - 1)}\right). \tag{3.6}$$

And that's it: The term in brackets in equation (3.6) is the compensating variation for the welfare loss from one dollar of expenditure on imports (which in the context of this model should be interpreted as one dollar of Manufactures trade deficit).

To estimate the quantitative importance of the actual deindustrialization, we then need only three numbers. First, we need a value for w. Proponents of the deindustrialization hypothesis, such as Lester Thurow, often use the figure of 30 percent for the wage premium in manufacturing. This is actually the difference in weekly earnings between manufacturing and nonmanufacturing workers and may well be an exaggeration of the true premium, as discussed in section 3.5, but let us accept it for now.

Second, we need the trade-induced fall in expenditure on manufactured goods E_{IM}, which we will tentatively identify with the trade deficit in such goods. In the 1990s to date the U.S. trade deficit in manufactured goods has averaged about 1.5 percent of GDP; let us use this as a baseline, with the understanding that it is very easy to scale the calculation up or down if you regard the structural deficit as smaller or larger.

Finally, we need the marginal propensity to spend on manufactured goods. Manufactures account for about 18 percent of U.S. value-added; together with a trade deficit of 1.5 percent, this gives an average propensity to spend of about 0.2. Lacking any particular reason to suppose that the marginal is very different from the average, we may therefore assign a value of $\mu = 0.2$.

Substituting $w = 1.3$, $E_{IM} = 1.5$, and $\mu = 0.2$ into (3.6), we arrive at an estimate of the real income loss due to the trade-induced loss of high-wage manufacturing jobs: 0.363 percent.

To put this estimate in context, consider what the proponents of the deindustrialization hypothesis believe that it explains. Depending on the particular measure used, ordinary workers in the United States experienced something between stagnation and a 15 percent fall in their wages between 1973 and 1993, compared with a 60 percent rise over the previous twenty years. The deindustrialization hypothesis assigns *primary* responsibility for that deterioration in performance to the loss of high-wage jobs to imports. Instead our estimate finds that the negative impact of trade is well under half of 1 percent—not one but two orders of magnitude too small to bear the weight being placed on it.

3.4   Critiques of the Estimates

When back-of-the-envelope estimates similar in spirit to the one reported in the previous section were published in Krugman (1994) and Krugman and Lawrence (1994), they immediately drew critical reaction from proponents of the deindustrialization hypothesis. The tone of these reactions might perhaps best be described as ranging from rage to blind fury. What were the nature of these criticisms?

Some of the critiques are not worth discussing at length. Thurow (1994) argued, in effect, that both E_{IM} and w were much larger than I (or he in his own earlier writings) had supposed. His large value of E_{IM} seems, however, to have been based on a simple and puzzling misreading of U.S. trade statistics, while his new, higher value of w was based on the wage loss experienced by individual workers losing their jobs—an obviously flawed procedure because fired workers would suffer losses even in an undistorted economy. Prestowitz (1994) argued that there are multiplier effects to the loss of good manufacturing jobs. While there is indeed a small multiplier effect implied by (3.6) (the decline in income due to loss of manufacturing jobs leads to a decline in demand for manufactures, which further reduces income, and so on—a sequence captured by the negative second term in the denominator), the mechanism he described seemed to involve nothing more than naive double-counting.

A more serious criticism, raised, for example, in a vitriolic letter circulated but never published by Charles McMillion, a senior editor at the *Harvard Business Review*, was that to the wages lost because workers are displaced from high-wage jobs we must add the depressing effect on the wages of the workers that remain. In effect, this is an argument that says that w is not constant and that it has been forced down by international competition.

It is easy to produce at least anecdotal evidence for a decline in w, perhaps tied to international trade; certainly during the 1980s many large firms sought "givebacks" from their workers, or began outsourcing large parts of their business to nonunion workers in smaller companies. It therefore seems extremely plausible to argue that the real costs of international trade have come from wage compression rather than the actual displacement of high-wage workers.

There is only one problem: While intuition may suggest that displacing high-wage workers and compressing their wages are similar in their economic effects, once one realizes that we are talking about a second-best problem we see that the parallel, however seductive, is misleading. If trade leads to less high-wage employment, it is in effect playing into and aggravating the effects of a distortion. If, on the other hand, trade drives down manufacturing wages, it is in effect *reducing* the distortion, and this *raises* real income for the nation as a whole (although not for the high-wage workers themselves).

This result is easiest to see if we consider the effects of a reduction in w in an autarkic economy—the situation illustrated by point A in figure 3.1. A reduction in w in such an economy will lower the relative price of manufactures and lead to a shift in the equilibrium southeast along the production possibility frontier; this unambiguously raises welfare. Indeed, if w is reduced to 1, the full optimum A' is achieved.

A reduction in w when the economy is already running a trade deficit in manufactures is slightly more complicated, but it is in fact even more favorable to real income. First, consider the effect on the economy's international trade. As long as the economy continues to produce both goods, relative prices will be tied down by w and relative labor requirements, and given these relative prices, trade flows will be determined by the rest-of-world offer curve. It is apparent on reflection that reducing w will mean that the trade vector QC is replaced by a new trade vector, $Q'C'$, which is both flatter and shorter, as shown in figure 3.2.

The economy's consumption pattern will also change: With a lower relative price of manufactures, it will consume more manufactures at any given level of utility. In figure 3.2 the consumption expansion path OE which passes through the original consumption point C is replaced by another, flatter path, OE'. The new equilibrium may be found by sliding Q' along the production possibility frontier until C' lies on OE'.

It is immediately apparent that welfare is higher at the new equilibrium. The gain occurs for two reasons: Not only is the wage distortion reduced, but there is also a terms of trade gain. Thus to the extent that import competition drives down manufacturing wages, the adverse impact of deindustrialization on welfare is actually diminished.

Admittedly, there will be distribution effects. In this model a fall in w raises the real wages of those workers who would not otherwise hold high-wage jobs, but it obviously reduces the real wages of those workers who would have held such jobs in any case; in principle the winners could compensate the losers, but as usual it is unrealistic to suppose that this

Services

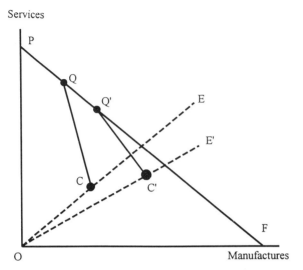

Figure 3.2
Reduction in wage distortion

happens in real life. We might make the point, however, that in the model the change in income distribution is actually equalizing—that is, it is the "labor aristocracy" that is hurt, while the less lucky workers gain.

Of course in the real economy there has been a substantial increase in inequality among workers, with in particular a rise in the premium associated with college education. (There has, on the other hand, been absolutely no change in the distribution of income between capital and labor.) There is a serious debate about how much of this increase in the education premium is due to globalization. The important point for this chapter is that this distributional issue is very different from the deindustrialization hypothesis, which focuses on the loss of high-wage jobs and not the ever-lower pay of low-wage jobs.

3.5 Qualifications on the Other Side

While many people are shocked if not outraged at an estimate that suggests that deindustrialization has lowered U.S. real income by no more than a few tenths of 1 percent, as a practical matter it may be argued that even this estimate is too high.

First, the true manufacturing wage premium is probably less than 30 percent. The 30 percent number is based on weekly earnings, whereas the high weekly earnings in manufacturing are primarily due to a longer work week than in services. If this difference reflects voluntary choice—for example, because the service sector contains more secondary earners—then it is the hourly rather than the weekly wage differential that should be used. It is also likely that *tradable* services such as insurance pay higher wages than the nontradable services that make up the bulk of the average. Overall, one can easily make a case that the true wage differential is half or less of the often-repeated 30 percent estimate.

Second, trade deficits in manufactured goods do not reduce value added in manufactures one for one, since not every dollar of manufactures sales is a dollar of value added. In Krugman and Lawrence (1994) we estimate that the reduction in manufacturing value added due to trade is in fact only 60 percent of the trade deficit. Thus the value of E_{IM} should be thought of as more like 0.9 than 1.5 percent of GDP.[2]

Third, to the extent that manufacturing trade deficits are matched not by exports of services but by capital inflows, they imply a future in which the United States will run manufactures trade surpluses—that is, a future of "reindustrialization" in which trade will presumably lead to a *larger* number of manufacturing jobs than would exist in its absence.

These considerations suggest that section 3.3's estimate of the income lost by displacement from high-wage jobs is, if anything, much too high. A better number might be 0.1 percent or less.

3.6 Conclusions

Critics of the economics profession, such as Robert Kuttner (1991), often seem to say that economists are so wedded to the assumption of perfect markets that they never think about the possible implications of market failure. They seem to believe that if there is any plausible case for the existence of a market failure, economic analysis places no constraints on the range of possible conclusions. In particular, if there is a theory that suggests that international trade *could* produce losses instead of gains, then one is free to indulge one's gut feeling that in fact expanded trade is a terrible thing, with devastating effects on the economy.

The reality, however, is that economists have thought long and hard about the consequences and policy implications of market failure—in the general theory of the second best, and especially in the theory of trade policy in the presence of domestic distortions. And that analysis does not say that anything goes: It places crucial limitations on the range of speculation, by forcing one to be specific about the mechanism through which distortions and trade interact. The existence of a theoretical possibility does not give the commentator a license to believe whatever he likes: Effects that are possible in principle may also be, fairly certainly, unimportant in practice.

In this chapter I have pointed out that a widely accepted view about the sources of American economic difficulties, the "deindustrialization hypothesis," is in fact a second-best, domestic distortions argument. Once one recognizes this, it is possible not only to think about the hypothesis clearly but to quantify its importance. And it turns out that even on favorable assumptions the deindustrialization hypothesis cannot bear more than a tiny fraction of the explanatory weight its proponents place on it.

Aside from the practical importance of this issue, the analysis in this chapter is a reminder of the enduring usefulness of great ideas in economics. When Jagdish Bhagwati developed his beautiful analysis of distortions and trade policy, the world was a very different place: Poor countries were poor, rich countries were rich, and the idea that the United States would fear deindustrialization would have seemed strange indeed. The insights and tools he introduced have proved to be more relevant now than ever before.

Notes

1. There is a quite different issue that is often confused with the deindustrialization argument: the claim that international trade leads to the loss of *low*-wage manufacturing jobs, with adverse consequences for the distribution of income. Most recent efforts to quantify this impact have suggested that it is real but limited in size; in any case that is not the issue in this chapter.

2. There is a possible counterargument, one that cannot be dealt with formally in a two-sector model. Suppose that the United States exports goods with substantially higher value added per worker than the goods it imports; this might be the case if the export goods are either physical- or (more likely) human-capital-intensive. Then even balanced trade might have a net negative impact on manufacturing employment. This seems to be what Sachs and Schatz (1994) had in mind in their insistence on carrying out an elaborate input-output analysis of the effects of trade on manufacturing employment. In the end, however, their results were very close to the back-of-the-envelope calculations in Krugman and Lawrence (1994).

References

Bhagwati, J. 1971. The generalized theory of distortions and welfare. In J. Bhagwati et al., eds., *Trade, Balance of Payments, and Growth: Papers in International Economics in Honor of Charles P. Kindleberger*. Amsterdam: North Holland.

Bhagwati, J., and Ramaswami, V. K. 1963. Domestic distortions, tariffs, and the theory of optimum subsidy. *Journal of Political Economy* 71 (February).

Bluestone, B., and Harrison, B. 1982. *The Deindustrialization of America*. New York: Basic Books.

Brecher, R. 1974. Optimal commercial policy for a minimum-wage economy. *Journal of International Economics* 4:139–49.

Cohen, S., and J. Zysman. 1987. *Manufacturing Matters*. New York: Basic Books.

Cuomo Commission on Trade and Competitiveness. 1988. *The Cuomo Commission Report*. New York: Simon and Schuster.

Johnson, H. G. 1965. Optimal trade intervention in the presence of domestic distortions. In R. Caves et al., eds., *Trade, Growth, and the Balance of Payments*. New York: Rand McNally.

Krugman, P. 1994. Competitiveness: a dangerous obsession. *Foreign Affairs* 73:28–44.

Krugman, P., and Lawrence, R. 1994. Trade, jobs, and wages. *Scientific American* (April).

Kuttner, R. 1991. *The End of Laissez-Faire*. New York: Basic Books.

Lawrence, R. 1983. *Can America Compete?* Washington: Brookings.

Prestowitz, C. 1994. Playing to win. *Foreign Affairs* 73:186–89.

Sachs, J., and Shatz, H. 1994. Trade and jobs in US manufacturing. *Brookings Papers on Economic Activity* 1.

Thurow, L. 1994. Microchips, not potato chips. *Foreign Affairs* 73:189–92.

II TRADE AND INCOME DISTRIBUTION

4 Industry or Class Cleavages over Trade Policy? Evidence from the British General Election of 1923

Douglas A. Irwin

4.1 Introduction

The Stolper-Samuelson relationship between output prices and factor rewards is central to any discussion of the political economy of trade policy. This relationship describes the economic stakes faced by the various factors of production that will ultimately interact in the political arena in the actual determination of policy.

These factors will have different economic interests—and therefore will be aligned in different political coalitions—depending upon the configuration of factor intensity, substitutability, and specificity across sectors. If factors are perfectly mobile across sectors, as assumed in the Heckscher-Ohlin model, for example. economic interests differ between factors of production (e.g., labor and capital) regardless of their industry of current employment. If factors are imperfectly mobile across sectors, then economic interests will be organized along industry lines with different factors of production (e.g., labor and capital in the steel industry) seeking the same policy.

Economists and political scientists have tried to assess whether trade-related political behavior takes place more along sectoral (industry) lines or along factor (class) lines. Magee (1978) examined testimony before the House Ways and Means Committee on the Trade Reform Act of 1973 and found that in 19 of 21 industries, trade unions (representing labor) took the same position as management and trade associations (representing the owners of capital). Rogowski (1989), by contrast, argues that political alignments in various countries over the last century can be best interpreted through the mobile factor Heckscher-Ohlin framework, although he performs no explicit test of this view.[1]

This chapter provides some additional evidence on such political "cleavages" in the context of a simple institutional mechanism for observing economic interests: a direct election. The British general election of 1923, an election that hinged on the issue of free trade and protection, provides a revelation mechanism such that the economic interests of the electorate can potentially be determined from cross-sectional voting patterns. Because the costs of voting are low, elections can increase the participation of free-trade segments of the electorate that, owing to the free-rider problem, are commonly thought to be underrepresented in the political process. Thus elections provide a setting relatively free from the complications of political structure, where, for example, the power of interest group lobbying and the ability of coalitions to organize can be decisive, and thereby provide a sharper view of the underlying economic interests of the electorate than would otherwise be the case.[2]

Furthermore this particular election provides a reasonably fair opportunity to distinguish between the two hypotheses because either an industry or a factor alignment among voters is a plausible source of the election outcome. The institutional rigidities of the British interwar labor market often discussed by economic historians, such as Thomas (1992), suggest imperfect intersectoral mobility that would define economic interests in terms of industry of employment. Alternatively, Pulzer's (1967, 98) widely quoted claim—"class is the basis of British party politics; all else is embellishment and detail"—is generally accepted by political scientists as describing elections prior to World War II and points to electoral divisions among unskilled labor, skilled labor, and the upper classes.

This chapter addresses this question by exploiting data from the British census of 1921, which divides the population into categories of occupation (by industry) and categories of economic class (by income and/or skill level). These data are then related to cross-county variation in voting for the contending political parties to determine which set of characteristics best describes the election outcome. The results indicate that county differences in the occupational structure of the electorate account for the election outcome far better than differences in class structure.

I hope the selection of this topic needs little motivation for Jagdish Bhagwati or admirers of his delightful book *Protectionism* (1988), which in analyzing current trade policy issues is also richly informed by the British experience of the past century and a half. Despite voting in the midst of a deep economic slump, the electorate reaffirmed its support for free trade in the 1923 election. This outcome preserved, for nearly a decade more, free trade as the principal basis of Britain's commercial policy, a policy that was introduced by parliament in 1846 with the repeal of the Corn Laws (as Bhagwati discusses in *Protectionism*) and was withdrawn by parliament in 1932 with the passage of the Import Duties bill.

Section 4.2 presents some historical background on the general election of 1923. Section 4.3 provides econometric evidence on how voting patterns in England relate to the employment or class characteristics of constituents in a given county. Section 4.4 summarizes the results and speculates about their implications for our understanding of the political economy of trade policy.

4.2 Historical Background

During the half century of prosperity that followed the repeal of the Corn Laws in 1846, Free Trade (as it was often spelled) was taken as an article of faith in British politics. Britain's manufacturing superiority ensured that sizable export industries lent the policy their unquestioned support. The consumer and labor interest in cheap food provided an even broader base of popular backing. Indeed, for the second half of the nineteenth century, free trade was essentially a closed political question. Although support for the policy wavered slightly during the 1880s, a period of economic instability and growing import competition due to foreign industrialization, proposals for tariff reform (e.g., reciprocity) failed to make any serious impression until the turn of the century.[3]

The few opponents of free trade—an eclectic group of protectionists, imperialists, and landed aristocrats—found their home in the Conservative party, the traditional supporters of agricultural protection. Because these opponents had quite different interests, however, the meaning of "tariff reform" as advocated by the Conservatives was never entirely clear: Protectionists wanted higher tariffs for bargaining purposes or to halt import penetration, imperialists wanted higher tariffs to create preferences to unite the empire, and the aristocracy wanted higher tariffs on agricultural goods to preserve their position in society. All that one could really conclude is that tariff reformers rejected "free trade dogma" and wanted to introduce a higher tariff in some form or another.

By the turn of the century, these varied groups within the Conservative party grew in strength as foreign competition intensified and imperial sentiments deepened. This enabled them to seize opportunities to bring their proposals to the top of the political agenda. In three elections in the first quarter of the twentieth century—1906, 1910, and 1923—the Conservatives sought electoral support under the banner of "tariff reform." Each time they failed. In 1903 the Conservative party split over Joseph Chamberlain's scheme of tariffs on food imports to create imperial preferences and tariffs on manufactured imports to protect domestic producers.

Conservatives fought the 1906 general election on Chamberlain's platform but were crushed by the reinvigorated Liberal party, long-time supporters of free trade, as analyzed in Irwin (1994). In January 1910, in an election campaign dominated by the controversy over the powers of the House of Lords, the Conservatives again rallied around the cause of tariff reform. They met electoral defeat once again, though by a lesser margin than in 1906.

The situation was somewhat different in 1923. In the years after World War I, the central problem in Britain was unemployment. The jobless rate jumped from under 5 percent in 1920 to over 15 percent in 1922, substantially above what it had been during the pre-war era. The underlying cause of the severe downturn was the reversal of the brief, inflationary boom that immediately followed the war. Unemployment soared as declines in money wages could not keep pace with falling prices. The political parties lacked any compelling proposals to deal with the situation, and hence the Conservatives turned once again to import protection.

This turn was facilitated by the experience with widespread controls and regulations on foreign trade that had been introduced during the war. The postwar coalition government retained some of these protectionist measures, such as the Safeguarding of Industries Act of 1921, although Capie (1983) finds that these tariffs affected rather few goods and were relatively minor in impact. After the collapse of Lloyd George's coalition in 1922 prompted a general election, the Conservatives (under Andrew Bonar Law) captured a majority of seats in the House of Commons. Bonar Law had pledged during the campaign not to engage in tariff reform, but poor health forced his replacement as prime minister by Stanley Baldwin, a tariff reformer, in May 1923. Baldwin felt bound by Bonar Law's pledge during the life of the current parliament.

But as the unemployment rate ticked upward again in the third quarter of 1923, Baldwin became convinced that higher tariffs were the cure to Britain's maladies. In October at the Conservatives's annual party conference, Baldwin declared:

Now from what I have said I think that you will realize that to me, at least, this unemployment problem is the most crucial problem of our country. I regard it as such. I can fight it. I am willing to fight it. I cannot fight it without weapons.... And I have come to the conclusion myself that the only way of fighting this subject is by protecting the home market. (Quoted in Snyder 1944, 141)

For this reason Baldwin soon dissolved parliament and sought from the electorate a mandate to pursue tariff revision. Of course there was also a political motivation for this move. Baldwin sought to strengthen his hand by choosing an issue that might unite the Conservatives and split the Liberals.

According to A. J. P. Taylor (1965, 208), the general election of 1923 "was the only election in British history, fought solely and specifically on Protection." Once a radical cause for reformers, free trade had long been the status quo and, in light of contemporary economic conditions, appeared to be a rather tired and outdated symbol of *laissez-faire*. Free trade had lost its special aura in British politics, and departures from it were no longer believed to have grievous economic consequences. The widespread feeling of resignation about adopting protection is nicely captured in a cartoon (reproduced below in figure 4.1) from *Punch* in November 1923, just weeks before the election.

Soon after the Conservatives's conference, Baldwin endorsed three principles: (1) a tariff on imports of foreign manufactured goods, (2) tariff preferences for the commonwealth, and (3) no import duties on wheat or meat. The National Union of Manufactures welcomed Baldwin's proposals and sought to generate public support for a policy of selective protection. According to Snyder (1944, 154), this group maintained that 36,043 jobs would be created among its member firms if Baldwin's proposal to protect the home market was implemented. Several regional chambers of commerce and other industries beset by import competition also lined up behind the Conservatives.

Agriculture was a more sensitive issue. Free traders demolished previous attempts at tariff reforms by stigmatizing any policy with even a remote chance of increasing the price of foodstuffs as the "stomach tax" or the "dear loaf" policy. This played on the fears of the working classes, which found food taxes quite unpalatable. Free-trade Conservatives in Lancashire and Manchester typically found tariff reform proposals hard to swallow for this reason and, recalling previous electoral defeats, were skeptical of Baldwin's enterprise. But Baldwin had specifically avoided pledging tariff protection to agriculture to avoid alienating the labor vote. Yet at the same time Conservatives in agricultural districts were outraged at their neglect and demanded some form of relief.

In his election address to constituents, Baldwin formally outlined his platform. Imposing duties on imported manufactured goods to aid

Figure 4.1
Cartoon from *Punch*

employment in industry, he argued, would at the same time (1) raise revenue to pay for unemployment relief, (2) protect industries afflicted by unfair foreign competition, (3) help reduce foreign tariffs on British exports through negotiations, (4) establish substantial preferences for the commonwealth. "It is not our intention, in any circumstance, to impose any duties on wheat, flour, oats, meat (including bacon and ham), cheese, butter, or eggs," Baldwin stated (Craig 1975, 46).

In an effort to win rural districts, however, agriculture would be assisted with "a direct measure of support" through "a bounty of £1 an acre on all holdings of arable land exceeding one acre." Baldwin explained that "the main object of that bounty is to maintain employment on land and so keep up the wages of agricultural labour." This subsidy would promote landed interests but not increase the price of food and annoy labor as a tariff would.

Tremendous uncertainty remained about the criteria for determining which industrial and agricultural products would benefit from Baldwin's scheme. Baldwin refused to divulge which manufactures would receive protection. Instead he asked a select group of tariff reformers to draw up a "secret tariff." The list of "nonessential" foods, which were never completely identified, could be taxed to help establish preferences for the empire. In one instance, apples were deemed nonessential and could thereby receive protection through tariff preferences, but orchards also counted as arable land and could receive the £1 per acre subsidy. The following election verse (from Hirst 1927, 19) mocks, in Baldwin's voice, some of the confusion surrounding the campaign proposals:

I'm a plain and simple countryman. This tariff bothers me.
I cannot make my meaning clear for other folks to see.
For instance, when a heckler asks—and asking seems to scoff—
'Why put a tax on apples and from cider take it off?'
I'm blessed if I can answer, when I'm out in Worcestershire,
Where people grow the apples and so want them to be dear.

My Bewdley Tariff works all right in Bewdley; but we find
That every other county seems to need a different kind.
Dundonians want free honey, with a tax on marmalades;
Brum would prohibit foreign guns, and Sheffield razor blades.
The politicians prime me; but their primings disagree.
On one side there is Derby, on the other Amery.

I try to keep the whole thing vague; but through the screen of smoke
A swarm of puzzling questions seem to penetrate and poke.
What taxes are protective, and what are preferential?
And what are raw materials, and what are foods essential?
And then at last a poser comes, perplexing and belated:—
'If apples are protected, why are orchards compensated?'
This is 'the mildewed straw' that breaks my patient camel's back.
So send me home to Astley Hall and let me have the sack.
Those die-hards put me in this fix, and made me tariff faker.
Better retire, resume the squire, and earn a pound an acre.

The two main opposition parties, Labour and the Liberals, rejected the turn toward protection, emphatically denying that higher tariffs were a remedy for higher unemployment. According to Labour's election manifesto:

The Labour Party challenges the Tariff policy and the whole conception of economic relations underlying it. Tariffs are not a remedy for Unemployment. [Unemployment is a recurrent feature of the existing economic system, common to every industrialised country, irrespective of whether it has Protection or Free Trade.] They are an impediment to the free interchange of goods and services upon which civilized society rests. They foster a spirit of profiteering, materialism and selfishness, poison the life of nations, lead to corruption in politics, promote trusts and monopolies, and impoverish the people. They perpetuate inequalities in the distribution of the world's wealth won by the labour of hands and brain. These inequalities the Labour Party means to remove. (Craig 1975, 47–48)

The Liberals once again championed their old cause of free trade:

Trade restrictions cannot cure unemployment. Post-war conditions do not justify such restrictions; they merely render it more disastrous. High prices and scarcity can only lower the standard of living, reduce the purchasing power of the country, and thereby curtail production. An examination of the figures shows that the suggested tariff cannot possibly assist those trades in which unemployment is most rife. The last thing which taxation on imports can provide is to provide more work for those engaged in manufacture for export. (Craig 1975, 51)

Despite their similar views on trade policy, Labour and the Liberals fought the election separately because they could not agree on other issues, such as remedies for unemployment and the capital levy. Both, however, argued that import tariffs would not reduce unemployment among those in export industries.[4] They also exploited working class fears by questioning whether the Conservatives could be trusted not to put taxes on food imports.

Table 4.1
Industry position in international trade, 1924 (in millions £)

	Gross output	Exports/ production	Imports/ consumption	Trade balance
Agriculture	779.2	5.7	40.9	−464.5
Mining	274.7	57.9	13.1	78.5
Bricks, etc.	75.7	16.2	10.7	4.8
Chemicals	142.4	18.0	10.3	12.2
Metals	499.4	23.5	11.0	70.5
Electrical	74.5	13.7	3.6	7.8
Scientific instruments	62.3	11.9	11.4	0.3
Machinery	156.2	28.5	7.7	35.2
Leather	54.7	10.5	19.6	−6.1
Textiles	992.5	27.1	9.3	194.3
Wood	82.3	2.3	5.4	−2.7
Paper	170.4	5.1	7.8	−4.8

Sources: *Final Report on the Third Census of Production of the United Kingdom* ([1924] 1930). Customs and Excise Office (1924).

Table 4.1, indicating the international trade position of select industries, provides the first evidence on the possible political economy stances of voters employed in various sectors.[5] Agriculture, leather, wood, paper, and (to a lesser extent) scientific instruments all appear to face the greatest import competition. Thus in the case of agriculture, for example, the possibility of subsidies and perhaps even import duties was certain to reinforce the Conservative capture of votes in those districts. Conversely, export industries such as mining, metals, machinery, and textiles might be thought to show broad support for free trade.

Yet the broad sectoral aggregation of these commodities masks a high degree of import penetration in particular segments of an industry. This evidence should be supplemented with contemporary observations on the political stance of various groups. Many business groups remained large net exporters and were skeptical of Baldwin's proposals. The National Association of Merchants and Manufactures, the National Chamber of Trade, and the Chamber of Shipping among others all opposed Baldwin.

But even export industries that traditionally supported free trade had reconsidered their position in light of growing import competition. Despite its large net export position, the textile industry was no longer a stronghold of free trade sentiment. In the weeks before the election, parts

Table 4.2
General election results, 1922 and 1923 (England only)

	Share of 1922 vote (MPs elected)	Share of 1923 vote (MPs elected)
Conservative	41.5 (336)	39.8 (245)
Liberal	26.9 (80)	29.6 (126)
Labour	28.8 (97)	29.7 (139)
Other	2.8 (9)	0.6 (4)
Total	100.0 (514)	100.0 (522)

Source: Craig (1971, 3–5).

of the industry (woolens, worsteds, and hosiery) had sought protection under the Safeguarding of Industries Act. The scores of unemployed textile workers in Lancashire and elsewhere, according to Snyder (1944, 151), "made it possible for the factory owners, who had swung over in large numbers to the side of protection, to influence their workers." Iron and steel manufacturers consistently sought protection after World War I, arguing that tariffs were necessary prevent the dumping that they claimed imperiled the industry. Representatives of the iron and steel industry contended that protection would not increase prices to users because scale economies could be realized, but those users (such as the shipbuilding industry) were skeptical of such claims. The protectionist case was also championed by new, emerging industries such as automobiles.

The result of the general election (for England alone), held on December 6, 1923, is presented in table 4.2. The Conservatives captured virtually the same share of the vote as they had in 1922, losing just 1.7 percentage points. The combined share of Labour and the Liberals rose 3.3 percentage points, mainly at the expense of smaller parties. These slight shifts obscure a dramatic change in parliamentary representation. The Conservatives lost almost 100 seats (and their majority) in parliament, paving the way for the first Labour government headed by J. Ramsay MacDonald. Thus what needs to be explained is not only the shift in the aggregate support for the three parties but also the composition of their support across counties.

4.3 An Analysis of the 1923 Voting Patterns

Mayer's (1984) analysis of democratic voting on tariffs points to three consideration that should be addressed before analyzing the vote directly: (1) general equilibrium structure of the economy, (2) distribution of (nonhuman) factor ownership (e.g., land and capital), (3) franchise restrictions and voter eligibility. The first issue will be taken up in the context of the econometric results; the second and third deserve immediate consideration.

The distribution of factor ownership matters in that wages may not be the most important source of income for certain classes of voters. In this case occupation may be a misleading indicator about where true economic interests lie. In Britain, however, the overwhelming majority of the population were wage earners whose only source of income was from their current occupation. According to the 1921 Census, 90 percent of the occupied population (over 12 years of age) were wage and salary workers (employees), 6 percent self-employed, and 4 percent employers. Furthermore the distribution of income was severely unequal, indicating a high concentration of land and capital ownership. In 1923, according to Atkinson and Harrison (1978, 141), the top 1 percent of the population held 61 percent of the total wealth, the top 5 percent held 82 percent, the top 10 percent held 89 percent, and the top 20 percent held 94 percent.

The Representation of the People Act of 1918 enfranchised all men above the age of 21 and all women above the age of 30. A residency qualification of 6 months affected those who had recently moved between districts, only a small fraction of the electorate. As described below, the census data will be adjusted in an attempt to exclude those not in the electorate.

The econometric approach taken in this chapter is similar to that in my 1994 paper analyzing the 1906 election: Cross-county voting patterns will be related to census data on constituents in each county. The dependent variable is the log of the odds ratio, $\ln[p_i/(1 - p_i)]$, where p_i is the proportion of voters in county i who voted for the free-trade parties (Labour and the Liberals are combined here). Election data by district from Craig (1969) has been summed to the county level (using Craig 1972) to match the census data.

The independent variables are the occupational or skill characteristics of the constituents in each county taken from the 1921 Census of England.

For occupations, the Census Office (1923) produced data on the distribution of 32 occupational groups for men and women (aged 12 and higher) in 51 English counties.[6] To make these data conform more closely to the potential electorate, the sample has been adjusted using census information on the age distribution of each occupational category. The final sample includes the occupations of men aged 20 and higher and women aged 25 and higher. For each occupational category, the Registrar-General (1927) reports the class distribution (skill or income level) within five categories: an upper and middle class, a skilled labor class, an unskilled labor class, and two intermediate categories between them. To calculate the class composition of a district, the skill distribution of each occupational category is assumed to be identical across districts.

Basic features of the data are available in table 4.3. The first two columns indicate the overall size and concentration (across counties) of the occupational categories. Large shares of total employment indicate which industries that potentially weigh heavily in the election outcome. Agriculture and mining, for example, account for 14.3 and 3.8 percent of the electorate sample, respectively. Although the tariff debate concentrated on the manufacturing sector (21.4 percent of the electorate sample), their views could be overwhelmed by those employed in the service sector (comprising 60.5 percent of the sample). Concentration is important in that the outcome in certain counties may hinge on small groups clustered in one region. Mining, metals, and textiles are concentrated in this way. The last five columns indicate the distribution of skills or economic class in each occupational category as determined by the Registrar-General.

The fact that these data are based on an occupational rather than an industrial classification creates a problem. Because laborers, stationary engineers, clerks, and others are not given an industrial affiliation even though they worked for a specific industry, the interest of these workers in promoting the industry in which they were employed will be missed. Fortunately this concern applies to just a few of the available occupational categories in the service sector. The deficiency is mitigated to the extent that these workers had general rather than industry-specific skills. In this case they might be more mobile than others; for example, a clerk employed by the textile industry might have less of a stake in that industry than a textile worker.

The following equation, relating the county vote to characteristics of the electorate in that county, is estimated by weighted least squares to account

Table 4.3
Census data on occupations in England, 1921

	Share of employment	Concentration[a]	Skill level I	II	III	IV	V
Fisherman	0.3	12.0	0.00	0.00	0.00	1.00	0.00
Agriculture	14.0	3.0	0.00	0.30	0.21	0.46	0.02
Mining	3.6	8.0	0.00	0.01	0.62	0.36	0.01
Mine products	0.2	4.7	0.00	0.05	0.06	0.23	0.66
Brick, pottery, etc.	0.6	9.2	0.00	0.06	0.64	0.08	0.21
Chemicals	0.3	5.0	0.00	0.11	0.44	0.45	0.00
Metal workers	7.1	2.7	0.00	0.04	0.74	0.22	0.00
Electroplate/precious metals	0.1	35.1	0.00	0.14	0.85	0.01	0.00
Electrical	0.6	2.5	0.00	0.05	0.85	0.10	0.00
Scientific instruments	0.1	3.0	0.00	0.10	0.90	0.00	0.00
Leather goods	0.3	3.4	0.00	0.12	0.79	0.09	0.00
Textile workers	2.1	9.9	0.00	0.07	0.76	0.17	0.00
Textile products	4.4	4.2	0.00	0.18	0.77	0.05	0.00
Makers of food, etc.	1.7	2.7	0.00	0.18	0.56	0.26	0.00
Wood and furniture	3.0	2.2	0.00	0.05	0.78	0.11	0.06
Paper and printers	1.1	2.7	0.00	0.11	0.78	0.08	0.03
Builders	3.5	2.0	0.00	0.11	0.35	0.14	0.40
Painters	1.2	2.2	0.00	0.06	0.88	0.00	0.06
Workers in other materials	0.2	6.0	0.00	0.05	0.80	0.15	0.00
Workers in mixed materials	0.5	2.9	0.00	0.09	0.84	0.02	0.05
Gas, water, electric workers	0.2	2.1	0.06	0.05	0.16	0.40	0.33
Transport and communications	7.2	2.1	0.01	0.08	0.44	0.34	0.13
Commerce, finance, insurance	8.0	2.0	0.12	0.57	0.27	0.00	0.04
Government and defense	3.0	3.4	0.05	0.46	0.37	0.12	0.00
Professionals	5.1	2.1	0.55	0.38	0.07	0.00	0.00
Entertainment	0.5	3.0	0.00	0.13	0.81	0.06	0.00
Personal service	13.8	2.2	0.00	0.32	0.56	0.12	0.00
Clerks	2.8	2.4	0.04	0.96	0.00	0.00	0.00
Warehousemen, storekeepers	0.8	2.6	0.00	0.00	0.66	0.34	0.00
Stationary engine drivers	0.7	2.7	0.00	0.00	0.52	0.48	0.00
Other workers (laborers)	4.9	2.0	0.00	0.03	0.08	0.89	0.00
Unoccupied and retired	8.1	2.0	—	—	—	—	—

Sources: Census Office (1923); Registrar-General (1927, ciii–cxiv).
Note: *Defnition of Skill Level*: (I) Upper and middle, (II) intermediate, (III) skilled, (IV) intermediate, (V) unskilled.
a. Herfindahl index of geographic concentration is $100 \times \sum s_i$, where s_i is the share of an employment category in district i.

Table 4.4
Sectoral voting

Sector (share of employment)	$\ln[p_i/(1 - p_i)]$	$\ln[p_i/(1 - p_i)]$	$\Delta \ln[p_i/(1 - p_i)]$
Constant	9.08	3.26	−0.25
	(2.45)	(1.69)	(0.12)
Agriculture	−0.21	−0.13	−0.09
(14.3)	(5.67)	(4.70)	(2.88)
Mining	0.01	0.01	0.01
(3.8)	(0.22)	(0.45)	(0.46)
Manufacturing	−0.19	−0.21	−0.22
(22.4)	(1.71)	(2.67)	(2.42)
Services	−1.23	−0.25	0.32
(59.5)	(3.34)	(0.87)	(1.08)
Lagged log of odds ratio	—	0.62	—
		(6.81)	
Unweighted $\bar{R}^2$	0.49	0.70	0.03
F	43.3	79.1	12.8
Unweighted s.e.	0.24	0.18	0.23

Note: t statistics in parentheses.

for the unequal size of each county and to correct for heteroskedasticity:[7]

$$\ln\left[\frac{p_i}{1 - p_i}\right] = \alpha + \sum_{j=1}^{n} \beta_j \ln(X_{ji}) + \varepsilon_i,$$

where p_i is the proportion of vote in county i for the free trade Labour and Liberal parties, X_{ji} is the proportion of occupation or class j in county i, and ε_i is the error term.

The first set of results is reported on table 4.4. In this table, broad sectoral aggregates are constructed from the occupational data. In the first specification the log of the odds ratio is regressed on the four sectoral aggregates (agriculture, mining, manufacturing, and services). The results indicate that all sectors but mining are strongly negatively correlated with voting for the free trade parties. Since a large component of support for free trade is captured by the constant terms, these results are largely uninformative.

The second and third specifications analyze the change or the "swing" in the 1923 election patterns from those in the previous (1922) election. The second specification includes the lagged value of the log of the odds ratio from the 1922 election, while in the third the dependent variable is the difference in the log of the odds ratios. These specifications may be

Table 4.5
Class voting

	$\ln[p_i/(1-p_i)]$	$\ln[p_i/(1-p_i)]$	$\Delta\ln[p_i/(1-p_i)]$
Constant	7.30	2.81	0.73
	(1.21)	(0.61)	(0.15)
(I) Upper and middle	−1.77	−0.40	0.23
	(2.74)	(0.74)	(0.45)
(II) Intermediate	0.53	0.20	0.05
	(0.77)	(0.38)	(0.08)
(III) Skilled labor	0.07	−0.04	−0.08
	(0.15)	(0.11)	(0.24)
(IV) Intermediate	−0.66	−0.37	−0.23
	(1.23)	(0.95)	(0.57)
(V) Unskilled labor	−0.28	−0.07	0.02
	(0.73)	(0.26)	(0.06)
Lagged log of odds ratio	—	0.68	—
		(6.03)	
Unweighted $\bar{R}^2$	.32	.62	.03
F	23.2	41.1	6.1
Unweighted s.e.	0.39	0.21	0.25

Note: t statistics in parentheses.

informative for the following reason: While there is substantial persistence in both regional voting trends and regional employment composition, voting patterns can be expected to shift at the margin as economic interests (which were not as important in previous elections) replace other considerations in affecting voter behavior.

Three patterns emerge from these regressions: (1) Counties with employment concentration in agriculture and manufacturing swung toward the Conservative party in the 1923 election compared with the prior election, (2) counties heavily populated with those employed in mining did not swing toward the Liberals or Labour, primarily because those counties were already overwhelming represented in parliament by those parties, and (3) the net contribution by service employment is ambiguous. Although the estimate in the last equation is imprecise, the coefficient on services is positive and, given the overwhelming share of the electorate in this category, might account for the election outcome in this specification.

Table 4.5 analyzes the county vote pattern by economic class. The only information that can be gleaned from the first specification is that counties with a concentration of upper and middle income voters tended to vote

Conservative, but this does not carry over to the other specifications that control for the prior voting pattern. If class considerations were important in determining the election outcome, one would expect to see a positive coefficient on unskilled labor, but this is not apparent. The first specification is also the best test of the class hypothesis since other specifications that control for past voting behavior would also be dominated by class considerations. Yet this table is completely uninformative about the determinants of the 1923 election or why the results differed from the previous election. One is tempted to draw the conclusion that skill levels and income classes are not good explanatory variables for the voting patterns in the 1923 election. However, this conclusion must be tempered by the recognition that problems may exist with the original social grading of occupational categories as undertaken by the Registrar-General or with the assumption that the within-occupation distribution of class is the same across counties.

Table 4.6 breaks down the vote by occupational category, including only those (14) groups in traded goods industries. Focusing on the third specification, we find that regressors explain 26 percent of the variation in the difference of the log of the odds ratio, much more than previous regressions were able to and adjusting for the different number of regressors which the occupational data allow. Counties with occupational concentrations in agriculture, metals, and textile workers appear to have swung toward the Conservatives compared to the previous election; coefficients on these variables are also statistically significant and are in line with the discussion in the previous section. Those working with mine products supported free trade, although this pattern is not so evident among mine workers themselves. In earlier specifications at least, counties with concentrations of those working on textile products were correlated with votes for the free-trade parties. Thus, in both textiles and mining, there is slight evidence of the following divergence in economic interests: namely downstream-user industries favor free trade to acquire their inputs from the source at the lowest possible cost, while upstream producers (even if net exporters) may be facing some import competition and would desire tariff protection.

As in the 1906 general election results, the constant terms also weigh in positively and significantly, indicating broader support for the free-trade parties than is captured by these occupational categories. A plausible interpretation for this result is that many voters in service sectors, which

Table 4.6
Occupation voting (traded goods industries)

	$\ln[p_i/(1-p_i)]$	$\ln[p_i/(1-p_i)]$	$\Delta\ln[p_i/(1-p_i)]$
Constant	1.37	1.58	1.69
	(1.56)	(2.93)	(2.57)
Agriculture	−0.22	−0.14	−0.01
	(3.96)	(3.76)	(2.10)
Mine workers	0.01	−0.01	−0.02
	(0.50)	(0.65)	(1.21)
Mine products	−0.01	−0.01	0.03
	(0.40)	(1.24)	(1.90)
Bricks	−0.03	−0.03	−0.03
	(0.55)	(0.86)	(0.69)
Chemicals	0.02	0.00	−0.01
	(0.82)	(0.08)	(0.51)
Metals	0.25	−0.03	−0.18
	(1.69)	(0.26)	(1.62)
Electrical	−0.40	−0.06	0.13
	(2.43)	(0.52)	(1.07)
Scientific	−0.06	−0.09	−0.10
	(0.55)	(1.27)	(1.20)
Leather	−0.19	−0.05	0.03
	(2.19)	(0.91)	(0.39)
Textile workers	−0.01	−0.02	−0.03
	(0.28)	(2.00)	(2.38)
Textile products	0.24	0.07	−0.02
	(2.12)	(1.00)	(0.24)
Food	−0.11	0.01	0.08
	(0.75)	(0.10)	(0.69)
Wood	−0.42	−0.26	−0.17
	(1.32)	(1.32)	(0.71)
Paper	0.11	−0.02	−0.09
	(0.66)	(0.18)	(0.72)
Lagged log of odds ratio	—	0.64	—
		(7.72)	
Unweighted $\bar{R}^2$	0.58	0.81	0.26
F	12.0	33.9	5.2
Unweighted s.e.	0.26	0.18	0.25

Note: t statistics in parentheses.

Table 4.7
Occupation voting (traded and nontraded goods industries)

	$\ln[p_i/(1-p_i)]$	$\ln[p_i/(1-p_i)]$	$\Delta\ln[p_i/(1-p_i)]$
Constant	2.63	0.21	−3.67
	(1.17)	(0.11)	(1.31)
Agriculture	−0.21	−0.18	−0.11
	(3.53)	(3.43)	(1.44)
Mine workers	−0.00	−0.00	0.00
	(0.21)	(0.11)	(0.09)
Mine products	−0.02	−0.00	0.02
	(1.28)	(0.18)	(1.31)
Bricks	−0.02	−0.01	0.08
	(0.60)	(0.35)	(0.16)
Chemicals	0.02	0.00	−0.02
	(1.04)	(0.27)	(0.86)
Metals	0.00	−0.03	−0.08
	(0.04)	(0.27)	(0.50)
Electrical	0.06	−0.05	0.04
	(0.30)	(0.32)	(0.17)
Scientific	−0.23	−0.19	−0.14
	(2.32)	(2.37)	(1.09)
Leather	−0.12	−0.06	0.03
	(1.96)	(1.16)	(0.43)
Textile workers	−0.06	−0.05	−0.05
	(3.15)	(3.67)	(2.21)
Textile products	0.07	0.05	0.02
	(0.64)	(0.57)	(0.16)
Food	0.24	0.16	0.04
	(1.68)	(1.37)	(0.20)
Wood	−0.06	−0.02	0.03
	(0.22)	(0.11)	(0.09)
Paper	0.11	0.02	−0.10
	(0.98)	(0.30)	(0.72)
Building	1.02	0.76	0.33
	(2.81)	(2.48)	(0.73)
Painters	−0.92	−0.64	−0.18
	(3.37)	(2.71)	(0.55)
Gas, water, electricity	0.22	0.15	0.05
	(1.16)	(1.00)	(0.22)
Transport and communications	0.05	0.09	0.17
	(0.17)	(0.45)	(0.54)
Commerce, finance, insurance	−0.36	0.01	0.61
	(0.82)	(0.03)	(1.11)
Government and defense	−0.05	−0.06	−0.07
	(0.57)	(0.08)	(0.66)

Table 4.7 (continued)

	$\ln[p_i/(1 - p_i)]$	$\ln[p_i/(1 - p_i)]$	$\Delta\ln[p_i/(1 - p_i)]$
Professionals	−0.49	−0.18	0.33
	(1.27)	(0.53)	(0.68)
Entertainment	0.25	0.19	0.10
	(1.70)	(1.61)	(0.58)
Clerks	0.39	0.25	0.04
	(2.49)	(1.91)	(0.19)
Laborers	−0.57	−0.39	−0.10
	(2.07)	(1.70)	(0.30)
Lagged log of odds ratio	—	0.38	—
		(3.67)	
Unweighted $\bar{R}^2$	0.72	0.82	0.32
F	20.7	30.3	3.1
Unweighted s.e.	0.25	0.14	0.28

Note: t statistics in parentheses.

are relatively uniformly distributed across England, voted against protection to keep the price of their inputs or consumption articles inexpensive. This hypothesis is explored further in table 4.7, which includes occupational categories from the nontraded goods sector (services). While these results are less informative than those in table 4.6, one result remains pronounced: the swing of textiles workers toward the Conservatives. None of the standard accounts of professionals in the city of London and elsewhere supporting free trade is evident, although clerks do seem to be related to voting for free trade.

A formal test to discriminate between the two competing models—class versus occupational voting—confirms what one already suspects from the results, namely that the occupational regressors (in traded goods industries) explain the election outcome better than the class regressors in choosing between the third specifications in tables 4.5 and 4.6. Davidson and MacKinnon's (1981) J test allows us to assess H_0 (the occupational model is appropriate) against H_1 (the class/skill model is appropriate) by an indirect linear combination of the two models (with α the weight on the second model). In the first case we cannot reject the hypothesis that H_0 is true because including the fitted values from the class model enter with $\hat{\alpha} = 0.87$ with a t ratio of 1.07. This does not preclude the possibility that we also cannot reject H_1. Reversing the test, however, we can reject H_1 because $\hat{\alpha} = 6.98$ with a t ratio of 6.07. Thus the occupation model dominates the class model.[8]

These results conform to our current understanding of labor markets in interwar Britain. Thomas (1992) argues that insider-outsider models of unemployment fit the British experience of the 1920s and 1930s well. As he notes:

Those workers who lost jobs in the traditional staple industries (coal, shipbuilding, iron and steel, textiles), especially those with well-developed, industry specific skills, took on the character of outsiders to the vibrant sectors of the labour market, such as services, light engineering, and vehicles. It is no accident that most of the long-term unemployed (57% in 1936) came from the staple sectors. These workers were unlikely to find work in either their own trades or elsewhere. They had very low reemployment probabilities from the very moment of dismissal, joining an extremely long queue at the exchanges, made up of individuals with distressingly similar career histories. (Thomas 1992, 300)

This description and the empirical results presented above are consistent with the political divisions suggested by the imperfect labor mobility variant of the specific factor model, as developed by Mussa (1982) and Baldwin (1984). There is less support for the notion that distinct class differences were driving voting patterns, at least in this election where the outcome would directly affect important economic interests.

Were occupational characteristics decisive in determining the election outcome for many counties? We can answer this question from the second specification in table 4.6 by calculating $\hat{p}_i - \bar{p}_i$, the predicted value of p_i minus the predicted mean value of p (as when the county had sample-average occupational characteristics). This measures the portion of the county's vote that can be attributed to the particular distribution of occupations there. After computing $y = p_i - (\hat{p}_i - \bar{p}_i)$, where p_i is the actual percentage Liberal-Labour vote in the county, if either $p_i > 0.5$ and $y < 0.5$ or $p_i < 0.5$ and $y > 0.5$, then occupational factors were decisive in shifting the election outcome in that country.[9]

Of the 51 counties in the sample, occupational voting patterns proved decisive in 13 counties (25 percent). This calculation tells more about the sources of support for the Conservatives than for the Labour or Liberal parties because deviations must be made from $\bar{p}_i$, the average level of support for the Labour and the Liberals. In 10 of the 13 cases the particular configuration of occupations shifted the vote to the Conservatives. The Conservatives dropped from having majorities in 25 to 12 counties after the two elections, a decline of 13 of which 3 can be attributed to specific occupational concentrations. This is not to say that industry or occupational considerations were not important in other counties, but these results cannot be distinguished from those in counties having sample average characteristics.

4.4 Conclusions and Speculations

This chapter has provided additional evidence for viewing the political economy of trade policy through the lens of the Mussa (1982) and Baldwin (1984) models of imperfect factor mobility. Even in an economy noted for its class stratification, such class sentiments were not sufficient to overcome strong, underlying economic interests when those interests were at stake. This chapter has not made any direct test of those models or any direct test of factor mobility itself. Rather, in terms of observable political behavior, however determined, the specific-factors type of models conform better to the evidence than those models making strong factor mobility assumptions.

In defense of the political economy implications of the Heckscher-Ohlin model with perfect factor mobility, some economists argue that the short-term interests of factors will dominate longer-term interests if policy decisions are viewed as short-term or are easily reversed. This ignores the point that policy reversals are costly; witness the fact that within five years the repeal of the highly controversial Corn Laws, it was accepted as a policy decision with no further attempt to overturn it.

The failure of the protectionist "tariff reformers" in the first quarter of this century in Britain was also not independent of the institutional mechanism by which decisions about commercial policy were made. Since the costs of voting are arguably lower than the costs of lobbying, the free-rider problems often said to afflict dispersed free-trade interests are absent in direct voting. Democratic voting thereby affects the configuration of interests that are represented in the political arena, which in turn affects the political outcome. In the British case the electorate repeatedly established (in the 1906, 1910, and 1923 elections) the equilibrium political outcome as free trade. When higher tariffs were finally introduced during the Great Depression, they came not as a result of such an election but through a legislative vote in a Conservative-dominated parliament.[10] Why Conservative parliaments did not simply enact such legislation earlier without seeking an electoral mandate, of course, is a story for another paper.

Notes

I wish to thank David Frankel, Gene Grossman, and Mark Thomas for their helpful comments on an earlier draft of this paper.

1. In this context, Alt and Gilligan (1994) provide an overview of how economic interests and political organization costs affect the formation of trade policy.

2. Legislative voting, a common method of determining commercial policy prior to World War II, provides imperfect information on such political economy cleavages because of uncertainty about whether such votes reflect the ideology of legislators, log rolling within or between political parties, the pressure of particular interest groups, or the economic interests of constituents.

3. Bhagwati and Irwin (1987) examine the parallels and contrasts between the British debate over reciprocity and foreign unfair trade practices in the late nineteenth century and the similar American debate in the late twentieth century.

4. During the campaign John Maynard Keynes made his famous pronouncement that a tariff to remedy unemployment was "the Protectionist fallacy in its grossest and crudest form."

5. British trade data are available in greater detail than presented in this table, but are aggregated for comparability with the production and consumption data from the Census of Production.

6. The sample has been confined to England alone, which accounted for 82 percent of the votes cast. Wales was uniformly in favor of Labour and the Liberals (in this and in the 1922 election) with several uncontested seats. Scotland conducted a separate census with different census categories.

7. The weights are equal to $w_i = \{p_i/n_i(1 - p_i)\}^{1/2}$, where n_i is the total vote count in each county.

8. While the occupational voting regressions have many more independent variables, the class voting regressions have fewer "grouped" variables which also tends to increase the goodness of fit.

9. This is a stringent standard. For example, if $p_i = \hat{p}_i = 0.60$ and $\bar{p}_i = 0.55$, then even though the model accounts for the actual vote in the county, the occupational patterns there were not sufficiently different from an average county to change whether it would have voted Liberal or not. On the other hand, if $p_i = \hat{p}_i = 0.48$ and $\bar{p}_i = 0.55$, then the concentration of occupations in the county was sufficient to swing it from voting Liberal or Labour to voting Conservative.

10. Since there was, strictly speaking, a national government, the Tories could delude themselves and the electorate that this was a national and not a party decision.

References

Alt, James E., and Michael Gilligan. 1994. The political economy of trading states: Factor specificity, collective action problems and domestic political institutions. *Journal of Political Philosophy* 2:165–92.

Atkinson, A. B., and A. J. Harrison. 1978. *Distribution of Personal Wealth in Britain.* Cambridge: Cambridge University Press.

Baldwin, Robert. 1984. Rent seeking and trade policy: An industry approach. *Weltwirtschlaftliches Archiv* 129:662–77.

Bhagwati, Jagdish. 1988. *Protectionism.* Cambridge: MIT Press.

Bhagwati, Jagdish, and Douglas Irwin. 1987. The return of the reciprocitarians: U.S. trade policy today. *World Economy* 10:109–30.

Capie, Forrest. 1983. *Depression and Protection: Britain between the Wars.* London: George Allen and Unwin.

Census Office. 1923. *Census of England and Wales, 1921, General Report.* London: His Majesty's Stationery Office.

Craig, F. W. S. ed. 1969. *British Parliamentary Election Results, 1918–1949.* Glasgow: Political Reference Publications.

Craig, F. W. S. ed. 1971. *British Parliamentary Election Statistics.* 2d ed. Chichester: Political Reference Publications.

Craig, F. W. S. ed. 1972. *Boundaries of Parliamentary Constituencies, 1885–1972.* Chichester: Political Reference Publications.

Craig, F. W. S. ed. 1975. *British General Election Manifestos, 1900–1974.* London: Macmillan.

Customs and Excise Office. 1924. *Annual Statement of the Trade of the United Kingdom, 1923,* vol. 1. London: His Majesty's Stationery Office.

Davidson, Russell, and James G. MacKinnon. 1981. Several tests for model specification in the presence of alternative hypotheses. *Econometrica* 49:781–93.

Final Report on the Third Census of Production of the United Kingdom (1924). London: His Majesty's Stationery Office, 1930–32.

Hirst, Francis W. 1927. *Safeguarding and Protection in Great Britain and the United States.* New York: Macmillan.

Irwin, Douglas A. 1994. The political economy of free trade: Voting in the British general election of 1906. *Journal of Law and Economics* 37:75–108.

Magee, Stephen P. 1978. Three simple tests of the Stolper-Samuelson theorem. In Peter Oppenheimer, ed., *Issues in International Economics.* Stockfield, England: Oriel Press.

Mayer, Wolfgang. 1984. Endogenous tariff formation. *American Economic Review* 74:970–985.

Ministry of Labour. 1926. *18th Abstract of Labour Statistics of the United Kingdom.* London: His Majesty's Stationery Office.

Mussa, Michael. 1982. Imperfect factor mobility and the distribution of income. *Journal of International Economics* 12:125–41.

Pulzer, Peter G. J. 1967. *Political Representation and Elections in Britain.* London: George Allen and Unwin.

Registrar-General. 1927. *England and Wales, 1921. Part II: Occupational Mortality, Fertility, and Infant Mortality. Decennial Supplement.* London: His Majesty's Stationery Office.

Rogowski, Ronald. 1989. *Commerce and Coalitions: How Trade Affects Domestic Political Alignments.* Princeton: Princeton University Press.

Snyder, Rixford Kinney. 1944. *The Tariff Problem in Great Britain, 1918–1923.* Stanford Studies in History, Economics, and Political Science, vol. 5, no. 2. Stanford: Stanford University Press.

Taylor, A. J. P. 1965. *English History, 1914–1945.* Oxford: Oxford University Press.

Thomas, Mark. 1992. Institutional rigidity in the British labour market. In S. N. Broadberry and N. F. R. Crafts, eds., *Britain in the International Economy.* Cambridge: Cambridge University Press.

5 Liberalizing Multinational Investment: The Stolper-Samuelson Question Revisited

Richard A. Brecher and Ehsan U. Choudhri

5.1 Introduction

In recent years considerable attention has been focused on liberalization of commodity trade and direct investment between high- and low-wage countries. The prospect of such liberalization has heightened the concern that income levels of (unskilled) labor in the former countries would be threatened by import competition from and transfer of plants to the latter. Although the first of these two threats has been extensively discussed by Bhagwati (1994) and others[1] in relation to the Stolper-Samuelson question, there is relatively little analysis of the second.[2]

To reduce this lacuna in the literature, the present chapter develops and applies a simplified version of Helpman and Krugman's (1985, ch. 12) model of multinational firms. We retain their key assumptions that a differentiated good is produced under monopolistic competition and that firms can geographically separate their headquarters from their plants.[3] Instead of their two-good framework, however, our model includes only one good, since this simpler setup suffices to raise the Stolper-Samuelson question associated with multinational investment.

Before we introduce such investment, section 5.2 sets up our basic model of free trade between two countries with different relative endowments of capital and labor.[4] To generate multinational investment, section 5.3 allows firms headquartered in either country to operate plants abroad, while assuming that headquarter services can be neither sold nor leased.

Since we assume also that these services are more capital intensive than plant output, a tax on international investment has a Stolper-Samuelson type of effect on marginal products. Real wage rates, however, respond also to tax-induced changes in the number of product varieties and the terms of trade. We are nevertheless able to show that reducing a small tax on multinational investment unambiguously causes the real wage to fall in the capital- and rise in the labor-abundant country. The wage of the former relative to the latter country moreover is shown to decrease for a tax reduction of any magnitude. Some concluding remarks about our analysis are offered in section 5.4.

5.2 Basic Model

This section develops the basic model that is used in the next section to examine how restrictions on foreign investment affect real wage rates. The model has two countries, two primary factors (capital and labor), and one differentiated good produced under monopolistic competition. Each variety of the good requires its own single unit of a specialized input (headquarter services).[5] The specialized input is produced at a firm's headquarters, while the differentiated good is produced in plants. Location of its headquarters determines the firm's nationality. In the present section, firms headquartered in one country are not allowed to set up plants in the other country. All varieties of the differentiated good, however, are freely tradable.

Each consumer has an SDS (Spence 1976; Dixit and Stiglitz 1977) utility function with elasticity of substitution equal to $\sigma > 1$. The variety space is continuous so that σ also represents the price elasticity of demand for each variety. On the technology side, the production functions for headquarters and plants are each strictly quasi-concave, as well as homogeneous of degree one in the two primary factors. At any common wage/rental ratio, the capital/labor utilization ratio is higher in headquarter than in plant production. Throughout the world, technology is the same for all headquarters and for all plants, while all consumers have the same tastes. The capital/labor endowment ratio, however, is higher for the home than for the foreign country.

We first derive the equilibrium conditions for the home economy. For simplicity of exposition, assume that the firm would incur a small extra cost to operate each additional plant.[6] The firm avoids this cost by operating only a single plant, given our assumption that returns to scale (in primary factors) are constant for plants.

Minimizing the cost of producing one unit of headquarter services implies that

$$w = \phi[f_H(k_H) - k_H f_H'(k_H)],$$ (5.1)

$$r = \phi f_H'(k_H),$$ (5.2)

where w and r are the nominal wage and rental rates in the home country; $f_H(k_H)$, $f_H'(k_H)$, and k_H, respectively, represent the average product of labor, marginal product of capital, and capital/labor ratio of home headquarters; and ϕ denotes the shadow price of headquarter services at home.[7] Since ϕ is independent of the level of plant output, it also represents each firm's fixed cost.

Maximization of profits implies that

$$w = m[f_Q(k_Q) - k_Q f'_Q(k_Q)], \tag{5.3}$$

$$r = m f'_Q(k_Q), \tag{5.4}$$

where m is the marginal revenue; while $f_Q(k_Q)$, $f'_Q(k_Q)$, and k_Q, respectively, are the average product of labor, marginal product of capital, and capital/labor ratio in home plants.[8] Thus factor prices equal marginal revenue products in plant production [according to (5.3) and (5.4)], and equal shadow values of marginal products in headquarter production [as stated by (5.1) and (5.2)].

Assuming flexibility of w and r, we have full employment of both factors. Thus

$$\overline{K} = L_Q k_Q + L_H k_H, \tag{5.5}$$

$$\overline{L} = L_Q + L_H, \tag{5.6}$$

where $\overline{K}$ and $\overline{L}$ are the economy's endowments of capital and labor, while L_Q and L_H represent the quantities of labor employed by all plants and headquarters at home.

The model represented by (5.1)–(5.6) is formally equivalent to the production side of a two-sector Heckscher-Ohlin-Samuelson model, with π ($\equiv \phi/m$) serving as the product-price ratio, and $L_Q f_Q(k_Q)$ and $L_H f_H(k_H)$ representing outputs of the two sectors (plant value added and headquarter services). Given this equivalence, π determines k_Q, k_H, all marginal products, and aggregate output levels $Q(\pi)$ for plants and $H(\pi)$ for headquarters along the economy's production-possibility frontier. Since this frontier has the usual properties, $Q'(\pi) < 0$ and $H'(\pi) > 0$.

Since there are zero profits (due to free entry) under monopolistic competition, fixed (headquarter) cost must equal the difference between total revenue and variable (plant) cost of the firm, so

$$\phi = (p - m)x, \tag{5.7}$$

where x is the output scale of each plant, and p denotes the price of the good. (In understanding this equation, note that profit maximization makes marginal revenue equal to marginal cost, which equals average variable cost under constant returns to scale at the plant level.) Given the standard relationship that $m = p(1 - 1/\sigma)$, (5.7) determines the plant scale as

$$x = \pi(\sigma - 1). \tag{5.8}$$

In view of this equation, the equilibrium number of home plants is

$$n(\pi) \equiv \frac{Q(\pi)}{\pi(\sigma - 1)}, \tag{5.9}$$

with $n'(\pi) < 0$. As the number of home plants equals the number of headquarters in the present case,

$$H(\pi) = n(\pi). \tag{5.10}$$

This equation uniquely determines π.

The home country's equilibrium is illustrated in figure 5.1, where AB is the production-possibility curve at home, line CD has a slope of $-\pi$, and home production occurs at point G. Thus, $\overline{OF}$ represents the left-hand side of (5.10); while the (equal) right-hand side is given by $\overline{FD}\ [=\overline{GF}/(\overline{GF}/\overline{FD})]$ if, for simplicity of illustration, we set $\sigma = 2$ in (5.9).

Relations analogous to (5.1)–(5.10) hold for the foreign country, with a star denoting each foreign variable. Since the foreign country is relatively abundant in labor, the well-known Rybczynski reasoning implies that $Q^*(\pi^*)/H^*(\pi^*) > Q(\pi)/H(\pi)$ if $\pi^* = \pi$. Thus (5.9), (5.10), and their foreign counterparts imply that $\pi^* > \pi$.

This result is illustrated in figure 5.1, where line C^*D^* is parallel to CD, and G^* is the point at which foreign production would occur if π^* were equal to the equilibrium value of π. (To avoid clutter, the diagram omits the foreign production-possibility frontier, to which line C^*D^* is tangent at point G^*.) Assuming, for the sake of concreteness, that the endowment of labor is greater in the foreign than in the home country while both countries have the same endowment of capital, note that point G^* lies northwest of G by the Rybczynski theorem. Thus $\overline{OF^*} < (\overline{OF} = \overline{FD} <)\overline{F^*D^*}$, which implies that $H^*(\pi^*) < n^*(\pi^*)$ if π^* were represented by (minus) the slope of line C^*D^*. Therefore, to satisfy the foreign counterpart of (5.10), we need a steeper π^* line (not drawn), implying that $\pi^* > \pi$ when both countries are in equilibrium.

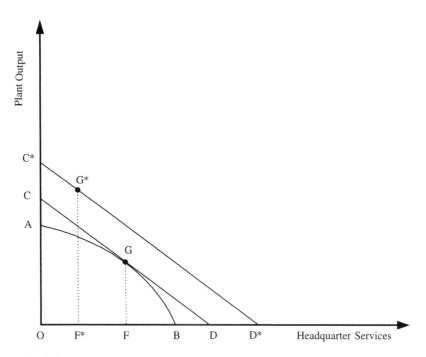

Figure 5.1
Home country equilibrium

Before discussing this result's implications for real-wage differences, we now derive a relation between p/p^* and π^*/π. With E and E^* representing aggregate expenditure in the home and foreign economies, market clearing implies that

$$x = (E + E^*)\frac{p^{-\sigma}}{np^{1-\sigma} + n^*p^{*1-\sigma}}, \tag{5.11}$$

where the right-hand side of this equation is the free-trade demand for each variety according to the SDS utility function.[9] Use (5.11) and the corresponding equation for the foreign economy to obtain $x^*/x = (p/p^*)^{\sigma}$. At the same time (5.8) and its foreign counterpart imply that $x^*/x = \pi^*/\pi$. Thus

$$\frac{p}{p^*} = \left(\frac{\pi^*}{\pi}\right)^{1/\sigma}. \tag{5.12}$$

Since $\sigma > 1$ and $\pi^* > \pi$, (5.12) implies that $p > p^*$ and (because $m/p = m^*/p^*$) that $\phi < \phi^*$.

According to the Stolper-Samuelson theorem, w/m is a monotonic decreasing function of π. Since $m/p \ (\equiv 1 - 1/\sigma)$ is constant, we also have

$$\frac{w}{p} = \omega(\pi),\tag{5.13}$$

with $\omega'(\pi) < 0$. Given the SDS utility function, the price index for converting nominal income into utility can be expressed as

$$\tilde{p} = [n(\pi)p^{1-\sigma} + n^*(\pi^*)p^{*1-\sigma}]^{1/(1-\sigma)}.\tag{5.14}$$

Equations (5.12)–(5.14) can now be used to express the home real wage as

$$\frac{w}{\tilde{p}} = \omega(\pi)\left[n(\pi) + n^*(\pi^*)\left(\frac{\pi^*}{\pi}\right)^{(\sigma-1)/\sigma}\right]^{1/(\sigma-1)}.\tag{5.15}$$

Noting that $\omega^*(\pi^*) \equiv \omega(\pi^*)$ because the two countries have the same technology, and that $\tilde{p}^* = \tilde{p}$ under free trade, we can similarly express the foreign real wage as

$$\frac{w^*}{\tilde{p}^*} = \omega(\pi^*)\left[n(\pi)\left(\frac{\pi}{\pi^*}\right)^{(\sigma-1)/\sigma} + n^*(\pi^*)\right]^{1/(\sigma-1)}.\tag{5.16}$$

Since $\pi^* > \pi$ and hence $\omega(\pi^*) < \omega(\pi)$, (5.15) and (5.16) clearly imply that the real wage is higher in the home than in the foreign country. (By similar reasoning the real rental rate is lower at home.) Thus, in the present model, free trade does not equalize real factor incomes.[10]

5.3 Multinational Investment

We now allow firms headquartered in either country to operate plants in both countries. Under our free-trade assumption, however, each firm continues to operate only a single plant. A multinational operation arises if a firm sets up its plant abroad. We assume moreover that each country remains diversified in production—that it continues to produce both headquarter services and plant output.

In the presence of multinational firms, (5.1)–(5.9) and their foreign counterparts remain valid. Thus the numbers of plants and headquarters are still $n(\pi)$ and $H(\pi)$ in the home country, and $n^*(\pi^*)$ and $H^*(\pi^*)$ in the foreign country. In the presence of multinational investment (by single-plant firms), (5.10) is replaced by

$$H(\pi) + H^*(\pi^*) = n(\pi) + n^*(\pi^*). \tag{5.17}$$

Since ϕ was less than ϕ^* before the introduction of international investment, it is now profitable for some home firms to operate foreign plants.

First, suppose that there are no restrictions on multinational investment. In this case, under our assumption that production is diversified in both countries, $\phi = \phi^*$.[11] Thus, given (5.12) and recalling that $m/p = m^*/p^*$, we have $\pi = \pi^*$. As implied by this equality together with (5.15) and (5.16), the real wage rates in the two countries are equalized. Since multinational investment in our model is analytically equivalent to international trade in headquarter services, it is not surprising that free investment equalizes factor prices internationally.

We next examine how restrictions on foreign investment affect real wages in the two countries.[12] Without loss of generality, suppose that the foreign country imposes a tax on home multinationals, while the home country levies no tax.[13] Let τ^* be the foreign tax rate, expressed as a proportion of home headquarter cost (i.e., home investment). In the presence of this tax, the fixed cost to produce in the foreign country is $\phi(1 + \tau^*)$ for a home firm and ϕ^* for a foreign firm. Thus competition between home and foreign firms ensures that

$$\phi^* = \phi(1 + \tau^*), \tag{5.18}$$

for any nonprohibitive value of τ^*. In view of (5.12), (5.18), and the fact that $m/p = m^*/p^*$,

$$\frac{\pi^*}{\pi} = (1 + \tau^*)^{\sigma/(\sigma-1)}. \tag{5.19}$$

Since $H'(\pi) > 0 > n'(\pi)$ and $H^{*'}(\pi^*) > 0 > n^{*'}(\pi^*)$, (5.17) and (5.19) can be simultaneously solved for π and π^* as respectively decreasing and increasing functions of τ^*.

Thus, in accordance with (5.15) and (5.16), an increase in τ^* affects the real wage rate of each country via three channels. First, this increase raises $\omega(\pi)$ and lowers $\omega(\pi^*)$ by decreasing π and increasing π^*. This channel represents the standard Stolper-Samuelson effect on marginal products.[14]

Second, the tax-induced change in π and π^* raises $n(\pi)$ and reduces $n^*(\pi^*)$, giving rise to what may be called the "variety effect" of the tax. Third, the tax increase raises π^*/π, by increasing the numerator while lowering the denominator of this ratio. Since π^*/π varies directly with p/p^* according to (5.12), this third channel represents the "terms-of-trade effect" of the tax.

To explore the relative magnitudes of the terms-of-trade and variety effects, the square-bracketed expressions in (5.15) and (5.16) can be written as follows, in view of (5.19):

$$v \equiv n(\pi) + (1 + \tau^*)n^*(\pi^*), \tag{5.20}$$

$$v^* \equiv \frac{n(\pi)}{1 + \tau^*} + n^*(\pi^*). \tag{5.21}$$

Differentiation of (5.20) and (5.21) with respect to τ^* yields

$$\frac{dv}{d\tau^*} \equiv n'\frac{d\pi}{d\tau^*} + (1 + \tau^*)n^{*\prime}\frac{d\pi^*}{d\tau^*} + n^*, \tag{5.22}$$

$$\frac{dv^*}{d\tau^*} \equiv \left(\frac{n'}{1 + \tau^*}\right)\frac{d\pi}{d\tau^*} + n^{*\prime}\frac{d\pi^*}{d\tau^*} - \frac{n}{(1 + \tau^*)^2}. \tag{5.23}$$

In each of these two identities, the sum of the first two components is the variety effect of the tax change. In general, this effect can be of either sign, since π and π^* move in opposite directions. The third component in each of (5.22) and (5.23) is the terms-of-trade effect, which is positive for the home but negative for the foreign country, since an increase in τ^* raises p/p^*.

For the special case in which $\tau^* = 0$ initially, the appendix shows that the general expressions for (5.22) and (5.23) become

$$\frac{dv}{d\tau^*} = (1 - \sigma\eta^*)(Q + Q^*)\frac{n^*}{(1 - \sigma\eta)Q + (1 - \sigma\eta^*)Q^*}, \tag{5.24}$$

$$\frac{dv^*}{d\tau^*} = (\sigma\eta - 1)(Q + Q^*)\frac{n}{(1 - \sigma\eta)Q + (1 - \sigma\eta^*)Q^*}, \tag{5.25}$$

where $\eta \equiv Q'\pi/Q$ and $\eta^* \equiv Q^{*\prime}\pi^*/Q^*$. Since η and η^* are both less than zero, the right-hand sides of (5.24) and (5.25) are positive and negative, respectively. In other words, the variety effect cannot outweigh the terms-of-trade effect in this special case. Thus, when the Stolper-Samuelson effect is also taken into account, a small tax on international investment (in the neighborhood of the tax-free equilibrium) must raise the real wage rate in the home but lower it in the foreign country. As this result clearly implies, reducing a small tax on multinational investment necessarily benefits foreign but hurts home labor.

An even stronger result holds for relative real-wage changes in response to a tax of any magnitude. Dividing (5.15) by (5.16) and using (5.19), obtain

$$\frac{w/\tilde{p}}{w^*/\tilde{p}^*} = (1 + \tau^*)\frac{\omega(\pi)}{\omega(\pi^*)}. \tag{5.26}$$

Thus any (large or small) decrease in τ^* lowers $w/\tilde{p}$ relative to $w^*/\tilde{p}^*$, since $\omega(\pi)/\omega(\pi^*)$ is reduced by the Stolper-Samuelson effects of the tax cut. In other words, liberalization of multinational investment unambiguously worsens the relative position of home versus foreign labor.

5.4 Concluding Remarks

Some interesting changes in our results arise if we relax the assumption that both countries are diversified in production. For example, suppose that all firms locate their headquarters in the home but operate plants only in the foreign country. With neither home plants nor foreign firms, the number of foreign (and world) varieties remains equal to the fixed number of home headquarters, $\bar{L}f_H(\bar{K}/\bar{L})$. Consequently, in the foreign country, the real wage is uniquely determined by the constant marginal product of labor, $f_Q(\bar{K}^*/\bar{L}^*) - (\bar{K}^*/\bar{L}^*)f_Q'(\bar{K}^*/\bar{L}^*)$. Although the marginal product of labor in the home country remains constant at $f_H(\bar{K}/\bar{L}) - (\bar{K}/\bar{L})f_H'(\bar{K}/\bar{L})$, we could show that a decrease in the tax on international investment raises ϕ/p^*, and hence increases the real wage at home. Thus, if both countries remain completely specialized in production, liberalizing multinational investment unambiguously benefits home without affecting foreign labor.

It is worth emphasizing that firms in our model have decreasing average costs without increasing returns to scale. If headquarter services are considered to be knowledge-related inputs (like product-specific research and development), our specification of the firm's technology is consistent with the standard replication argument that production functions should be homogeneous of degree one in all other inputs.[15] Under this specification, although the tax-induced changes in π and π^* lower x and raise x^* [in accordance with (5.8) and its foreign counterpart], these changes in scale do not have a direct impact on marginal products. Nevertheless, if increasing returns to plant scale were allowed, changes in this scale would affect marginal products, and this additional effect could modify our results.

Finally, our model of trade in a differentiated good could be used to shed light on an alternative type of foreign investment, in the form of international movements of physical capital. For example, we could show that reducing a small tax on these movements would necessarily benefit foreign but hurt home labor, and that a tax decrease of any magnitude would raise the foreign relative to the home real wage.

5.5 Appendix

First, we differentiate (5.9) and its foreign counterpart to yield

$$n' \equiv (\eta - 1)\frac{Q}{\pi^2(\sigma - 1)}, \tag{5.A1}$$

$$n^{*\prime} \equiv (\eta^* - 1)\frac{Q^*}{\pi^{*2}(\sigma - 1)}. \tag{5.A2}$$

Then, differentiating (5.17) with respect to τ^*, substituting (5.A1) and (5.A2) into the resulting equation, and using the well-known conditions that $\pi H' + Q' = 0 = \pi^* H^{*\prime} + Q^{*\prime}$ under profit maximization, we obtain

$$\frac{d\pi^*}{d\tau^*} = \left[\frac{\pi^{*2}Q(1 - \sigma\eta)}{\pi^2 Q^*(\sigma\eta^* - 1)}\right]\frac{d\pi}{d\tau^*}. \tag{5.A3}$$

Next, we differentiate (5.19) with respect to τ^*, note that $(1 + \tau^*)^{1/(\sigma-1)} = (\pi^*/\pi)^{1/\sigma}$ in view of (5.19), and use (5.A3) to derive

$$\frac{d\pi}{d\tau^*} = \frac{\sigma\pi^2(\pi^*/\pi)^{1/\sigma}}{(\sigma - 1)\pi^*[\pi^*Q(1 - \sigma\eta)/\pi Q^*(\sigma\eta^* - 1) - 1]}. \tag{5.A4}$$

Now, substituting (5.A1)–(5.A4) into (5.22) while using (5.19) and the foreign counterpart of (5.9), we see that

$$\frac{dv}{d\tau^*} = \frac{[\rho(\sigma\eta - 1)Q + \sigma\rho^{1/\sigma}(1 - \eta)Q + (\sigma - 1)Q^*](1 - \sigma\eta^*)n^*}{[\rho(1 - \sigma\eta)Q + (1 - \sigma\eta^*)Q^*](\sigma - 1)}, \tag{5.A5}$$

where $\rho \equiv \pi^*/\pi$. For the special case in which $\tau^* = 0$ (and hence $\rho = 1$) at the initial equilibrium, (5.A5) simplifies to (5.24), and similar reasoning leads to (5.25).

Notes

We are grateful for helpful comments and suggestions from Zhiqi Chen, Donald R. Davis, Robert C. Feenstra, Lawrence L. Schembri and Aileen J. Thompson. Research for the paper was supported by the Social Sciences and Humanities Research Council of Canada under Grant No. 410-93-0848.

1. For example, see Bhagwati (1995), Bhagwati and Dehejia (1994), and Brown, Deardorff, and Stern (1993).

2. For a journalistic treatment of both threats, see "War of the Worlds: A Survey of the Global Economy" in *The Economist*, vol. 333, no. 7883, October 1, 1994.

3. On this locational assumption, see also Helpman (1984) and Markusen (1984).

4. Although our two factors are called capital and labor in the Stolper-Samuelson tradition, they could be easily reinterpreted as skilled and unskilled labor, in light of recent concerns about the relative wages of these two types of labor. In any case, under our present formulation, capital can include human as well as physical types of this factor.

5. If the firm were instead permitted to choose an optimal level of headquarter services for its single variety, as assumed by Helpman and Krugman (1985, ch. 12), this level would still be a constant (independent of prices) under certain plausible assumptions. As in the Helpman-Krugman model, there are no economies of scope, since each firm's headquarters can service only one variety.

6. Dropping this assumption would leave our results essentially the same.

7. Letting λ_H denote the firm's use of labor in headquarter production, obtain (5.1) and (5.2) by choosing λ_H and k_H to minimize $w\lambda_H + rk_H\lambda_H$, subject to the constraint that $\lambda_H f_H(k_H) = 1$. As the Lagrange multiplier for this constraint, ϕ represents the marginal cost of headquarter services, which equals their average cost under our assumption that returns to scale are constant.

8. Let λ_Q denote the amount of labor that the firm uses in plant production, and represent the firm's revenue as a function $R[\lambda_Q f_Q(k_Q)]$ of its plant output, where $R' (= m) > 0$ and $R'' < 0$. Then, choose λ_Q and k_Q to maximize $R[\lambda_Q f_Q(k_Q)] - w\lambda_Q - rk_Q\lambda_Q - \phi$, thereby obtaining (5.3) and (5.4).

9. For a derivation of such a demand function, see Helpman and Krugman (1985, ch. 6).

10. This result is not surprising, since we have simplified the Helpman-Krugman (1985, ch. 12) model to include only one good. Under this simplification, international differences in relative factor endowments rule out factor-price equalization, until multinational investment is introduced in the next section.

11. If ϕ differed from ϕ^*, firms in the country with the higher fixed cost could not survive and headquarter production in this country would be eliminated, contrary to our diversification assumption.

12. Our focus is on labor's wage as distinct from its income, which could also include a share of tax revenue. On this income-wage distinction and its implications for the Stolper-Samuelson question, see Bhagwati (1959).

13. If this same tax were imposed by the home rather than the foreign country, none of our analysis would be affected, since our results about real wage rates do not depend on the international distribution of the tax revenue.

14. As also implied by Stolper-Samuelson reasoning, the tax-induced changes in π and π^* increase w/r and decrease w^*/r^*.

15. For a discussion of this argument, see Romer (1990).

References

Bhagwati, Jagdish. 1959. Protection, real wages and real incomes. *Economic Journal* 69:733–48.

Bhagwati, Jagdish. 1994. Free trade: Old and new challenges. *Economic Journal* 104:231–46.

Bhagwati, Jagdish. 1995. Trade and wages: Choosing among alternative explanations. *Federal Reserve Bank of New York Economic Policy Review* 1:42–47.

Bhagwati, Jagdish, and Vivek H. Dehejia. 1994. Freer trade and wages of the unskilled—Is Marx striking again? In J. Bhagwati and M. Kosters, eds., *Trade and Wages: Leveling Wages Down.* Washington: AEI Press.

Brown, Drusilla K., Alan V. Deardorff, and Robert M. Stern. 1993. Protection and real wages: Old and new trade theories and their empirical counterparts. Discussion paper 331, Institute of Public Policy Studies, University of Michigan. May.

Dixit, Avinash, and Joseph E. Stiglitz. 1977. Monopolistic competition and optimum product diversity. *American Economic Review* 67:297–308.

Helpman, Elhanan. 1984. A simple theory of international trade with multinational corporations. *Journal of Political Economy* 92:451–71.

Helpman, Elhanan, and Paul R. Krugman. 1985. *Market Structure and Foreign Trade: Increasing Returns, Imperfect Competition, and the International Economy.* Cambridge: MIT Press.

Markusen, James R. 1984. Multinationals, multi-plant economies, and the gains from trade. *Journal of International Economics* 16:205–26.

Romer, Paul M. 1990. Endogenous technological change. *Journal of Political Economy* 98:S71–S102.

Spence, Michael E. 1976. Product selection, fixed costs, and monopolistic competition. *Review of Economic Studies* 43:217–36.

6 Foreign Investment, Outsourcing, and Relative Wages

Robert C. Feenstra and Gordon H. Hanson

6.1 Introduction

One of the most controversial issues in the U.S. presidential campaign of 1992 was the impact of the proposed North American Free Trade Agreement (NAFTA) on employment and wages in the United States. Many observers feared that this legislation would lead to an exodus of U.S. companies across the border to take advantage of the lower wages in Mexico: the "giant sucking sound," to use the oft-cited phrase of Ross Perot. With the passage of this legislation in November 1993, the possible impact on unskilled workers in the U.S. remains an important issue. Initial studies for the 1980s have argued that trade competition, among other factors, will contribute to a fall in the relative employment and wages of unskilled workers (Revenga 1990; Murphy and Welch 1991; Borjas, Freeman, and Katz 1992).

Surprisingly, this conclusion is not obtained by the most recent studies, which focus on the accelerating decline in the employment and wages of production workers relative to nonproduction workers in the United States. Instead the proximate cause of this decline is thought to be biased technological change, due to the introduction of computers and other research and development activities. This view is expressed most strongly by Bound and Johnson (1992) and Berman, Bound, and Griliches (1994), who identify the decreasing ratio of production to nonproduction workers *within* industries as the crucial determinant of the wage and employment pattern. Lawrence and Slaughter (1993) argue that this decreasing ratio cannot be due to import competition: from the Stolper-Samuelson theorem, if import competition reduces the relative wages of production workers, then all industries should substitute *toward* this factor, whereas the data show substitution away from it. Thus both the shift away from production workers and their reduced relative wages must be due to another cause, of which biased technological change seems most likely.[1]

The average annual wages of nonproduction relative to production workers for the United States, which is used as a proxy for the skilled/unskilled wage ratio, are plotted in figure 6.1.[2] These data show the increase in the relative wages of nonproduction workers in the United States during the 1980s. For comparison, figure 6.1 also plots the ratio of

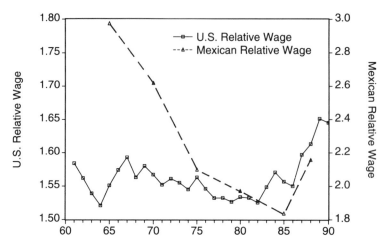

Figure 6.1
Relative wages for nonproduction/production workers

nonproduction/production wages for Mexico, computed from the Industrial Census for the period 1965 to 1988. This relative wage shows a sharp
increase after 1985, following a steady decline over the previous decades.
While the magnitude of these changes are very different (as reflected in the
differing scales), the timing of the increase in relative wages in the two
countries is surprisingly similar. Given the proximity and integration of
these economies, a model that explains the movement in the relative wage
for the United States should also account for the movement in Mexico.

    The similarity of these wage movements on both sides of the border
suggests that they are *not* due to trade liberalization directly, since in that
case we generally expect factor prices to move in opposite directions
across countries (as goods prices fall in the country formerly protected and
rise in the other). However, with the liberalization of foreign ownership
in Mexico, there has been a substantial movement of capital across the
border, which has its own impact on factor prices. We will argue that
capital mobility from the north to the south, or more generally, any
increase in the relative capital stock of the south, will lower the relative
wage of unskilled workers in *both* countries. This result holds also for
neutral technological progress in the south, which is complementary with
the earnings of skilled labor worldwide. These findings support the sugges-
tion of Bhagwati and Dehejia (1994, 55) that the increased globalization of

firms "could well be a contributing factor of some, perhaps growing, importance" in explaining the increasing wage gap, though our model is quite different from the process they have in mind.

The model we will use is described in sections 6.2 and 6.3; it has a single manufactured good produced from a continuum of intermediate inputs, which are in turn produced using skilled workers, unskilled workers, and capital. Capital has the same degree of substitution with either type of labor in the production of intermediate inputs. The structure of this model is very similar to the Hecksher-Ohlin model with a continuum of goods, as in Dornbusch, Fischer, and Samuelson (1980), except that we can interpret all the activities as occurring within a *single* industry. Assuming that trade does not lead to factor-price equalization, the equilibrium is described by the south producing and exporting a range of inputs up to some critical ratio of skilled to unskilled labor, with the north producing the remainder of the inputs. The northern inputs will include such activities as R&D and marketing, for example, which use little or no unskilled labor, while those activities that are more intensive in unskilled labor are "outsourced" to the south.

Growth of the relative capital stock in the south, or neutral technological progress relative to the north, will raise the critical ratio dividing the northern and southern activities. The activities transferred from the north to the south will be more skilled-labor intensive than those formerly produced in the south, but less skilled-labor intensive than those now produced in the north. It follows that the relative demand for skilled labor in *both* countries increases, which results in a higher relative wage for skilled workers. It is not the case, however, that unskilled workers in the north (or south) need be worse off in real terms because the increase in southern supply lowers the prices of goods available through trade, which may be enough to offset the wage reduction. Corresponding to the change in factor prices is an increase in the price index of Northern inputs relative to that of the South, so a modified Stolper-Samuelson result applies by comparing the country price indexes *within* each industry.

In section 6.4 we use the results of our model to reinterpret the evidence for the United States. Berman, Bound, and Griliches (1994) have argued that the magnitude of outsourcing—defined as the import of materials by U.S. firms—is too small to account for the observed wage and employment changes. Similarly Lawrence (1994) and Krugman (1994) argue that outsourcing and foreign direct investment through multinational firms is also too small to account for the changes. In contrast, we adopt a more general definition of outsourcing, which in addition to imports by U.S. multinationals, includes all imported intermediate or final goods that are used in the production of, or sold under the brandname of, an American firm. This definition of outsourcing corresponds to common usage and would include a very wide range of textiles and apparel, footwear, consumer electronics, and many other imports.

In our model, outsourcing increases the relative demand for skilled labor in both countries, and therefore acts as a type of "endogenous technical change" biased in favor of the skilled factor. Using the same data source as Berman, Bound, and Griliches (1994), we show that the increasing share of nonproduction workers in the United States is *positively and significantly* correlated with increasing imports: The rising import share over 1979–87 explains 15 to 33 percent of the shift toward nonproduction labor in U.S. manufacturing. Furthermore, using data from Lawrence and Slaughter (1993) and Lawrence (1994), we show that the modified Stolper-Samuelson result holds for the United States and other countries, so the commodity price movements are consistent with the factor price changes. This reinforces our view that trade and investment are an important part of the explanation for the pattern of wage and employment changes.

In section 6.5 we describe in more detail the movements in relative wages and employment in Mexico during the 1980s. A change in regulations during this period led to a very substantial inflow of foreign direct investment, particularly to the U.S.–Mexico border region. This is also the region where the greatest increase in the relative wages of nonproduction workers occurred. These observations support our theoretical model, under which the activities transferred to the border region would have a higher ratio of nonproduction/production workers than those previously in place. In section 6.6 we compare our results to other studies, and provide conclusions.

6.2   The Model

Our goal in this section is to construct a simple model that is consistent with the observations for the United States and Mexico, of rising relative wages for skilled workers. We will suppose that there is a single manufactured good, which is assembled from a continuum of intermediate inputs, indexed by $z \in [0, 1]$. Each unit of the input z uses $a_L(z)$ of unskilled labor and $a_H(z)$ of skilled labor, with the total usage of these factors in input z denoted by $L(z)$ and $H(z)$. We will arrange goods such that the ratio $a_H(z)/a_L(z)$ is *increasing* in z. In addition the production of each input requires capital $K(z)$, which substitutes for labor in a Cobb-Douglas production function:

$$x(z) = A_i \left[\min \left\{ \frac{L(z)}{a_L(z)}, \frac{H(z)}{a_H(z)} \right\} \right]^\theta [K(z)]^{1-\theta}, \tag{6.1}$$

where A_i is a constant that can differ between the north and south, $i = N, S$. Given these inputs, the final good Y is then costlessly assembled (in either country) according to the Cobb-Douglas function:

$$\ln Y = \int_0^1 \alpha(z) \ln x(z)\, dz, \quad \text{with} \quad \int_0^1 \alpha(z)\, dz = 1. \tag{6.2}$$

In addition to the "neutral" technological difference A_i, the north and the south differ in their supplies of the three factors. We will denote their endowments of unskilled labor, skilled labor and capital by L_i, H_i, and K_i, respectively, with the factor prices denoted by w_i, q_i, and r_i, for $i = N, S$. We will suppose that the technologies and factor endowments are sufficiently different so that factor prices are not equalized, with northern capital earning a lower rate of return ($r_N < r_S$), and the ratio of skilled/ unskilled wages being lower in the north ($q_N/w_N < q_S/w_S$). We will also let the supply of skilled and unskilled labor respond to the relative wages, with $L_i'(q_i/w_i) \le 0$ and $H_i'(q_i/w_i) > 0$. These supply responses may be due to more unskilled workers becoming skilled as the relative wage rises or may reflect excess supply from the rest of the economy, which we leave unspecified. Capital will flow between countries in response to the difference in the rates of return, though initially restrictions on foreign investment prevent this flow from occurring.

The minimum costs of producing one unit of $x(z)$ in country i takes the form,

$$c(w_i, q_i, r_i; z) = B_i [w_i a_L(z) + q_i a_H(z)]^\theta r_i^{1-\theta}, \tag{6.3}$$

where $B_i \equiv \theta^{-\theta}(1 - \theta)^{-(1-\theta)} A_i^{-1}$. For fixed wages, we will suppose that $c(w_i, q_i, r_i; z)$ is a continuous function of z. The locus of minimum costs for

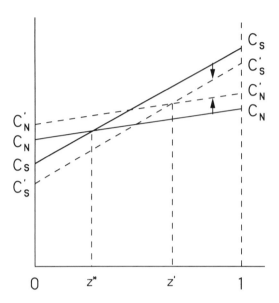

Figure 6.2
Determination of z^*

intermediate inputs produced in the north and south are graphed in figure 6.2 as $C_N C_N$ and $C_S C_S$, respectively. While the absolute slopes of these minimum cost lines are not determined, if inputs are produced in both countries (as we assume) then the relative slopes are determined: $C_S C_S$ must lie *above* $C_N C_N$ at high ratios of skilled to unskilled labor, indicating that the north has a cost advantage in that range (reflecting a lower relative wage of skilled workers), while the reverse holds at the low ratios. It can be verified that since capital enters with the same cost share $(1 - \theta)$ for all goods z in (6.2), costs are equalized at most at a single point, shown by z^* in figure 6.2 and satisfying

$$c_S(w_S, q_S, r_S; z^*) = c_N(w_N, q_N, r_N; z^*). \tag{6.4}$$

It follows that the activities $z > z^*$ will take place in the north, while the activities $z < z^*$ will take place in the south.

To determine the dividing point z^*, we utilize the full-employment conditions. The total demand for each factor is obtained by differentiating (6.3) with respect to its factor price, and integrating over all industries producing in each country. For the South, the full employment conditions for the two types of labor are given by

$$L_S\left(\frac{q_S}{w_S}\right) = \int_0^{z^*} B_S \theta \left[\frac{r_S}{w_S a_L(z) + q_S a_H(z)}\right]^{1-\theta} a_L(z) x_S(z)\, dz \qquad (6.5)$$

and

$$H_S\left(\frac{q_S}{w_S}\right) = \int_0^{z^*} B_S \theta \left[\frac{r_S}{w_S a_L(z) + q_S a_H(z)}\right]^{1-\theta} a_H(z) x_S(z)\, dz. \qquad (6.6)$$

An analogous expression can be written for capital, but instead, we will utilize the Cobb-Douglas production function in (6.1) to divide southern national income ($w_S L_S + q_S H_S + r_3 K_S$) into the labor share of θ and the capital share of $(1 - \theta)$. It follows that

$$r_S K_S = [w_S L_S + q_S H_S]\frac{1 - \theta}{\theta}. \qquad (6.7)$$

With demand for the intermediate inputs obtained from the Cobb-Douglas production function in (6.2), each input z receives the share of expenditure $\alpha(Z)$. The price of each input equals the minimum of the unit costs across the two countries. Letting E denote world expenditure on the final good Y, the demand for an input from the south is given by

$$x_S(z) = \frac{\alpha(z)E}{c_S(z)}, \qquad z \in [0, z^*). \qquad (6.8)$$

Then making use of the unit costs in (6.3) along with (6.8), the factor demands on the right side of (6.5) and (6.6) are simplified to obtain

$$L_S\left(\frac{q_S}{w_S}\right) = \int_0^{z^*} \theta \left[\frac{a_L(z)\alpha(z)E}{w_S a_L(z) + q_S a_H(z)}\right] dz \qquad (6.5')$$

and

$$H_S\left(\frac{q_S}{w_S}\right) = \int_0^{z^*} \theta \left[\frac{a_H(z)\alpha(z)E}{w_S a_L(z) + q_S a_H(z)}\right] dz. \qquad (6.6')$$

Notice that the return to capital r_S no longer appears in these expressions.

The equilibrium of the model is described by equations (6.4), (6.5'), (6.6'), (6.7), the analogous three full-employment conditions for the north, and the definition of world expenditure E as the sum of factor payments in both countries. This will give eight equations in eight unknowns—the three factor prices in each country $z*$ and world expenditure E. One equation can be dropped from Walras's law, and one variable can be chosen as numéraire. We will choose to normalize world expenditure at unity, $E \equiv 1$, so that all factor prices are being measured as shares of world factor income (equal to expenditure) in this industry. Then wages of each type of labor are simply determined as functions of $z*$ from (6.5′) and (6.6′), with the return to capital determined by (6.7), and $z*$ determined by (6.4).[3]

6.3   Effects of Southern Capital Growth

Relative Wages

We have assumed that the return to capital in the south exceeds that in the north, reflecting the scarcity or capital in the south. Suppose now that an amount of capital dK flows from the north to the south, earning the additional return $(r_S - r_N)dK > 0$. What will be the effect on relative wages?

Notice that for fixed $z*$, the wages of both types of labor are constant in (6.5′) and (6.6′), so the initial impact of the capital flow lowers the return to capital in the south from (6.7) and raises it in the north from the analogous condition there. This in turn lowers the southern cost locus $C_S C_S$ in figure 6.2 and raises the northern locus $C_N C_N$. Because the southern locus cuts the northern locus from below, this will *increase* the critical value of $z*$ to z' (at fixed wages), and the activities in the range $[z*, z')$ now will take place in the south rather than the north.

The activities in the range $[z*, z')$ are more skilled-labor intensive than any that formerly occurred in the south but less skilled-labor intensive than any that now occur in the north. Thus, at unchanged wages, this will increase the relative demand for skilled labor in *both* countries. This result can be verified by defining relative demand for skilled labor in the south as the ratio of (6.6′) and (6.5′)

$$D_S\left(\frac{q_S}{w_S}, z*\right) \equiv \frac{\int_0^{z*} a_H(z)\alpha(z)E/[w_S a_L(z) + q_S a_H(z)]\,dz}{\int_0^{z*} a_L(z)\alpha(z)E/[w_S a_L(z) + q_S a_H(z)]\,dz}. \tag{6.9}$$

The relative demand for skilled labor in the north, $D_N(q_N/w_N, z*)$, is defined by using the northern factor prices in evaluating the integrals in

(6.9) over $[z^*, 1]$. Letting $L_i(z^*) = \theta a_L(z^*)\alpha(z^*)E/[w_i a_L(z^*) + q_i a_H(z^*)]$ denote the unskilled labor used in z^* if it is produced only in country i, several properties of the relative demands are

LEMMA 6.1

i. $\partial \ln D_S/\partial z^* = [L_S(z^*)/H_S][a_H(z^*)/a_L(z^*) - H_S/L_S] > 0$, $\partial \ln D_N/\partial z^* = [L_N(z^*)/H_N][H_N/L_N - a_H(z^*)/a_L(z^*)] > 0$,

ii. $\partial \ln D_i/\partial \ln(q_i/w_i) < 0$, $i = N, S$.

Condition i follows directly from differentiation of (6.9) and the analogous relative demand for the north. These expressions are positive because the skilled/unskilled labor ratio at the critical value z^* exceeds the average for the south and is less than the average for the north. Condition ii states that the relative demand curves are a downward-sloping function of the relative wage. Although we provide a proof in the appendix, this condition actually follows directly from the well-behaved optimization problems solved by competitive markets in both countries. Letting $p_i(z) \equiv \min\{c_S(w_S, q_S, r_S; z), c_N(w_N, q_N, r_N; z)\}$ denote the prices of the intermediate inputs, competitive markets will maximize the value of industry production in each country, given the endowments (L_i, H_i, K_i):

$$E_i(L_i, H_i, K_i) \equiv \max_{x_i(z)} \int_0^1 p_i(z)x_i(z)\,dz, \qquad (6.10)$$

subject to the production functions (6.1) and the full-employment conditions in each country. Note that at the prices $p_i(z)$, the production of southern inputs $x_S(z)$ is chosen optimally as zero in (6.10) for $z \in (z^*, 1]$, and the production of northern inputs $x_N(z)$ is zero for $z \in [0, z^*)$. Since the production functions (6.1) are concave, as is the objective function in (6.10), the resulting industry-value functions $E_i(L_i, H_i, K_i)$ are a concave function of the factor endowments. The derivatives of the industry-value functions equal the factor prices, and then the downward-sloping relative demand for skilled labor follows from the concavity properties of $E_i(L_i, H_i, K_i)$.

Summing up, the capital flow will lead to an increase in z^*, which results in an increase in relative demand for skilled labor from A to B in figure 6.3. The situation in the north is analogous: The increase in z^* at fixed factor prices leads to a concentration of production in more skilled-labor

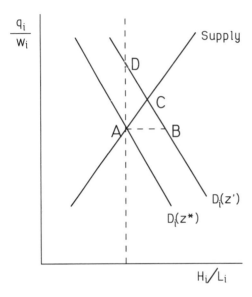

Figure 6.3
Labor market equilibrium

intensive activities, which raises the relative demand for skilled labor. The result is that the relative wage (q_i/w_i) in *both* countries increases. Of course these factor price changes feed back into figure 6.2, shifting both the cost loci. Under a stability condition that is verified below, we find that z^* will still increase after these factor prices changes are taken into account. We then obtain

PROPOSITION 6.1   With a capital flow from the north to the south:

i. the relative wage of skilled labor in *both* countries increases;

ii. the ratio of skilled/unskilled labor used in total production in each country is unchanged or increases.

Both these results follow from figure 6.3, where the equilibrium moves from A to C. The ratio of skilled/unskilled labor used in production in each country equals the relative supply $H_i(q_i/w_i)/L_i(q_i/w_i)$, which will increase if either of these factor supplies respond to the relative wage.

A further implication of the capital flow is that *variance* of the ratio of nonproduction/production workers across activities within the south increases, if the factor supplies are fixed. This is seen from figure 6.2, where the south moves into the range of activities $[z^*, z')$ that are more skilled-labor intensive than any inputs formerly produced. If the supplies of skilled and unskilled labor are fixed, then full-employment of these factors can occur only if employment at the lowest-skilled activities also increases, with less employment in the middle of the range $[0, z')$. Thus there is an expansion of the production of activities using both the highest and lowest ratios of skilled/unskilled labor, which corresponds to an increase in the variance of this ratio within the industry. We will confirm this prediction using data for Mexico in section 6.5.

To determine the pattern of factor price changes more fully, we can add w_S times (6.5′) plus q_S times (6.6′), and the analogous conditions for the north, to obtain

$$w_S L_S + q_S H_S = \theta \int_0^{z^*} \alpha(z)\,dz \tag{6.11a}$$

and

$$w_N L_N + q_N H_N = \theta \int_{z^*}^1 \alpha(z)\,dz. \tag{6.11b}$$

From these conditions we see that the increase in z^* implies that payments to labor (expressed as a fraction of total factor payments) will increase in the south but decline in the north. In this sense southern labor gains relative to northern labor. These results can also be expressed by letting $\lambda_{Li} = w_i L_i / (w_i L_i + q_i H_i)$ denote the share of unskilled labor in total wage payments in country i, with $\lambda_{Hi} = 1 - \lambda_{Li}$ denoting the share of skilled labor. Letting $\hat{z} = dz/z$ denote a logarithmic change, the implications of increasing z^* in (6.11) are summarized by

PROPOSITION 6.2   With a capital flow from the north to the south:

i. $\lambda_{LS}\hat{w}_S + \lambda_{HS}\hat{q}_S > 0 > \lambda_{LN}\hat{w}_N + \lambda_{HN}\hat{q}_N$;

ii. $\hat{q}_S > \max\{0, \hat{w}_S\}; \hat{w}_N < \min\{0, \hat{q}_N\}$.

Result i follows directly from differentiating (6.11), and it shows that southern workers obtain a larger overall share of global factor payments at the expense of northern labor. Note that the first inequality in i can be stated as $q_S > \lambda_{LS}(\hat{q}_S - \hat{w}_S)$, which is positive because the relative wage of skilled workers rises. This implies that skilled workers in the south will obtain a greater share of global factor payments, and establishes the first result in ii. The second result in i is obtained by working with the inequalities in i for the north and implies that unskilled workers in the north must obtain a smaller share of global factor payments. Despite this, we will argue below that all workers can gain from the capital flow.

Stability Condition and Real Wages

We still need to confirm the stability condition used in our results above, that the capital flow will lead to an increase in z^* even with factor prices changing endogenously. It turns out that a careful examination of this stability condition will allow us to generalize the above results to apply to *any* increase in the southern capital stock relative to the northern (not necessarily due to capital mobility) and also to technological progress in the south relative to the north.

Let us consider changes in the capital endowments $\hat{K}_i$ and in the technological parameters $\hat{A}_i$, $i = N, S$. Then in the appendix we show that

LEMMA 6.2   The change in z^* due to a change in capital endowments and technology is

$$dz^* = \Delta[(1 - \theta)(\hat{K}_S - \hat{K}_N) + (\hat{A}_S - \hat{A}_N)],$$

where

$$0 < \Delta < \left[\frac{\alpha(z^*)}{E_N} + \frac{\alpha(z^*)}{E_S}\right]^{-1}. \tag{6.12}$$

Thus growth in the relative southern capital stock ($\hat{K}_S > \hat{K}_N$) or in its technology ($\hat{A}_S > \hat{A}_N$) will ensure that the critical value z^* increases, leading to the changes in factor prices discussed in propositions 6.1 and 6.2. Formally, we state this as

COROLLARY

i. The pattern of relative wage and employment changes in propositions 6.1 and 6.2 hold for any increase in the southern capital stock relative to that in the north, or any increase in the technology parameter A_S relative to A_N.

ii. If the south is sufficiently small relative to the north, then the change in z^* is also small, and all workers in both countries gain from the capital flow or any absolute increase in the southern capital stock or technology parameter.

From part i the changes in wage and employment patterns that we have identified are not dependent on capital mobility across countries but apply more generally to any neutral increase in relative supply from the south. This generalization is important because, as noted by Bhagwati (1995, 46), more foreign direct investment entered the United States during the 1980s than exited, which would cast doubt on the applicability of our results if they relied solely on capital mobility. It is quite possible than the inbound foreign investment employed a higher ratio of skilled/unskilled labor than the outbound, as with foreign companies acquiring firms in Silicon Valley for their R&D expertise, for example. It follows that the *net flow* of capital is not sufficient to determine the impact on relative employment and wages. But regardless of the net flow of capital, the rapid growth of economies outside the United States—such as in the border region of Mexico, and the newly industrialized countries more generally—is enough to cause the "outsourcing" of intermediate inputs and the corresponding increase in the relative wage of skilled workers.

Although the gap between the wages of skilled and unskilled labor increases in both countries, it is not necessarily the case that any of these factors are worse off in real terms, as indicated by part ii. To obtain the *real return* to any factor, we need to determine the change in the price index for the final good Y, denoted by π. Multiplying this price index by aggregate output, we should obtain total expenditure, so $E = \pi Y$. With the normalization $E \equiv 1$, it can be confirmed that the increase in total output Y due to the capital flow is precisely $\hat{Y} = (r_S - r_N)\, dK > 0,$[4] so the price index π will fall by an equivalent amount: $\hat{\pi} = -\hat{Y} = -(r_S - r_N)\, dK < 0$. Notice that this fall in the price index is related to the initial differences in the return to capital but *not* to the extent of change in the critical value z^*.

However, the change in the factor prices reported in proposition 6.2 are all related to the extent of change in z^*. As the south becomes very small relative to the north, so that $E_S \to 0$ in (6.12), then we also have that $dz^* \to 0$. In that case the capital flow would have only a minimal effect on the wages in each country as a share of total factor payments. However, the capital flow will still result in a reduced price index π, so that the real returns w_i/π and q_i/π are *increased*, $i = N, S$. Thus all workers gain in real terms. This conclusion is also obtained for any absolute increase in the southern capital stock or technology parameter.

The result that all workers can gain is surprising and contradicts our intuition from a one-good model that in the country where capital is leaving, the marginal product of labor—and their real wage—must fall. However, the intuition that some workers must lose does not extend to a two-good, two-factor model, for example, where each country is fully specialized in its export good. In that case a capital flow from the north to the south will lower the northern wage in terms of its own good and also lower the relative price of the southern good. It is straightforward to show that if the elasticity of substitution in consumption is less than or equal to that in production, then the wage of northern labor in terms of the southern good will *rise*. Under this same condition, if the share of the two goods in consumption for all workers equal their world production shares (i.e., tastes are the same across countries), then both northern and southern workers necessarily gain in terms of their cost of living index. Thus we see that even in a conventional two-good trade model, capital mobility can improve the conditions of all workers. The same result is obtained in our model if the change in z^* is sufficiently small, as occurs when the southern country is small.

Terms of Trade

The bounds on the magnitude of dz^* in (6.12) can be used to establish a modified version of the Stolper-Samuelson theorem in this model. With the south exporting inputs in the range $z \in [0, z^*)$, and the north exporting those in the range $z \in (z^*, 1]$, the *terms of trade* is the ratio of the price index for inputs from each country. We will define the input price index implicitly, by taking the ratio of the nominal and real values of production. The nominal value of production $E_i(L_i, H_i, K_i)$ was given by (6.10). Let us define the $F[L_i, H_i, K_i; \bar{p}(z)]$ as the "real" value of production, evaluated at some fixed prices $\bar{p}(z)$:

$$F_i[(L_i, H_i, K_i; \bar{p}(z)] = \max_{x_i(z)} \int_0^1 \bar{p}(z)x_i(z)\,dz. \tag{6.13}$$

Then we will define the price index for country $i = N, S$ as

$$\pi_i[L_i, H_i, K_i; \bar{p}(z)] \equiv \frac{E_i(L_i, H_i, K_i)}{F_i[L_i, H_i, K_i; \bar{p}(z)]}, \tag{6.14}$$

and the terms of trade are $\pi_N/\pi_S = (E_N/F_N)/(E_S/F_S)$.

Obviously, when evaluating "real" production at the equilibrium prices, then $\pi_i[L_i, H_i, K_i; p(z)] \equiv 1$. Keeping $\bar{p}(z)$ fixed at the initial equilibrium prices $p(z)$, we can consider a small change in the price schedule $p(z)$, and in the endowments (L_i, H_i, K_i) and technology parameters A_i, to obtain the following change in the price index π_i:

$$
\begin{aligned}
\hat{\pi}_i &= \frac{1}{E_i}\left[\int_0^1 p(z)\, dx_i(z)\, dz + \int_0^1 dp(z) x_i(z)\, dz\right] - \frac{1}{F_i}\left[\int_p^1 \bar{p}(z)\, dx_i(z)\, dz\right] \\
&= \frac{1}{E_i}\left[\int_0^1 dp(z) x_i(z)\, dz\right] \\
&= \int_0^1 \hat{p}(z)\gamma_i(z)\, dz, \tag{6.15}
\end{aligned}
$$

where

$$\gamma_i(z) \equiv \frac{p(z)x_i(z)}{E_i}.$$

The first line in (6.15) follows by definition of the price index in (6.13), the second line follows because we are evaluating $F_i[L_i, H_i, K_i; \bar{p}(z)]$ at $\bar{p}(z) = p(z)$, and the third line follows by definition of γ_i as the shares of production for each intermediate input z. From the last line, we can interpret $\hat{\pi}_i$ as a weighted average of the (percentage) change in inputs prices, where the weights $\gamma_i(z)$ equal zero for $z \in [0, z^*)$ and $i = N$, or for $z \in (z^*, 1]$ and $i = S$. Thus the change in the terms of trade π_N/π_S is

$$\hat{\pi}_N - \hat{\pi}_S = \int_{z^*}^1 \hat{p}(z)\gamma_N(z)\, dz - \int_0^{z^*} \hat{p}(z)\gamma_S(z)\, dz.$$

This is simply the difference in a weighted average of the change in input prices for each country. The question we wish to address is whether this change in this terms of trade can be related to change in relative wages.

With the normalization $E \equiv 1$, the values of industry production E_i in (6.10) can be written alternatively as shares of world production, $E_N = \int_{z^*}^1 \alpha(z)\, dz$ and $E_S = \int_0^{z^*} \alpha(z)\, dz$. Then $\hat{E}_N - \hat{E}_S = -\{[\alpha(z^*)/E_N] +$

$[\alpha(z^*)/E_S]\} \, dz^*$. Furthermore the change in the "real" outputs due to changes in capital and technology are simply $\hat{F}_i = \hat{A}_i + (1 - \theta)\hat{K}_i$, $i = N$, S. Then by definition of the terms of trade $\pi_N/\pi_S = (E_N/F_N)/(E_S/F_S)$, it follows that

$$\hat{\pi}_N - \hat{\pi}_S = [(1 - \theta)(\hat{K}_S - \hat{K}_N) + (\hat{A}_S - \hat{A}_N)] - \left[\frac{\alpha(z^*)}{E_N} + \frac{\alpha(z^*)}{E_S}\right] dz^*,$$

which is *positive* whenever $[(1 - \theta)(\hat{K}_S - \hat{K}_N) + (\hat{A}_S - \hat{A}_N)] > 0$, from (6.12). Thus we have established

PROPOSITION 6.3   Corresponding to the increase in the relative wage of skilled labor in both countries, there is an increase in the price index of the northern inputs relative to that of the south.

Given that all the inputs produced in the north are more skilled-labor intensive than those in the south, this result is in the same spirit as the Stolper-Samuelson theorem. In contrast to that theorem, however, the northern and southern price indexes refer to the intermediate inputs used in the production of a given final output. In practice we could measure these indexes as the price deflators for domestic value added as compared to imports, either within a given industry, or aggregated across the entire economy. Note that in our model the assembly of the aggregate output Y requires no additional factors beyond the intermediate inputs, so that value added in this activity is zero; thus it can be done in either country and will not affect the price deflators for value added. A comparison of domestic and import prices for the United States and other industrialized countries will be made in the next section.

6.4   Reinterpretation of U.S. Evidence

Domestic and Import Prices

The results we have obtained above offer some guidance on how to interpret the existing evidence on U.S. wages and employment. We begin by reexamining the price evidence of Lawrence and Slaughter (1993). They have found that the prices of U.S. imports that are intensive in production workers *did not fall* relative to imports that are intensive in nonproduction workers, and for this reason they argue that the rising relative wages of nonproduction workers could not be attributed to the price movements.

Table 6.1
Employment-weighted percentage changes in wholesale and import prices

	Domestic prices	Import prices
United States (1980–89)		
All manufacturing industries		
Nonproduction weights	33.1	26.0
Production weights	32.3	28.1
Japan (1980–90)		
All manufacturing industries		
Nonproduction weights	−5.60	−18.23
Production weights	−3.90	−17.29
Without office machines		
Nonproduction weights	−7.09	−18.69
Production weights	−4.72	−17.50
Also without petroleum products		
Nonproduction weights	−6.98	−18.45
Production weights	−4.66	−17.39
Germany (1980–90)		
All manufacturing industries		
Nonmanual weights	23.98	15.24
Manual weights	26.03	17.07
Without office machines		
Nonmanual weights	24.79	15.38
Manual weights	26.21	17.11
Also without petroleum products		
Nonmanual weights	24.97	15.70
Manual weights	26.28	17.24

Sources: Lawrence and Slaughter (1993, tables 3 and 4); Lawrence (1994, table 4).
Note: Nonproduction and nonmanual weights weight each industry's price change by that industry's share of total manufacturing employment of nonproduction and nonmanual workers, and similarly for production and manual worker weights. Industries are defined at the three-digit SIC level for the United States, and generally correspond to the two-digit SITC level for Japan and Germany.

Lawrence (1994) finds similar evidence for Japan and Germany. Their results for these countries are reproduced in table 6.1.

The first rows of table 6.1 report the percentage change in U.S. domestic and import prices, where the aggregate price change is obtained as a weighted sum of the three-digit SIC price changes, using the employment of either nonproduction or production workers as weights. For domestic prices these alternate weighting schemes make little difference, but for import prices the average price change using nonproduction workers as weights is *lower* than the change using production workers as weights. This indicates that the prices of imports intensive in production labor *rose* slightly relative to the prices of imports intensive in nonproduction labor:

just the opposite of the expected Stolper-Samuelson pattern. Exactly the same result is obtained by comparing the domestic or import prices with the differing weighting schemes for Japan and Germany, even after office machines and also petroleum products are excluded from the aggregate indexes.

However, the difference between the price indexes obtained with production and nonproduction weights—which is of principal interest to Lawrence and Slaughter—seems to be of second order compared to the direct comparison of the domestic and import prices in table 6.1: For all countries and indexes the domestic prices rose by more than the import prices. This is precisely the pattern of price changes reported in proposition 6.3, and it is fully consistent with an increase in the relative wages of nonproduction workers. This modified Stolper-Samuelson result recognizes that the factor intensities of northern production and imports from the south within the same industry are likely to differ, with the domestic industry employing a higher ratio of nonproduction workers. Thus the increase in the price of domestic production relative to imports is fully consistent with the increase in the relative wage of these workers.

Outsourcing

We have seen in figure 6.3 that the transfer of activities from the north to the south—or the increase in z^*—increases the relative demand for skilled labor in both countries. In this sense, the transfer of activities acts as a form of "endogenous technical change." Our model thus provides a simple formalization of the idea that trade will induce a shift in the factor intensities in production, as discussed by Wood (1994, 1995). While Berman, Bound, and Griliches find very substantial evidence of a change in the skilled/unskilled ratio across many U.S. industries, they reject outsourcing as a possible explanation. In their working paper (1993, 19–20) they note that the 1987 *Census of Manufactures* reports that foreign materials constitute only 8 percent of all materials purchased in manufacturing. Based on this figure, they calculate that replacing all outsourcing with domestic activity would raise manufacturing employment of production workers by only 2.8 percent.

There are several reasons, however, why this calculation may underestimate the extent of outsourcing. First, an imported intermediate input could be processed and resold several times between firms, but it would only be counted as an "import" when it first enters the United States. This means that there could be double counting in the "domestic materials" as compared to imports, so the 8 percent figure may be biased downward. Second, the value of "imported materials" in the 1987 *Census of Manufactures* includes only the "cost of materials, parts, components, containers, etc.," but *explicitly excludes* the "cost of products bought and sold as such" and "contract work done for you by others."[5] This means that the measure of outsourcing obtained from the Census excludes all offshore assembly and goods purchased on an OEM (original equipment manufacturer) basis. For example, Nike currently employs 2,500 person in the United States for marketing and other headquarters services, while about 75,000 persons are employed in Asia producing shoes that are sold to Nike.[6] Since these shoes are finished products when they enter the United States, they would not be counted as "materials" nor included in the Census measure of outsourcing. The same is true for General Electric, which currently imports all of the microwaves marketed under its brandname from Samsung in Korea (Magaziner and Patinkin 1989), but these imports occur as finished products rather than as materials. Activity of this sort is certainly typical of footwear (Yoffie and Gomes-Casseres 1994, case 7), textiles (Waldinger 1986; Gereffi 1993), electronics (Alic and Harris 1986), and many other industries in the United States, and they must be included in any valid measure of outsourcing.

A related question about what constitutes outsourcing arises in Lawrence (1994), who focuses on the imports of U.S. multinational firms as one measure of outsourcing. Similarly Krugman (1994) argues that flows of foreign direct investment through multinational firms is also too small to account for the observed wage or employment changes. In contrast, we adopt a more general definition of outsourcing, which in addition to imports by U.S. multinationals, includes all imported intermediate or final goods that are used in the production of, or sold under the brandname of, an American firm. The reason the brandname is important is that some of these U.S. firms will also be engaged in manufacturing activities and therefore included in the *Census of Manufactures*. As these firms choose to import rather than produce domestically, the composition of their work force between production and nonproduction workers will certainly be affected. In our model such outsourcing occurs due to growth in the relative southern capital stock or neutral technological progress in that country relative to the north.

Table 6.2
Annual rates of change in U.S. variables, selected periods

Variable[a]	1953–73	1973–79	1979–87
ΔS_N	0.070	0.208	0.431
$\Delta \ln(K/Y)$	0.241	1.159	0.813
$\Delta \ln(P/Y)$	−0.445	−0.463	−0.557
$\Delta \ln(E/Y)$	1.281	2.589	1.858
$\Delta \ln Y$	4.095	2.221	1.800
ΔS_M	0.249	0.290	0.656

Source: NBER productivity (Bartelsman and Gray 1994) and trade database (Abowd 1991).
Note: Data are weighted by the average share of the industry wage bill in manufacturing.
The sample consists of 450 four-digit SIC manufacturing industries for all variables except
ΔS_M, in which case data is available for 436 manufacturing industries (435 in 1979–87).
a. Variables are defined as
$\Delta S_N = 100 \times$ annual change in nonproduction workers' share of wage bill,
$\Delta \ln Y = 100 \times$ annual change in natural log of real output,
$\Delta \ln(K/Y) = 100 \times$ annual change in ln(capital stock/real output),
$\Delta \ln(P/Y) = 100 \times$ annual change in ln(plant/real output),
$\Delta \ln(E/Y) = 100 \times$ annual change in ln(equipment/real output),
$\Delta S_M = 100 \times$ annual change in imports/(shipments + imports).

If our more general definition of outsourcing is accepted, the question
is whether this can account for a significant part of the shift towards
nonproduction workers in the United States. To determine this, we extend
the regressions presented by Berman, Bound, and Griliches (1994), in
which changes in the share of nonproduction labor in the total wage bill is
explained on the basis of various industry variables. They did not include
imports as an explanatory variable, whereas we shall include the change
in the import share.[7] The data are a panel of 450 four-digit SIC industries
in the United States, which is an revised version of that used by Berman,
Bound, and Griliches.[8] The mean values for the variables over several time
periods are presented in table 6.2.[9] We see that the annual increase in the
share of nonproduction labor in the wage bill doubled from 0.21 to 0.43
percent between the 1973–79 period and 1979–87. Capital is measured
both as an aggregate, and separately as plant and equipment. Production
became more capital intensive over all the periods shown, but this is
explained by the growth of equipment/output rather than plant/output as
the growth of output continually slowed over the time periods. It is notable that the annual increase in the import share also doubled from 0.29 to
0.66 percent between 1973–79 and 1979–87 (the aggregate value of the
import share was 8.3 percent in 1979 and 13.1 percent in 1987).

Table 6.3
Regression results with import share. Dependent variable: Annual change in nonproduction workers' share in wage bill (ΔS_N), 1959–73, 1973–79, 1979–87 combined.

Regression	1	2	3	4	5
$\Delta \ln(K/Y)$		0.012		0.066	
		(0.004)		(0.007)	
$\Delta \ln(P/Y)$			−0.018		0.057
			(0.005)		(0.010)
$\Delta \ln(E/Y)$			0.027		0.020
			(0.005)		(0.006)
$\Delta \ln Y$				0.051	0.060
				(0.005)	(0.006)
ΔS_M	0.170	0.173	0.098	0.056	0.095
	(0.029)	(0.029)	(0.034)	(0.036)	(0.038)
1973–79	0.138	0.126	0.105	0.180	0.231
	(0.081)	(0.083)	(0.084)	(0.096)	(0.097)
1979–87	0.299	0.291	0.311	0.425	0.463
	(0.083)	(0.083)	(0.085)	(0.096)	(0.098)
Constant	0.024	0.020	−0.002	−0.172	−0.205
	(0.058)	(0.059)	(0.060)	(0.071)	(0.071)
R^2	0.058	0.073	0.107	0.311	0.309

Note: Equations are weighted by the average share of industry wage bill in manufacturing. The sample consists of the 436 (435 in 1979–87) four-digit SIC industries for which import data are available.

In table 6.3 we report the results from regressing the annual change in the share of nonproduction workers on a constant, dummy variables for the 1973–79 and 1979–87 periods, other variables used by Berman, Bound, and Griliches, and the change in the import share. The first equation in table 6.3 shows the result of just including the import share and time dummies. The coefficient of 0.17 on the import share is highly significant, and is also economically important: Multiplying this by the annual growth rate of 0.656 percent for the import share, we obtain an impact of 0.11 percent on the share of nonproduction labor, or about *one-quarter* of the annual change in this variable over 1979–87. The same estimate is obtained when the change in the capital/output ratio is included. However, when plant and equipment are included separately in regression 3, the coefficient on the change in the import share drops to 0.098. Again multiplying this by the annual growth rate of 0.656 percent, we obtain an impact of 0.064 percent annually on the share of nonproduction labor, or 15 percent of the annual change over 1979–87. When the growth in output is included along with the capital/output labor in regression 4, the import coefficient drops further, but when output growth is included along with plant and equipment in regression 5, we again find that rising imports explains about 15 percent of the increase in the share of non-production labor.

In table 6.4 we repeat the same regressions, but using only the 1979–87 period. When the change in the import share is included alone, or with the capital/output ratio, then its coefficient of 0.225 explains fully *one-third* (0.225 × 0.656/0.431) of the increase in the share of nonproduction labor. The import coefficient is entirely insignificant when plant and equipment are entered separately (regression 3) but becomes significant again when the output variable is included. If we are willing to ignore the highly imprecise estimate in regression 3, then the range of coefficients obtained indicate that the growth of imports over 1979–87 explains 15–33 percent of the increase in the share of nonproduction labor, which is slightly wider than the range we obtain over the entire 1959–87 period.

It would be of interest to extend this estimation to later years, especially since the wages of nonproduction workers rose so much at the end of the 1980s. While the nonproduction share and other domestic variables are available for later years, this is not the case for the import data, which are available only on an SIC basis until 1985. For the data used in tables 6.2–6.4, we have followed Berman, Bound, and Griliches (1994, note 7) in extrapolating the import data forward to 1987, treating the annual growth of import shares over 1979–85 and 1979–87 as identical. Obviously there is little point in estimating these regressions over later time periods until the import data are concorded to the domestic SIC data, as described for the years before 1985 in Abowd (1991).

Extending the data forward would also allow the estimation to be performed separately within individual industries (or narrow groups), since there is no reason for the coefficients of the import shares and other variables to be identical across industries, as we have presumed. This point can be emphasized by plotting the values for the change in the nonproduction share of the wage bill (ΔS_N) against the change in the import share (ΔS_M), over 1979–87, as in figure 6.4; both variables are weighted by the share of the industry wage bill in total manufacturing, averaged over the two years 1979 and 1987, and then multiplied by 100. This is the same weighting scheme that was used in the regressions in table 6.4. It means that only those SIC industries that have a large change in the

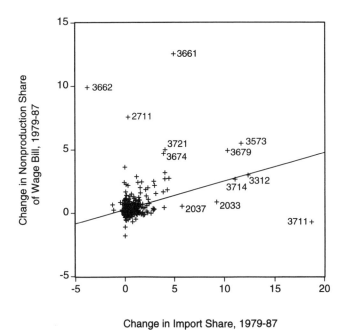

Figure 6.4
Scatter plot

Table 6.4
Regression results with import share. Dependent variable: Annual change in nonproduction workers' share in wage bill (ΔS_N), 1979–87 only.

Regression	1	2	3	4	5
$\Delta \ln(K/Y)$		0.013		0.096	
		(0.005)		(0.006)	
$\Delta \ln(P/Y)$			−0.083		0.062
			(0.006)		(0.015)
$\Delta \ln(E/Y)$			0.104		0.047
			(0.007)		(0.008)
$\Delta \ln Y$				0.066	0.074
				(0.003)	(0.007)
ΔS_M	0.225	0.225	0.019	0.119	0.136
	(0.030)	(0.030)	(0.027)	(0.023)	(0.028)
Constant	0.287	0.277	0.178	0.156	0.158
	(0.054)	(0.053)	(0.043)	(0.040)	(0.039)
R^2	0.115	0.126	0.429	0.527	0.538

Note: Equations are weighted by the average share of industry wage bill in manufacturing. The sample consists of the 435 four-digit SIC industries in 1979–87 for which import data are available.

shares, and are also reasonably large within total manufacturing, will be important. The regression line shown in figure 6.4 has the slope 0.225, as in the first regression of table 6.4.

It is evident from the figure 6.4 that there is an enormous variation across industries in the relation between the change in the import shares and the change in the nonproduction share of the wage bill. Moving in a clockwise direction, the SIC industries labeled in figure 6.4 are as follows:

1972 SIC number	Description
3662	Radio and TV communications equipment
3661	Telephone and telegraph apparatus
2711	Newspapers
3721	Aircraft
3674	Semiconductors and related devices
3573	Electronic computing equipment
3679	Electronic components, not elsewhere classified
3312	Blast furnaces and steel mills
3714	Motor vehicle parts and accessories
2033	Canned fruits and vegetables
2037	Frozen fruits and vegetables
3711	Motor vehicles and passenger car bodies

Except for the first and last industries listed, the others all show a positive relation between the increase in the nonproduction share of the wage bill and rising imports, though the magnitude of this relation varies considerably. The first industry above (radio and TV communications equipment) has a very large increase in the nonproduction wage-bill share, but a fall in imports, and conversely for the last industry (motor vehicles and car bodies).[10] Prominent in the list above are various industrial machinery, electronic and transportation industries (SIC 35, 36, and 37). Also present are canned and frozen fruits and vegetables (SIC 203), which has experienced a significant outflow of foreign investment to Mexico as processing of these products occurs closer to the growing sites (Feenstra and Rose 1993). Curiously absent from the list, however, are textile, apparel, and footwear industries (SIC 22, 23, and 31). These observations under-

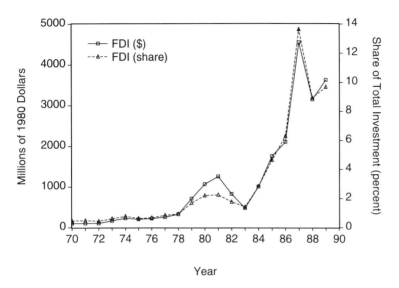

Figure 6.5
Foreign direct investment into Mexico

score the importance of investigating the link between imports and wages using an industry-by-industry approach.

6.5 Evidence from Mexico

Foreign Investment

During the 1980s Mexico experienced a dramatic increase in foreign capital inflows. Figure 6.5 shows foreign direct investment (FDI) in Mexico, and FDI as a share of total fixed capital investment. The measure of FDI we use is that calculated by the Mexican National Commission on Foreign Investment, which collects data directly from foreign firms on new investments and reinvestments from retained earnings (Nacional Financiera 1990). Between 1983 and 1989 the level of FDI in Mexico increased from $478 million to $3,635 million; the share of FDI in total investment increased from 1.4 percent to 9.7 percent.

The boom in FDI is attributable, at least in part, to reforms by the Mexican government during the 1980s that eased restrictions on foreign ownership. Mexico has a long history of regulating the activities of multinational enterprises. Restrictions on foreign investment reached their height in the 1970s, when the government began to strictly enforce a 49 percent foreign ownership cap on equity holdings in a given firm. Following the onset of the Mexican debt crisis in 1982, the government reversed its policy and began to eliminate impediments to foreign capital. In particular, the government waved the 49 percent foreign ownership cap for many new investors. A new foreign investment law passed in 1989 formally lifted the 49 percent cap and opened most sectors of the economy to FDI (Whiting 1992).

A large share of the FDI in Mexico has gone into in-bond assembly operations, known as *maquiladoras*, which are an example of foreign outsourcing by multinationals. Not all maquiladoras are foreign owned but the majority appear to be; of the 100 largest maquiladoras in 1990, 88 were majority-owned by foreign entities.[11] While we do not have data on the portion of FDI that has gone into maquiladoras, we do have data that show that the FDI boom coincided with a large expansion in assembly operations. Figure 6.6 shows total maquiladora employment from 1978 to 1990, both in the number of workers and as a share of manufacturing

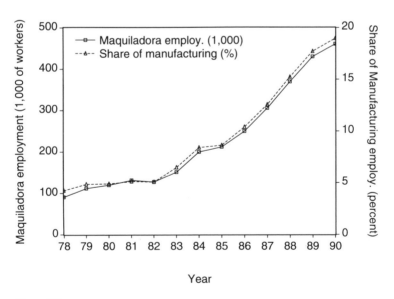

Figure 6.6
Maquiladora employment

employment. During the period 1978 to 1983, assembly employment grew at an average annual rate of 10.2 percent; during the period 1983 to 1990, it grew at an average annual rate of 15.9 percent.[12] The share of maquiladora workers in total manufacturing employment increased dramatically from 4.9 percent in 1980 to 19.0 percent in 1990. Maquiladora activities are concentrated in states along the Mexico–U.S. border: In 1990 the border region accounted for 90.3 percent of total assembly employment.

Relative Wages and Employment

Mexico's FDI boom represents a natural experiment of sorts, since it was large in relation to total capital investment and in the employment generated. The model we developed in the previous sections predicts that such capital inflows will increase the demand for skilled workers relative to that of unskilled workers and cause the relative wages of skilled workers to increase. This prediction was confirmed for Mexico as a whole from the Industrial Census data in figure 6.1. Since much of the foreign investment has been concentrated in the Mexico–U.S. border region, the relative-demand effects should be strongest for border states. Hence it is the border where we expect to observe the largest changes in relative wages.

We report data on the wages and employment of skilled and unskilled workers in Mexico from a panel of 2,354 manufacturing plants for the period 1984 to 1990 surveyed by the Mexican Ministry of Trade (SECOFI).[13] This sample classifies employees either as production workers or as nonproduction workers. Table 6.5 shows that there has been a dramatic increase in the wage of nonproduction relative to production workers in the SECOFI sample of plants. Between 1984 and 1990 the ratio of average hourly nonproduction and production wages increased from 1.93 to 2.55; the ratio of average annual earnings showed a similar change.[14] These data reinforce the conclusion from Figure 6.1 of rising relative wages in the latter half of the 1980s, which reverses a prolonged period of falling relative wages.

Despite the magnitude of the relative-wage changes, there were only small changes in the relative employment of nonproduction and production workers in Mexico during the 1980s. Table 6.6 shows the ratio of nonproduction and production employment for the SECOFI panel of plants. Between 1984 and 1990 the ratio of aggregate employment in the SECOFI sample of plants increased from 0.431 to 0.433; the ratio of

Table 6.5
Average annual real wages in manufacturing, 1984–90 (values are in 1980 pesos)

Year	Nonproduction workers		Production workers		Nonproduction/ production	
	Annual earnings	Hourly wages	Annual earnigs	Hourly wages	Annual earnings	Hourly wages
1984	138,793	62.127	72,528	32.191	1.914	1.930
1985	143,692	63.856	74,952	32.783	1.917	1.948
1986	137,444	60.641	68,525	29.929	2.006	2.027
1987	134,474	59.014	67,559	29.243	1.991	2.018
1988	122,241	53.557	57,781	24.729	2.116	2.166
1989	145,487	64.278	62,755	26.809	2.318	2.398
1990	160,502	70.460	64,935	27.691	2.472	2.545

Source: Calculations based on SECOFI sample data.
Note: Real wages are nominal annual remuneration per worker and per hour worked, deflated by the June consumer price index. All figures are weighted averages, where weights are the plant share of national employment or hours.

aggregate total hours declined from 0.427 to 0.421. While average relative employment did not change, the variance in relative employment within industries changed considerably. The fifth and final columns of table 6.6 report the weighted-average standard deviation in relative employment for four-digit industries, where weights are industry shares of total employment. The standard deviation of relative employment increased by approximately 25 percent between 1984 and 1990. This is consistent with the pattern of production and employment changes that occur in our model. As noted in section 6.2, when the south moves into new activities that are more skilled-labor intensive than those previously performed, an increase in the variance of skilled/unskilled labor in activities within the industry is expected. This prediction is confirmed by the standard deviations in table 6.6.

One striking feature of Mexico's wage structure is that relative wages and changes in relative wages vary considerably across regions within the country. Table 6.7 shows relative average hourly wages and relative average annual earnings for the SECOFI sample by region.[15] Not only does the border have the highest relative wages in any given year, but that region also experienced the largest increased in relative wages over the period 1984 to 1990. The region with the next highest relative wages and the next highest increase in the relative wage is the north.

Table 6.6
Relative employment in manufacturing, 1984–90

	Number of production and nonproduction workers				Thousands of hours worked			
	Production workers	Nonproduction	Mean ratio	Standard deviation of ratio[a]	Production workers	Nonproduction	Mean ratio	Standard deviation of ratio[a]
1984	234,851	545,477	0.431	0.398	524,666	1,229,016	0.427	0.395
1985	239,847	560,738	0.428	0.374	539,713	1,282,056	0.421	0.392
1986	242,189	550,963	0.440	0.401	548,925	1,261,465	0.435	0.414
1987	241,528	545,937	0.442	0.446	550,368	1,261,272	0.436	0.438
1988	243,741	549,839	0.443	0.468	556,327	1,284,741	0.443	0.458
1989	248,840	566,737	0.439	0.474	563,229	1,326,644	0.425	0.456
1990	250,066	577,405	0.433	0.492	569,629	1,353,991	0.421	0.492

Source: Calculations based on SECOFI sample data.
a. Ratio computed by first calculating the standard deviation of the ratio of production/nonproduction workers or hours across plants within each four-digit industry. A weighted sum of these standard deviations is taken where the weights are the four-digit industry share of total employment or total hours.

Table 6.7
Nonproduction/production wages by region

Region	Year	Hourly wage	Log change 1984–90	Annual wage	Log change 1984–90
Border	1984	2.007		1.970	
	1985	2.121		2.103	
	1986	2.192		2.123	
	1987	2.271		2.220	
	1988	2.409		2.442	
	1989	2.579		2.611	
	1990	3.019	0.408	3.020	0.427
North	1984	2.002		2.061	
	1985	2.020		2.052	
	1986	2.012		2.015	
	1987	1.778		1.787	
	1988	1.697		1.868	
	1989	2.408		2.482	
	1990	2.620	0.269	2.632	0.245
Center	1984	1.798		1.695	
	1985	1.740		1.731	
	1986	1.825		1.849	
	1987	1.799		1.770	
	1988	1.860		1.849	
	1989	2.041		2.045	
	1990	1.980	0.096	2.036	0.183
Mexico City	1984	1.931		2.023	
	1985	1.908		1.986	
	1986	2.005		2.036	
	1987	1.934		2.007	
	1988	2.086		2.134	
	1989	2.279		2.402	
	1990	2.523	0.267	2.605	0.253
South	1984	1.889		1.943	
	1985	1.892		1.928	
	1986	1.989		2.042	
	1987	1.994		2.060	
	1988	2.147		2.224	
	1989	2.357		2.465	
	1990	2.473	0.269	2.573	0.281

Source: Calculations based on SECOFI sample data.

Table 6.8
Relative wages by region, controlling for industry

Region	Mean for 1984–90[a]		Log change for 1984–90[b]	
	RLWGE1	RLWGE2	RLWGE1	RLWGE2
Border	0.0539 (0.0281)	0.0575 (0.0288)	0.0561	0.0506
North	0.0356 (0.0762)	0.0552 (0.0727)	−0.0484	−0.0801
Center	−0.0263 (0.0159)	−0.0340 (0.0154)	−0.0484	0.0130
Mexico City	−0.0134 (0.0127)	−0.0161 (0.0089)	0.0345	0.0163
South	−0.0169 (0.0193)	−0.0129 (0.0190)	0.0111	−0.0024

Source: Calculations based on SECOFI sample data.
Note: Figures are the regional weighted sums of variables defined below, where the weights are plant share of the regional wage bill, and the relative wage is the nonproduction/ production wage. Industries are defined at the four-digit level. RLWGE1 = log plant relative annual wage − log industry relative annual wage; RLWGE2 = log plant relative hourly wage − log industry relative hourly wage.
a. Means and standard deviations (in parentheses) are taken over the seven years for which the weighted sums are calculated.
b. The log change is the difference between the weighted sum of RLWGE1 or RLWGE2 for each region between 1984 and 1990.

One explanation for the regional variation in relative wages may be that the border, for whatever reason, contains a relatively high concentration of industries that are relatively intensive in the use of skilled labor. To control for the effects of industry composition on regional relative wages, we calculate the regional average wage differential, which is defined as the weighted sum of the log difference between the plant's relative wage and the industry average relative wage, where weights are the plant share of the regional wage bill. Table 6.8 reports the results. Controlling for industry, we still find that the border has the highest relative wages and the largest increase in the relative wage. This confirms our expectations about the regional effects of FDI on Mexico's wage structure.

The boom in FDI was certainly not the only shock to the Mexican economy in the 1980s. Two events of particular importance for the labor market were the liberalization of trade, which was initiated in 1985, and the relaxation of minimum wages, which began in 1983. We regard the trade liberalization as an additional cause of the foreign investment boom, since firms entering Mexico would be able to import inputs at lower tariffs and could also be anticipating the future reduction of U.S. and Canadian trade barriers under the NAFTA. Thus the liberalization of trade and foreign investment are highly complementary, and we will not attempt to disentangle these effects.

The relaxation of minimum wages, by contrast, does not appear to have been an important factor in the relative wage movement. During the 1980s the Mexican government chose not to increase minimum wages in line with inflation. The result was a decrease in the real product minimum wage by 30.8 percent between 1984 and 1990. Bell (1994) studies minimum wages and labor demand in Mexico over the period 1984 to 1990 using the SECOFI sample data. She finds that in 1984, the year minimum wages were most binding, only 1.9 percent of manufacturing plants had an average production worker wage at or below the minimum. She also finds no evidence of a negative correlation between minimum wages and employment. These results suggest that the decline in minimum wages do not account for the fall in the relative wage of production workers.

6.6   Conclusions

For the United States the regression results reported in section 6.4 indicate that 15 to 33 percent of the shift towards nonproduction labor within U.S. manufacturing industries over 1979 to 1985 is explained by the rising import share. This figure can be compared to the estimated impact of computers from Berman, Bound and Griliches (1994), who find that 40 percent of the increase in the share of nonproduction labor can be attributed to the rapid introduction of computers during the 1980s. (These authors find also find that just under 40 percent of the shift toward nonproduction labor can be explained by R&D expenditures.) While the impact of trade in these estimates is less than the impact of computers, we have not considered several other ways that trade competition can affect wages and employment.

First, trade has an impact on wages and employment through the amounts of skilled versus unskilled labor embodied in exports and imports, which can be modeled as (hypothetical) changes in the endowments of these factors. Borjas, Freeman, and Katz (1992) find that trade flows between 1980 and 1980 can explain up to 15 percent of the increase in the earnings differential between college-educated workers and those with only high-school education in the United States. Leamer (1993) obtains a somewhat higher estimate of 20 percent as the amount of income transferred away from low-skilled workers in the United States in 1985, and this can be attributed to trade. On the employment side, Wood (1994) suggests that no less than 20 percent of the decline in the demand for unskilled relative to skilled workers in developed countries over 1960 to 1990 is due to trade, with three-quarters of this decline taking place during the 1980s. Most recently Sachs and Shatz (1994) estimate that as much as 40 percent of the difference between the employment growth during 1950 to 1978 and employment decline during 1978 to 1990 in U.S. manufacturing can be attributed to the impact of trade. The employment decline during the latter period has been disproportionately on production workers.

Second, it is quite possible that a cross-sectional analysis of industry changes misses some of the impact of trade. We have already seen this in our data for Mexico, where there was little change in the ratio of production to nonproduction workers within individual industries or manufacturing overall (table 6.6) but substantial changes in employment and wages across regions of the country (table 6.7), especially the border with the United States. This suggests that *regional variation* may be able to pick up effects of trade that cross-industry data does not. This is confirmed for Mexico in Feenstra and Hanson (1995), who find that over 50 percent of the increase in the share of skilled labor in total wages is explained by growth in FDI in the border region. Borjas and Ramey (1993) have used data on wages across metropolitan areas in the United States to study the impact of trade in durable goods, and they obtain a lower bound of 10 percent as the impact of trade on wages. Furthermore *time-series variation* within each industry can be expected to give a more accurate description of the impact of imports, since there is no reason for the amount of outsourcing to be similar across industries.

Finally, variation in plants within each industry can also show greater changes than the industry data. We found this was true for the Mexican plant-level data, which showed increases in the variance of nonproduction/ production employment across plants within each industry (table 6.6), consistent with our theoretical model. For the United States, Bernard and Jensen (1996) have used plant-level data to decompose the increase in relative nonproduction employment into "within" versus "between" plant effects. They obtain much higher estimates of the "between" effect than found by Berman, Bound, and Griliches (1994) using industry-level data, and furthermore these effects are dominated by the changes in employment at *exporting plants*. Their results reinforce our conclusion that in addition to technological change, trade and investment are important contributing factors to the decline in the relative wages and employment of unskilled workers in the United States.

6.7 Appendix

Proof of Lemma 6.1

Part i follows from differentiation of (6.9) and the analogous relative demand for the north. To establish part ii for the south, we can differentiate (6.9) and rewrite terms to obtain

$$\frac{\partial \ln D_S}{\partial \ln(q_S/w_S)} = \int_0^{z^*} [g_L(z) - g_H(z)] f_H(z) \, dz,$$

where

$$f_j(z) \equiv \frac{a_j(z)}{a_L(z) + (q_S/w_S) a_H(z)},$$

$$g_j(z) \equiv \frac{\alpha(z) f_j(z)}{\int_0^{z^*} \alpha(z) f_j(z) \, dz} \quad \text{for} \quad j = H, L.$$

From our assumption that $a_H(z)/a_L(z)$ is increasing in z, it follows that (1) $f_H(z)$ is increasing in z and (2) $g_L(z)/g_H(z)$ is decreasing in z. In addition $\int_0^{z^*} g_j(z) \, dz = 1$ so that there exists at least one point $z^0 \in (0, z^*)$ at which $g_L(z^0) = g_H(z^0)$. From result 1, it follows that $g_L(z) > g_H(z)$ for $z < z^0$, and $g_L(z) < g_H(z)$ for $z > z^0$, and that

$$\int_0^{z^0} [g_L(z) - g_H(z)] \, dz = - \int_{z^0}^{z^*} [g_L(z) - g_H(z)] \, dz > 0.$$

In addition, from result 1 we have that $f_H(z) < f_H(z^0)$ for $z < z^0$, and $f_H(z) > f_H(z^0)$ for $z > z^0$. Combining these various results, we obtain

$$\int_0^{z^*} [g_L(z) - g_H(z)] f_H(z) \, dz < \int_0^{z^0} [g_L(z) - g_H(z)] f_H(z^0) \, dz$$

$$+ \int_{z^0}^{z^*} [g_L(z) - g_H(z)] f_H(z^0) \, dz = 0,$$

which establishes that $\partial \ln D_S / \partial \ln(q_S/w_S) < 0$. The proof for the northern relative demand curve is similar.

Proof of Lemma 6.2

The stability condition can be obtained by totally differentiating condition (6.4), allowing for changes in the capital stocks K_i and the technology parameters A_i, $i = N, S$. We let $\theta_{Li}^* \equiv w_i a_L(z^*)/[w_i a_L(z^*) + q_i a_H(z^*)]$ denote the share of unskilled labor in the total wage bill of the critical input z^*, $i = N, S$, with $\theta_{Hi}^* = 1 - \theta_{Li}^*$ denoting the share of skilled labor. The share of the wage bill in total costs of production for each input is θ. Then differentiating (6.4) we obtain

$$\left(\frac{\partial \ln C_S}{\partial z^*} - \frac{\partial \ln C_N}{\partial z^*}\right) dz^* = \theta[(\theta_{LN}^* \hat{w}_N + \theta_{HN}^* \hat{q}_N) - (\theta_{LS}^* \hat{w}_S + \theta_{HS}^* \hat{q}_S)]$$

$$+ (1 - \theta)(\hat{r}_N - \hat{r}_S) + (\hat{A}_S - \hat{A}_N), \qquad (6.A1)$$

using $\hat{A}_i = -\hat{B}_i$. The term in brackets on the left is the difference between the slopes of the $C_S C_S$ locus and the $C_N C_N$ locus at the point z^*, which is positive. Other terms in this expression can be simplified as follows:

1. With the normalization $E \equiv 1$, the values of industry production E_i in (6.10) can be written alternatively as shares of world production, $E_N = \int_{z^*}^{1} \alpha(z) dz$ and $E_S = \int_0^{z^*} \alpha(z) dz$. Then the changes in the returns to capital are computed from (6.7) and (6.11) as $\hat{r}_N = -\hat{K}_N - [\alpha(z^*)/E_N] dz^*$ and $\hat{r}_S = -\hat{K}_S + [\alpha(z^*)/E_S] dz^*$.

2. The change in the labor costs of producing the critical input z^* in the north, $(\theta_{LN}^* \hat{w}_N + \theta_{HN}^* \hat{q}_N)$ can be rewritten as

$$(\theta_{LN}^* \hat{w}_N + \theta_{HN}^* \hat{q}_N) = (\lambda_{LN} \hat{w}_N + \lambda_{HN} \hat{q}_N) + (\theta_{HN}^* - \lambda_{HN})\frac{\partial \ln(q_N/w_N)}{\partial z^*} dz^*$$

$$= \left\{-\left[\frac{\alpha(z^*)}{E_N}\right] + (\theta_{HN}^* - \lambda_{HN})\frac{\partial \ln(q_N/w_N)}{\partial z^*}\right\} dz^*,$$

where the first line follows because the cost shares and factor shares each sum to unity, and the second line follows from (6.11b). The cost share of skilled labor used in z^* in the north is less than the average for the economy, $\theta_{HN}^* < \lambda_{HN}$, and also $\partial \ln(q_N/w_N)/\partial z^* > 0$ as illustrated in figure 6.3, so that the final term in the brackets above is negative.

3. Similarly for the south we have

$$(\theta_{LS}^* \hat{w}_S + \theta_{HS}^* \hat{q}_S) = \left\{ \left[\frac{\alpha(z^*)}{E_S} \right] + (\theta_{HS}^* - \lambda_{HS}) \frac{\partial \ln(q_S/w_S)}{\partial z^*} \right\} dz^*.$$

The cost share of skilled labor used in z^* in the south exceeds the average for the economy, $\theta_{HS}^* > \lambda_{HS}$, and also $\partial \ln(q_S/w_S)/\partial z^* > 0$, so the final term in the brackets above is positive.

Substituting these various results in (6.A1), (6.12) is established with

$$\Delta^{-1} = \left[\left(\frac{\partial \ln C_S}{\partial z^*} - \frac{\partial \ln C_N}{\partial z^*} \right) + \left(\frac{\alpha(z^*)}{E_N} + \frac{\alpha(z^*)}{E_S} \right) \right.$$

$$\left. + \theta \left((\theta_{HS}^* - \lambda_{HS}) \frac{\partial \ln(q_S/w_S)}{\partial z^*} - (\theta_{HN}^* - \lambda_{HN}) \frac{\partial \ln(q_N/w_N)}{\partial z^*} \right) \right]$$

$$> \left(\frac{\alpha(z^*)}{E_N} + \frac{\alpha(z^*)}{E_S} \right),$$

where the final inequality follows from the signs established above.

Notes

The authors thank Peter Lindert, David Richardson, Alwyn Young, Adrian Wood, and various seminar participants for helpful comments.

1. This conclusion is reiterated by Krugman and Lawrence (1994), but has been challenged by Borjas and Ramey (1993), Leamer (1994), Sachs and Shatz (1994), and Wood (1994), among others. Davis (1992) compares wage trends in the United States with various trading partners, and Berman, Machin, and Bound (1994) compare the employment shifts across countries. See also the discussion in the "The Global Economy," *The Economist*, October 1, 1994, 14–24.

2. These data are taken from Lawrence and Slaughter (1993) and Sachs and Shatz (1994). While there are problems with the production/nonproduction classification (Leamer 1994), there is evidence suggesting that in practice the classification is successful in tracking employment by skill category (Berman, Bound, and Griliches 1994; Sachs and Shatz 1994).

3. We do not impose trade balance in this industry across countries, since the allocation of expenditure across the countries will have no impact on factor prices or the critical value z^*.

4. This is obtained by differentiating (6.2) with respect to the capital flow K, holding fixed z^* and the quantities of labor in the various activities z (from the envelope theorem), and simplifying the resulting expression using (6.8).

5. Specifically, the question asked to the sample of firms in the 1987 *Census of Manufacturers* (U.S. Bureau of the Census 1991, app. D, pp. D-25,26) was "What percentage (approximate) of the total materials used as reported in item (a) [i.e., cost of materials, parts, components, containers, etc.] is accounted for by foreign sources? Materials used should not include items partially fabricated abroad which reenter the country usually under Items 806 and 807, of

Schedule 8 of TSUSA." Also excluded are materials in the categories: "(b) cost of products bought and sold as such; (c) cost of fuels consumed for heat or power; (d) cost of purchased electricity; and (e) cost of contract work done for you by others."

6. "Shoe and Tell," *The New Republic*, September 12, 1994.

7. Borjas, Freeman, and Katz (1992, 223) also included the change in the import share in regressions explaining the relative employment share of production workers in the United States. We will follow Berman, Bound, and Griliches (1994) in using the share of nonproduction workers in the total wage bill as the dependent variable.

8. The domestic data is taken from the NBER productivity database (Bartelsman and Gray 1994), while the import data is taken from the trade database (Abowd 1991).

9. We follow Berman, Bound, and Griliches in weighting the data by the share of the industry wage bill in manufacturing averaged over the years 1959 and 1973 for the 1959–73 change, 1973 and 1979 for the 1973–79 change, and 1979 and 1987 for the 1979–87 change.

10. If we exclude SIC 3711 (motor vehicles and car bodies) from the regressions in tables 6.3 and 6.4, then our results are strengthened, and we find that 20 to 40 percent of the increase in the share of nonproduction labor in the wage bill is explained by rising imports.

11. "Las maquiladoras mas importantes de Mexico," *Expansion*, October 24, 1990, 35–52.

12. While the majority of production workers in maquiladoras are female, this share has been declining over time, from 77.3 percent in 1980 to 63.1 percent in 1988. Despite this declining share, we will see that the relative wage of production workers has been falling in assembly plants.

13. The sample contains medium and large plants that account for approximately 30 percent of Mexican manufacturing employment in any given year.

14. The data we report are averages over manufacturing plants; they do not control for changes in the composition of the labor force, but similar results have been found in studies that use microlevel data (Feliciano 1993; Bell 1994). The drop in annual earnings for 1988 in table 6.5 is due to the very high rate of inflation from June 1987 to June 1988, which are the dates for the consumer prices indexes used to deflate earnings.

15. The border contains states that abut the United States; the north contains the next tier of northern states; the center contains states surrounding Mexico City; Mexico City contains the two states the capital occupies; and the south contains all states south of the capital.

References

Abowd, John M. 1991. Appendix: The NBER immigration, trade, and labor markets data files. In George J. Borjas and Richard B. Freeman, eds., *Immigration, Trade and the Labor Market*. Chicago: University of Chicago Press, pp. 407–420.

Alic, John A., and Martha Caldwell Harris. 1986. Employment lessons from the electronics industry. *Monthly Labor Review* 109:27–36.

Bell, L. A. 1994. The impact of minimum wages in Mexico and Columbia. Presented at the World Bank Labor Markets Workshop. July.

Berman, Eli, John Bound, and Zvi Griliches. 1993. Changes in the demand for skilled labor within U.S. manufacturing: Evidence from the annual survey of manufactures. Working paper 4255. National Bureau of Economic Research.

Berman, Eli, John Bound, and Zvi Griliches. 1994. Changes in the demand for skilled labor within U.S. manufacturing: Evidence from the annual survey of manufactures. *Quarterly Journal of Economics* 109:367–98.

Berman, Eli, Stephen Machin, and John Bound. 1994. Implications of skill based technological change: International evidence. Mimeo. Boston University, University College, London,
and University of Michigan.

Bernard, Andrew B., and J. Bradford Jensen. 1996. Exporters, skill upgrading, and the wage
gap. *Journal of International Economics*, forthcoming.

Bhagwati, Jagdish. 1995. Trade and wages: Choosing among alternative explanations.
Economic Policy Review 1:42–47.

Bhagwati, Jagdish, and Vivek Dehejia. 1994. International trade theory and wages of the
unskilled. In Jagdish Bhagwati and Marvin H. Kosters, eds., *Trade and Wages: Leveling
Wages Down?* Washington: American Enterprise Institute, pp. 36–75.

Borjas, George J., Richard B. Freeman, and Lawrence F. Katz. 1992. On the labor market
effects of immigration and trade. In George J. Borjas and Richard B. Freeman, eds., *Immigration and the Workforce*. Chicago: University of Chicago Press.

Borjas, George J., and Valerie A. Ramey. 1993. Foreign competition, market power, and
wage inequality: Theory and evidence. Working paper 4556. National Bureau of Economic
Research.

Bound, John, and George Johnson. 1992. Changes in the structure of wages in the 1980's: An
evaluation of alternative explanations. *American Economic Review* 82:371–92.

Davis, Stephen. 1992. Cross-country patterns of changes in relative wages. In Olivier Jean
Blanchard and Stanley Fischer, eds., *NBER Macroeconomics Annual, 1992*. Cambridge: MIT
Press, pp. 239–91.

Dornbusch, Rudiger, Stanley Fischer, and Paul A. Samuelson. 1980. The Heckscher-Ohlin
trade model with a continuum of goods. *Quarterly Journal of Economics* 95:203–24.

Feenstra, Robert C., and Gordon H. Hanson. 1995. Foreign direct investment and relative
wages: Evidence from Mexico's maquiladoras. Mimeo. University of California, Davis and
University of Texas, Austin.

Feenstra, Robert C., and Andrew K. Rose. 1993. Trade with Mexico and water use in
California agriculture. In Peter M. Garber, ed., *The Mexico–U.S. Free Trade Agreement*.
Cambridge: MIT Press, pp. 189–218.

Feliciano, Z. 1993. Workers and trade liberalization: The impact of trade reforms in Mexico
on wages and employment. Mimeo. Harvard University.

Gereffi, Gary. 1993. The role of big buyers in global commodity chains: How U.S. retail
networks affect overseas production patterns. In Gary Gereffi and Miguel Korzeniewicz,
eds., *Commodity Chains and Global Capitalism*. Westport, CT: Praeger, pp. 95–122.

Gray, Wayne B., and Eric J. Bartelsman. 1994. Productivity database. Mimeo. National
Bureau of Economic Research. August 24 and September 9.

Krugman, Paul. 1994. Does third world growth hurt first world prosperity? *Harvard Business
Review* 72:113–121.

Krugman, Paul, and Robert Z. Lawrence. 1994. Trade, jobs, and wages. *Scientific American*
(April):44–49.

Lawrence, Robert Z., and Matthew J. Slaughter. 1993. International trade and American
wages in the 1980s: Giant sucking sound or small hiccup? *Brookings Papers on Economic
Activity: Microeconomics*, 2:161–226.

Lawrence, Robert Z. 1994. Trade, multinationals, and labor. Working paper 4836. National
Bureau of Economic Research.

Leamer, Edward E. 1993. Wage effects of a U.S.–Mexico free trade agreement. In Peter M.
Garber, ed., *The U.S.–Mexico Free Trade Agreement*. Cambridge: MIT Press, pp. 57–162.

Leamer, Edward E. 1994. Trade, wages and revolving door ideas. Working paper 4716. National Bureau of Economic Research.

Magaziner, Ira C., and Mark Patinkin. 1989. Fast heat: How Korea won the microwave war. *Harvard Business Review* 67:83–92.

Murphy, Kevin M., and Finis Welch. 1991. The role of international trade in wage differentials. In Marvin Kosters, ed., *Workers and Their Wages*. Washington: AEI Press, pp. 39–69.

Nacional Financiera. 1990. *La Economia Mexicana en Cifras*. Mexico City: Nacional Financiera.

Revenga, Ana L. 1992. Exporting jobs? The impact of import competition on employment and wages in U.S. manufacturing. *Quarterly Journal of Economics* 107:255–84.

Sachs Jeffrey D., and Howard J. Shatz. 1994. Trade and jobs in U.S. manufacturing. *Brookings Papers on Economics Activity* 1:1–84.

U.S. Bureau of the Census. 1991. *1987 Census of Manufactures*, MC87-S-1, Subject Series, General Summary: Industry, Product Class, and Geographic Area Statistics. Washington: GPO.

Waldinger, Roger D. 1986. *Through the Eye of the Needle*. New York: New York University Press.

Whiting, V. 1992. *The Political Economy of Foreign Investment in Mexico: Nationalism, Liberalism, and Constraints on Choice*. Baltimore: Johns Hopkins University Press.

Wood, Adrian. 1994. *North–South Trade, Employment and Inequality*. Oxford: Oxford University Press.

Wood, Adrian. 1995. Trade, technology, and the declining demand for unskilled labor. *Journal of Economic Perspectives* 9:57–80.

Yoffie, David B., and Benjamin Gomes-Casseres. 1994. *International Trade and Competition*. New York: McGraw-Hill.

7 Pure and Mixed Price and Income Compensation Schemes: Breaking Political Roadblocks to Trade Reform

Earl L. Grinols

It is not enough that there be potential compensation; compensation must actually be made. Otherwise, imagine a situation where the rich get richer and the poor poorer, and the rich can compensate the poor while still getting richer, yet they do not. Surely, no people in their right mind, or certainly their true hearts, would approve of the policy change, in that event.[1]—Jagdish Bhagwati

7.1 Introduction

The political economy of trade deals with the natural interest of producers, consumers, suppliers of labor, and other special factors to adjust the political process of trade policy-making to their own benefit. Often this activity takes the form of preventing trade liberalizations that, while helpful to the many, are harmful to the few. Rather than a calculus based on aggregate net benefits, the decision-making process becomes driven by the unfortunate calculus of degree of political power.

While trade theorists have long recognized that free trade and trade liberalization are rarely beneficial to everyone in the economic system, this has not dissuaded them from seeking conditions under which a trade liberalization might be accomplished with harm to no one, and with gains to some or all. After all, if it can be shown that a trade liberalization is unharmful to the owners of firms, the owners of labor and other factors, and to consumers as *individual* households the raison d'être for opposition to efficiency-inducing trade changes disappears. Rather than clip the weed of protectionism, we sever it at the tap root of self-interest.

Given the importance of the question of how unharmful changes might be effected, it is interesting that the positive results that are known are of relatively recent vintage. Grandmont and McFadden (1972) show that a group of autarkic countries can move to free trade without harm to any consumer or need for cross-country transfers. Internal financing ensures that every household is better off, or no worse off, after the change than before. Working from the insight of Vanek (1962, 1965) and Kemp (1965), Kemp and Wan (1976) show that for a group of countries initially engaged in trade, there must exist an unspecified set of cross-country transfers among countries forming a customs union such that no one is harmed and those inside the union gain. In Grinols (1981, 1986, 1987) I show that the necessary and sufficient cross-country transfers—in the sense that they apply under all conditions—must equal $p_1 \cdot z_0^k$ where z_0^k is country k's initial trade vector and p_1 is post union internal prices. I extend the result to cover all five types of growth (technological change, factor augmentation, receipt of a transfer, formation of a customs union, removal of impediments to efficient resource allocation) and to deal with the presence of foreign ownership. Individual consumers are shown to be better off by a revealed preference argument. It follows that growth, however derived, is not immiserizing with appropriate policy, thus addressing two other concerns—immiserizing growth and perverse effects of growth from foreign ownership—associated with the name of Bhagwati.

Dixit and Norman (1980, 1986) raise the question of policy implementability when the policy requires information from consumers about quantity choices. They show under appropriate conditions that if there exists a good for which all consumers who trade it are on the same side of the market, it is possible for government to influence consumer prices in such a way that no one loses and some or all gain. Their proposal, a form of pure price compensation, substitutes information about preferences for existence of the right kind of good. The different requirements for implementability do not come without cost, however. Their plan requires that the government acquire stocks of goods representing all of the economy's production efficiency gains, some or nearly all of which will be wasted in ensuring that no one is harmed. More recently Hammond and Sempere (1995) prove the existence of an income compensation scheme whereby the government budget can be structured so that all commodity stocks that might be acquired by the government are instead privately consumed, consumers face the same prices as before but have higher incomes.

Thus, in contrast to the recent past, we now have available at least three types of compensation plans—a pure price compensation plan, a pure income compensation plan, and a mixed price and income compensation plan—any one of which is capable of ensuring that efficiency gains can be distributed in such a way that no one is harmed. Dixit-Norman fix income and use the government surplus to adjust consumer prices in a favorable direction. Hammond-Sempere fix consumer prices and use the government surplus to adjust consumer income in a favorable direction. Grinols and Grandmont-McFadden allow prices and incomes to vary but use the government surplus to ensure that their joint variation is in a favorable direction.

Letting E denote the initial equilibrium and using initials to represent equilibria selected by each of the plans, it can be shown that Pareto improvement is possible in each step from E to D to H to G but that gains in the reverse direction are not possible.

A simple Pareto dominance ranking therefore suggests that we should employ in the chain the highest ranked policy that can be achieved. However, this returns us to the question of implementability. Since a review of implementability requires a clear description of each policy (which we now have), it is appropriate to begin the job of classifying the type of information that different policies require and ask whether it is realistic to assume that it can be obtained by government. In this process the incentive compatibility of agents to reveal true information about preferences, production technology, consumption, production, and income is an important consideration but not the only consideration. This chapter attempts to begin the process of taxonomy of information requirements. No doubt refinements by other scholars will be needed before we have a sufficiently clear understanding of how one type of information differs from another in some metric of implementability or government accessibility.

Unfortunately, the chapter's findings are negative. By asking what information applies to the initial situation/equilibrium upon which government works, what incentives agents have to misrepresent information needed by the government to implement D, H, and G schemes, we conclude that none of the policies is likely to have claim to great usefulness in the practical sense.

To justify this assessment, section 7.2 briefly summarizes the different approaches that are available. Section 7.3 then discusses the information requirements they imply, and section 7.4 concludes with an evaluative discussion and suggests one avenue of response.

7.2 Nonharmful Efficiency Gains

In this section I describe the three basic price, income, and price-income policies for ensuring Pareto-improving growth. Although I will refer primarily to the formation of a customs union, the theory applies to any of the five sources of production expansion or efficiency improvement: (1) technical change, (2) factor augmentation, (3) receipt of a transfer,

(4) removal of impediments to resource allocation, or (5) formation of a customs union. The theorems derive from Dixit-Norman (1980, 1986), Hammond-Sempere (1995), Grinols (1981, 1986, 1987), and their antecedents. Here I wish to relate the results to one another, and to identify their similarities and differences.

The Framework

Consider a set of countries $k \in K$, where I^k is the set of households in country k and $i \in I \equiv \bigcup_{k \in K} I^k$ denotes household i. Goods are indexed by $n = 1, \ldots, N$. Let J^k be the set of all firms in country k, where $j \in \bigcup_{k \in K} J^k$ denotes firm j. $\{J^k\}$ are pairwise disjoint sets. The production set of firm j is $Y^j \subset \mathbb{R}^N$. Finally, the endowment of household i, if any, is $e^i \in \mathbb{R}^N$ and θ^{ij} is the share of firm j owned by household i. In equilibrium, we assume household i has unearned income m^i, which is derived from its ownership of factors and firms.

Given the above, define a partitioned world equilibrium allocation as the ordered tuple corresponding to the grouping of countries into the set consisting of union countries U and the rest of the world R,

$$\{((X^i, \succsim^i), (Y^j), (e^i, \theta^{ij}), (x_0^i, y_0^j, m_0^i), (z_0^k))_{i \in I^k, j \in J^k, k \in U}, (z_0^R)\}$$

where

$$x_0^i \in X^i,$$

$$y_0^j \in J^j,$$

$$\sum_{i \in I^k} x_0^i - \sum_{j \in J^k} y_0^j - \sum_{i \in I^k} e^i = z_0^k,$$

$$\sum_{k \in U} z_0^k + z_0^R = 0.$$

In this notation, $(X^i, \succsim^i)$ denotes the consumption set and preferences of household i, (x_0^i, y_0^j, m_0^i) denotes the consumption vector of household i in the initial situation 0, the production vector of firm j in the initial situation 0 (inputs are negative numbers by convention), and m_0^i is the income of household i in initial situation 0, respectively. z_0^k and z_0^R denote the vectors of excess demand of country k and the non-union rest of the world, respectively.

We make the following standard assumptions about consumers and producers:

a. $X^i \subset \mathbb{R}^N$ is closed, convex, and bounded below.

b1. $\succsim^i$ is represented by a continuous, quasi-concave preference function exhibiting local nonsatiation.

b2. Household i of nation k can subsist on goods available in nation k.

c. Every household has an allocation on which it can survive that is strictly smaller than x_0^i in each nonzero component.

d1. Y^j, and $Y^k \equiv \sum_{j \in J^k} Y^j \subset \mathbb{R}^N$ are closed, convex, and contain the nonpositive orthant $-\Omega$.

d2. $Y^k \cap (-Y^k) = \{0\}$.

e. $\theta^{ij} = 0$ if i, j are not in the same country.

f. There exists at least one commodity such that in the initial equilibrium one of the following holds: some households are net buyers and none are net sellers of it, and it is not a free good, or some households are net sellers and none are net buyers of it, and it is not the only valuable good.

Finally, let P be the $N - 1$ price simplex and $p_0^W \in P$ be initial world prices.

Weaker assumptions than **a–b** can be found in the cited references. In particular, the above imply for $p \in P$ that each consumer has a demand correspondence with the usual properties: $\xi^i(p, m^i) = \arg\max\{U^i(x^i) | x^i$ is in the budget set$\}$ is nonempty, convex valued for every $p \gg 0$ and m^i such that the budget set is nonempty. It is upper hemicontinuous whenever a cheaper consumption $\tilde{x}^i$, $p \cdot \tilde{x}^i < m^i$ is in the budget set, and $p \cdot x^i = m^i$ for all x^i in $\xi^i(p, m^i)$. On the production side the set of efficient points from bounded inputs is bounded for firms and the union as a whole. Condition **b** is the Weymark condition which will be needed only for the Dixit-Norman result.

By a customs union, we mean a set of countries U characterized by free international trade internal to the union and a common external tariff. Countries in the union may apply commodity and profits taxes to the transactions of their households and firms, but they may not apply import duties or restrictions to the goods of other member countries.

Price, Income, and Mixed Compensations

The characteristics of the three basic types of compensation plans can now be indicated in the following propositions.

PROPOSITION 7.1 *Pure Price Compensation.* Assume that all production
in countries $k \in U$ exhibits constant returns to scale. Let E_0 be an arbitrary partitioned world equilibrium allocation with consumer prices in
country k given by $p_0^k \in P$ and world prices given by p_0^W. Let countries U
form a customs union. Then there exists a new partitioned world equilibrium allocation D such that

i. For countries $k \in U$, consumer prices are $p_2^k = p_0^k + \alpha\pi$ while producers
maximize profits by choice of y_1^j at prices p_1. Household incomes are
unchanged from their initial levels m_0^i. π is a vector of price change such
that for sufficiently small positive scalar α the household's consumption
vector as a function of prices and income $x^i(p_0^k + \alpha\pi, m_0^i)$ is at least as
good as $x^i(p_0^k, m_0^i)$ for all i in union country k.

ii. Commodity taxes equal $\tau = p_2^k - p_1$ and the common external tariff is
$t = p_1 - p_0^W$.

iii. Union government purchases of commodities paid for from tax and
tariff revenues equal vector $g \gg 0$ which are then thrown away (i.e., commodities g are wasted).

iv. Every household in union countries has the same or higher welfare
than in E_0. If post union aggregate production satisfies $p_1 \cdot \sum_{k \in U} \sum_{j \in J^k} y_1^j$
$> p_1 \cdot \sum_{k \in U} \sum_{j \in J^k} y_0^j$, then some households will be strictly better off.

v. Income transfers to households in union countries are zero.

vi. Outside the union countries, prices, incomes, quantities and welfare
are unchanged from their levels in E_0.

The essential idea behind this proposition is a two-step procedure due
to Dixit and Norman, though in practice it would be implemented as a
single step. For the first step, fix the aggregate external trade flows of
union countries, $-z_0^R$, and all consumer prices and incomes through the
use of commodity taxation[2] and the common external tariff.

Let union countries move to an efficient production position with the
government using its tax revenues to buy the increased quantities produced of each good. In the second step, let the government use some of its
positive stocks to change the price of a good satisfying condition **b** so that
consumers are benefited by the price changes. For example, if there is a
good that some or all households buy, but none sell, then the government
can use its positive stocks of that good to lower the market price.

Instead of fixing incomes, and adjusting prices as in proposition 7.1, gains could be ensured by fixing prices and increasing incomes.

PROPOSITION 7.2 *Pure Income Compensation.* Let E_0 be an arbitrary partitioned world equilibrium allocation with consumer prices in country k given by $p_0^k \in P$ and world prices given by p_0^W. Let countries U form a customs union. Then there exists a new partitioned world equilibrium allocation H such that

i. For countries $k \in U$, consumer prices are p_0^k while producers maximize profit by choice of y_1^j at prices p_1. In union country k, household incomes equal $m_0^i + s^k$ for $s^k \geq 0$, where s^k is a poll subsidy from the government.

ii. Commodity taxes in union country k equal $\tau^k = (p_0^k - p_1)$, and the common external tariff is $t = (p_1 - p_0^W)$.

iii. Each union country government pays out in subsidies all of its revenues, which equal

$$p_1 \cdot \left(z_0^k + \sum_{j \in J^k} y_i^j \right) + (p_0^k - p_1) \cdot \sum_{i \in I^k} x_1^i - \sum_{i \in I^k} m_0^i.$$

iv. Union country k's share of common tariff revenues is $t \cdot z_0^k$.

v. Outside the union countries, prices, incomes, quantities and welfare are unchanged from their levels in E_0. If post union aggregate production satisfies $p_1 \cdot \sum_{k \in U} \sum_{j \in J^k} y_1^j > p_1 \cdot \sum_{k \in U} \sum_{j \in J^k} y_0^j$, then $s^k > 0$, all households in U are better off than in E_0, and no commodities are wasted.

The idea behind the pure income compensation plan is a simple but powerful observation. Holding consumer prices and incomes m_0^i fixed, we can imagine the government moving each household out on its income expansion path by bestowing a poll subsidy s^k on each household in k. As the subsidies increase, consumption will eventually equal $y_1 + \sum_{k \in U} z_0^k$, where y_1 is some production point on the aggregate production frontier of the union countries. Producer prices can then be set at p_1 to support production y_1 with the tax system used to support consumer prices p_0^k and incomes m_0^i at initial levels. The poll subsidies s^k are then paid out of government tax revenues, which just exhaust the available tariff and commodity tax revenues, while markets clear in physical commodities.

The obvious advantage of pure income compensation over the pure price compensation of proposition 7.1 is that proposition 7.2 moves the economy to a productively efficient point and wastes no quantities of goods. However, neither proposition 7.1 nor proposition 7.2 moves union countries to a distributively efficient point, since one plan leaves goods unused and the other does not guarantee uniform commodity prices for the households of union countries.

Proposition 7.3 mixes price and income compensation to move union countries to a productively efficient point that is also distributively efficient.

PROPOSITION 7.3   *Mixed Price and Income Compensation.* Let E_0 be an arbitrary partitioned world equilibrium allocation with consumer prices in country k given by $p_0^k \in P$ and world prices given by p_0^W. Let countries U form a customs union. Then there exists a new partitioned world equilibrium allocation G such that

i. For countries $k \in U$, consumer prices are p_1 and firms maximize profits by choice of y_1^j at prices p_1.

ii. Commodity taxes are zero and the common external tariff is $t = p_1 - p_0^W$.

iii. Tariff revenues are distributed to member countries from the union central authority in the amount $t \cdot z_0^k$.

iv. Every household has sufficient income to purchase its original consumption bundle x_0^i.

v. Outside the union countries, prices, incomes, quantities and welfare are unchanged from their levels in E_0.

If post union aggregate production satisfies $p_1 \cdot \sum_{k \in U} \sum_{j \in J^k} y_1^j > p_1 \cdot \sum_{k \in U} \sum_{j \in J^k} y_0^j$, then all households in U are strictly better off than in E_0 and no commodities are wasted.

The idea behind proposition 7.3 is that by freezing conditions outside union countries and letting union countries move to a Pareto-optimal competitive equilibrium internal to the union, union member countries k can generate income satisfying

$$\text{Union income} = p_1 \cdot \sum_{k \in U} x_1^k$$

$$= \sum_{k \in U} \sum_{i \in I^k} p_1 \cdot x_1^i$$

$$= \sum_{k \in U} \sum_{i \in I^k} p_1 \cdot \left(\sum_{j \in J^k} \theta^{ij} y_1^j + e^i + \text{Transfer}^i \right)$$

$$= \sum_{k \in U} \left\{ p_1 \cdot (y_1^k - y_0^k) + p_1 \cdot \left(y_0^k + \sum_{i \in I^k} e^i + z_0^k \right) \right.$$

$$\left. + \left(\sum_{i \in I^k} \text{Transfer}^i - p_1 \cdot z_0^k \right) \right\}$$

$$= p_1 \cdot \left(\sum_{k \in U} (y_1^k - y_0^k) \right) + p_1 \cdot \sum_{k \in U} x_0^k + \sum_{k \in U} (T^k - p_1 \cdot z_0^k)$$

$$> p_1 \cdot \sum_{k \in U} x_0^k$$

when each member country receives tariff revenues $T^k = p_1 \cdot z_0^k$ and Transfer^i is the transfer to household i. Distributing to household i income equal to $p_1 \cdot x_0^i$ plus a positive share of the surplus $p_1 \cdot (y_1^k - y_0^k) > 0$ by use of the transfer guarantees that each household will be better off with the final price-income pair (p_1, m_1^i) than with (p_0^k, m_0^i) in E_0. An existence proof is needed to show the ability to finance the needed transfers out of available revenues simultaneously to selecting prices p_1 and tariff t. In this case both prices and income to the household are allowed to vary.

Although propositions 7.1–7.3 are applied to customs union formation or enlargement—probably their most important trade liberalization application—the efficiency gains derive from moving production from the interior of the union production set to its frontier. The propositions therefore also apply to efficiency gains from other types of commercial policies that move production to the efficient frontier. In particular, moving from a pure price compensation equilibrium D to a pure income compensation equilibrium H moves the union countries from a production position inside the frontier to one on the frontier; thereby allowing a Pareto improvement.[3]

Applying proposition 7.3 to equilibrium H leads to another Pareto improvement. Since equilibrium G is Pareto optimal given the union's endowment and fixed trade vector, and proposition 7.1 requires a strict production efficiency gain for government collection of g to be positive, the reverse movement from equilibria of type G to H to D is not possible with Pareto gains in each step.

PROPOSITION 7.4   Given an arbitrary partitioned world equilibrium allocation E_0 and associated Pareto-superior pure price compensation equilibrium D, there exists a Pareto-superior pure income compensation allocation H. Likewise, given H, there exists a Pareto-superior mixed price-income compensation allocation G. Equilibria may therefore be ranked by Pareto improvement from E_0 to D to H to G. Pareto improvement moving from G to H, from H to D, or from D to E_0 is not possible.[4]

7.3 Implementability

The data needed to implement propositions 7.1–7.3 must include one or more of the following types of information:

Preferences, technology $(X^i, \succsim^i), (Y^j)$

Ownership rights (e^i, θ^{ij})

Prices (p_0^k, p_0^W, p_1, p_2)

Incomes (m_0^i)

Quantity choices $(x_0^i, y_0^j, z_0^k), (x_1^i, y_1^j, z_1^k)$

For example, the pure price compensation mechanism of proposition 7.1 holds unearned income m_0^i constant in order to ensure that welfare of each household improves upon a favorable adjustment in price, while the pure income compensation mechanism holds consumer prices p_0^k and unearned income m_0^i constant in order that welfare of each household in nation k improve when given a positive poll subsidy s^k. Past incomes and prices are directly observable, but future incomes and prices that would have prevailed in the absence of the policy change must be predicted from knowledge of other fundamentals in the economy such as preferences and technology. Likewise, mixed income-price compensation requires knowledge of quantities x_0^i in order to guarantee that household incomes exceed $p_1 \cdot x_0^i$ when prices are p_1. Prices, quantities, and value variables (economic variables that have dimensional units of dollars per unit time, e.g., income, revenues, or profits) are the observables in an economy, unlike preferences and technologies. As before, past quantities can be observed from household choices, but future quantities must be predicted from other fundamentals.

Prices

By their public nature, prices are often more easily observed that quantity or income information. Further, the need to predict what prices would have been in the absence of a policy change (i.e., in order to know p_0^k) have been argued to depend on *aggregate* demands and supplies rather than the specific technologies or preferences of individual firms or households. Since estimates of aggregate demand and supplies in many cases can be made without needing micro-agent information and agent revelations may be unable to influence the prices of interest, the problem of incentives to misrepresent can be circumvented. Misrepresentation is not fully avoided, however, in cases where the technology set and preferences must be known, past prices have not varied sufficiently to reveal all aspects of aggregate production or the demand curve, and the available revelation results for atomless economies without private production do not apply. Dixit-Norman (1981, 1986), and Weymark (1979) whose work they use, require that consumer incomes do not depend on producer prices. House-holds therefore have constant (in this case identically zero) lump-sum incomes. When firms earn positive profits, however, in the presence of decreasing returns to scale, it is possible that an individual household could be sole owner of the firm. We would not expect the government to know the technology of a specific firm, nor to be able to learn it from the sole owner without the prospect of incentive incompatibilities.[5] Without such knowledge the government cannot ensure that its chosen price change policy is unharmful to all households. In addition, not knowing future components of p_0^k, for example, means that one may not know what consumer prices p_2^k should be chosen in order that $\Delta p = p_2^k - p_0^k$ represent a move in the appropriate direction.[6]

However, rather than pursue information and revelation needs relating to price, it is more fruitful to address the implementation problems relating to incomes and quantities. Income needs are common to all three propositions.[7] If they can not be met, then none of the compensation plans has much hope of being implementable except in special cases.

Quantities and Income

Granting that needed information to implement price predictions can be obtained, a greater problem remains with respect to quantities and in-come. Pure price compensation and pure income compensation require that incomes be known in order to isolate households from the effect that different prices have on changing unearned income m_0^i (both require fixing m_0^i). As noted, joint stock firms may be owned by one or many shareholders. Thus knowing how future prices before and after a trade liberalization would affect a particular household's income means knowing how prices determine firm profits. This means knowing the technology of individual firms that may be owned by one or many shareholders and whose technology may be known to none or some of them, all of them, or even to nonshareholding households who sell factors to the firm such as the firm's managers. The connection between one firm's technology and m_0^i, as it relates to what future incomes would have been in the absence of the policy change, produce incentives to misrepresent individual technology as strong as the incentives to misrepresent individual preferences in compensation that depends on knowing x_0^i. In the absence of mechanisms to elicit true information about individual firms' technologies in cases where joint stock firms can be owned by one or many shareholders, pure income compensation plans cannot be implemented. We know such mechanisms cannot have the property that agents' benefits change in any way dependent on what they reveal.[8] The problem is virtually identical to the need to know x_0^i in a mixed compensation plan—a requirement equivalent to knowing future prices and how the household will respond—and thus is tantamount to learning individual preferences. Without having traveled very far in our investigation of implementability, we are therefore met by a roadblock that must be removed before further obstacles can be cleared.

In summary, while price information in some cases may be learned without the need to gain individual information about preferences and production technologies, income and quantity information in general require information about individual preferences and firm technology that may need to be elicited from one or many interested agents. That is, as an agent responder, I may not be able to affect prices by the information I give, but I certainly can affect what future compensation I receive at those prices by describing my firm's production set or my preferences.

It is the connection between m_0^i and individual firm technology and the connection between x_0^i and individual household preferences that lead to potential implementation problems with the need to know specific preferences or technologies.

7.4   Review

It may be that theorists will ultimately find conditions under which both individual preferences and firm technologies can be learned from self-interested private agents. As the realism of the models in which these questions are considered grows, however, other problems related to time, uncertainty, absence of markets, and even the failure of agents to fully know their own (future) preferences or technology are likely to leave the discussion of implementation in an unsatisfactory state. As a logical proposition, the difficulties are likely to be equally burdensome under any of the three types of compensation. Income information was found to present problems for pure price and income compensations in section 7.3, and quantity information presented problems for mixed price-income compensation.

Faced with this state of affairs, a sensible response is to return to the compensation question and critique our objectives from first principles. Bhagwati and policy economists are, no doubt, concerned primarily with two things: first, that beneficial trade liberalizations not be stopped by the roadblocks of special interest groups, and second, that liberalizations, once enacted, do not reduce the welfare of already-needy groups within the polity. As we have seen, the problems encountered thus far arise from the need to compensate every household to its future pre-policy utility levels for all time and relate to the link between household income and firm technology. The inability to know what lifetime consumption and income would have been, even if future prices can be known, is the source of the dilemma.

For example, consider the following scenario: You are the architect of a trade liberalization program that faces the anti-lobbying efforts of two firms who agree with you that the prices they face will be lower twenty years hence due to the change. You assure both firms that each will be compensated by government subsidies to make up for lower profits and that the income of each firm's owner or owners will not suffer due to the change. Firm one responds, however, that their company is engaged in research that will result in improved technology and higher profits in twenty years if the constellation of future prices are undisturbed from what they would have been in the pre-policy state. Since the firm would earn greater profits than you have predicted based on existing technology, they say the firm should be compensated more. Of course, the research is reported to you to be advantageous only for the price configuration that would have prevailed and so is not desirable to undertake if the policy goes into effect.

The second firm has a different problem. It claims that it cannot stay in business at the future prices. Thus, in the future, the government must cover all of its profits, not just some as you have assumed, though it will cease to exist. In other words, you believe that at the new prices the firm has the knowledge to do nearly as well as before, but the firm says that the technology to profitably deal with the new configuration of prices does not exist.

Rather than struggle with issues of this type—and there certainly are more ingenious implementation problems that one can envision—a nondoctrinaire and more fruitful approach might be to abandon the full-security-for-all-time stricture, and limit assurances to compensating individuals so that they are no worse off after the policy change than their current utility. In other words, "splice insurance" is given—no one loses in the overlap transition period between the old regime and the new, and in any future period compared to the period before implementation—but no assurances are given, nor deserve to be given, concerning even better guarantees into the infinite, potentially unforecastable, future. Attempting an overgenerous guarantee, and the ensuing wrangling over enforcing it, could very well lead to greater harm to the trade liberalization process than no guarantee at all.

In providing splice insurance, the overlap period can be chosen to be as long as needed, though presumably it would be limited to a time period that can be forecasted reasonably well. The advantages to providing splice insurance are that current utilities can be observed from observations of past consumptions and incomes. Moreover these observations can be chosen from past periods so that incentive incompatibility and information limitations can be avoided. Since future utilities, incomes, and consumption bundles do not need to be forecasted for all time, one avoids entirely the pointless task of arguing over predictions for which normal uncertainties that are independent of the proposed policy have the lion's share of the influence. The final point is that splice insurance may be all that is needed to satisfy "reasonable people in their right mind, or certainly their true hearts," in the words of Bhagwati. If roadblocks to trade reform can be broken without raising insolvable implementation problems in this manner, then that should be our objective.

Notes

1. Which way? Free trade or protection? Interview, Jagdish Bhagwati, *Challenge*, January–February, 1994, p. 21.

2. Dixit and Norman assume firms exhibit constant returns to scale so that firm profits are zero. Hence, holding consumer prices fixed implies that household incomes are fixed when producer prices change. If we allow firms to have nonzero profits, then the income to households is held constant in the presence of changing producer prices by a tax on profits. For the government to set these taxes appropriately, it must be able to predict firm profits as a function of producer prices—a requirement to which we return later.

3. Let $Y^U \equiv \sum_{k \in U} \sum_{j \in J^k} Y^j$ be the production set of union countries, and let $g \gg 0$ be the vector of commodities collected by the government in proposition 7.1. Starting from E_0 and moving to D implies that nonwasted union production is on the surface of the translated production set $Y^U - \{g\}$ but is strictly interior to Y^U itself. Moving from D to an equilibrium of type H à la proposition 7.2 shifts union production to the surface of Y^U, creating a production efficiency gain and consequent Pareto improvement when the gains are distributed as in proposition 7.2.

4. In moving from each step to the next, we presume that a strict production gain takes place to eliminate the special case where the equilibria might be identical.

5. A closely related situation arises when the household is the owner of factor services whose level of provision do not enter utility directly but whose provision earns the household income which is spent on consumption goods. Feenstra and Lewis (1994)(FL), for example, consider an economy with household-specific technologies for producing factor services that are then sold in the market. The situation they address presages the present difficulty, since, on one hand, the government is not likely to know the shadow prices of factors the household may provide to be able to correct for the income effects of its policy on household welfare, and fixing the prices of household factors can lead to factor immobility and a failure of the plan to generate welfare gains (see FL, proposition 1). They report that the situation "is similar to a firm having specific capital, in which case we would not expect the government to observe the return to this capital"; see Dixit and Norman (1980, 80).

6. Pure price compensation also requires knowing which good or composite has all consumers on one side of the market, and how far prices can be adjusted in the needed direction. These information requirements in some cases may be as great or greater than the need to know p_0^k.

7. Proposition 7.1 needs to use both income and price data, while proposition 7.3 needs to augment income with quantity data. Proposition 7.2 needs only income information because poll subsidies are automatically chosen to be positive and to exhaust government revenues under pure income compensation.

8. See, for example, Hammond (1979, 266).

References

Dixit, A., and V. Norman. 1980. *Theory of International Trade.* Cambridge: Cambridge University Press.

Dixit, A., and V. Norman. 1986. Gains from trade without lump sum compensation. *Journal of International Economics* 21:111–22.

Dixit, A., and V. Norman. 1987. On Pareto-improving redistributions of aggregate economic gains. *Journal of Economic Theory* 41:133–53.

Feenstra, R., and T. Lewis. 1991. Distributing the gains from trade with incomplete information. *Economics and Politics* 3:21–40.

Feenstra, R., and T. Lewis. 1994. Trade adjustment assistance and Pareto gains from trade. *Journal of International Economics* 36:201–22.

144   Earl L. Grinols

Grandmont, J.-M., and D. McFadden. 1972. A technical note on classical gains from trade. *Journal of International Economics* 2:109–25.

Grinols, E. 1981. An extension of the Kemp-Wan theorem on the formation of customs unions. *Journal of International Economics* 11:259–66.

Grinols, E. 1986. Foreign investment and economic growth: Characterization of a second-best policy for welfare gains. *Journal of International Economics* 21:165–72.

Grinols, E. 1987. Transfers and the generalized theory of distortions and welfare. *Economica* 54:477–91.

Hammond, P. 1979. Straightforward individual incentive compatibility in large economies. *Review of Economic Studies* 46:263–82.

Hammond, P. 1987. Markets as constraints: Multilateral incentive compatibility in continuum economies. *Review of Economic Studies* 54:399–12.

Hammond, P., and J. Sempere. 1995. Limits to the potential gains from economic integration and other supply-side policies. *Economic Journal* 105:1180–1204.

Kemp, M. 1964. *The Pure Theory of International Trade*. Englewood Cliffs, NJ: Prentice-Hall.

Kemp, M., and H. Wan. 1976. An elementary proposition concerning the formation of customs unions. *Journal of International Economics* 6:95–97.

Kemp, M., and H. Wan. 1986. Gains from trade with and without lump-sum compensation. *Journal of International Economics* 21:99–110.

Vanek, J. 1962. *International Trade Theory and Economic Policy*. Homewood, IL: Irwin.

Vanek, J. 1965. *General Equilibrium of International Discrimination: The Case of Customs Unions*. Cambridge: Harvard University Press.

Weymark, J. 1979. A reconciliation of recent results in optimal taxation theory. *Journal of Public Economics* 12:171–89.

III PERSPECTIVES ON POLITICAL ECONOMY

8 The Political Economy of Trade Policy: Integrating the Perspectives of Economists and Political Scientists

Robert E. Baldwin

Both economists and political scientists have developed theoretical frameworks for analyzing the manner in which economic and political factors interact to shape the foreign economic policies of governments.[1] The theme of this chapter is that our understanding of international political economy can be improved by integrating various elements in the approaches being followed by the two disciplines. A specific integrative framework is proposed, with trade policy being used to illustrate the general theme and the usefulness of the suggested framework.

Section 8.1 discusses the strengths and weaknesses of the approach followed by economists in analyzing how economic and political factors influence trade policies, while section 8.2 does the same for the framework utilized by political scientists. Sections 8.3 and 8.4 draw on elements in both approaches in outlining a political economy framework that tries to combine the strengths of each discipline. Section 8.5 summarizes the main conclusions.

8.1 The Political Economy Framework of Economists

Major strengths of economists' models of political economy are their well-defined behavior theory and solid microfoundations. Political markets are analyzed with the same behavior theory and group of actors that has been highly successful in explaining decision making in economic markets. For example, individuals are assumed to be rational in the sense of being able to order the set of private and public goods available in a consistent manner, and their preferences for these goods and services are assumed to depend only on their own consumption of these items. Each individual maximizes her welfare subject to her budget constraint and voting power. In their role as productive agents, individuals organize into firms, who seek to maximize their profits.

On the basis of this self-interest framework, economists view individuals and firms, who may organize into common economic interest groups, as the demanders of particular public policies, such as import protection, and public officials as the suppliers of these policies. Public officials, who also act out of economic self interest, seek to be (re)elected and therefore respond to the policy demands of individuals and firms, who provide the votes and campaign funds needed for their election.

The nature of the policies sought by individuals and firms depends on the effect of the policies on their economic welfare. For example, in the simple two-good, two-factor (capital and labor) Heckscher-Ohlin model of international trade, individuals earning their incomes as workers in a capital-abundant country will favor protectionist policies, since these policies will raise the price of the labor-intensive import good and thereby increase labor's real income. Individuals who are capitalists will favor free trade for the opposite reason. In contrast, in a simple two-good, specific-factors model where capital is immobile between the two sectors and labor possesses industry-specific skills, both workers and capitalists in the import-competing industry benefit from protection, while workers and capitalists producing the export good lose. (Baldwin 1984).

A variety of formal models have been developed to explain the determination of domestic or international policies within this economic self-interest framework.[2] Using a framework in which citizens vote directly on trade policy, Mayer (1984) shows that a country's trade policy depends on the relationship between the country's aggregate endowment ratio and the median voter's factor endowments. Stigler (1971), Peltzman (1976), and Hillman (1982) view the government as maximizing a political-support function by balancing the marginal gain in political support from those who benefit from domestic or international regulatory measures against the marginal loss in support from those who lose. Grossman and Helpman (1994) adopt this approach in developing a game-theoretic model aimed at explaining the structure of protection in which profit-maximizing special interest groups make political contributions designed to influence the government's choice of tariffs and subsidies, while the government maximize a welfare function that depends on total contributions collected and the economic welfare of voters. Other economists, such as Magee, Brock, and Young (1989), Findlay and Wellisz (1982), and Hillman and Ursprung (1988), analyze the protection-setting process as a competitive game between different political candidates. Hillman and Ursprung (1988) and Das (1986) include foreign governments and foreign private interests as participants in the political process by which a country's trade policy is determined.

In such economic self-interest models, the well-known free-rider problem associated with public goods is usually utilized to explain why individuals in their role as consumers do not organize and lobby against protection, although their combined losses usually exceed the gains of producers. Trade policy has the characteristic of a public good in the sense that a beneficiary from a policy such as free trade cannot be excluded from its benefits, even if the person does not contribute to the costs of obtaining the policy. Consequently, for each of the many small consumers of a particular product, the decision to contribute campaign funds to officials favoring free trade for this good has the structure of a prisoners' dilemma game. If each consumer believes her contribution is too small to affect the policy outcome, the individual will conclude that it is best not to contribute, regardless of whether all other consumers do or do not contribute. Thus the dominant strategy for each consumer is not to contribute in support of free trade.

Olson (1965) argues that a common-interest group is more likely to overcome the free rider problem and raise the funds needed for effective lobbying if the number of its members is small or if a large share of an industry's output is concentrated among a relatively small number of firms, since some members of the group will then have a significant economic stake in the policy outcome. Caves (1976), in contrast, minimizes the importance of a high degree of concentration among firms in accounting for effective lobbying by an industry and, instead, emphasizes the size of an industry in employment—and thus bloc-voting—terms. Olson (1983) has also argued that, before an industry organizes and undertakes lobbying activities, a crisis such as a significant increase in imports or decline in employment may be necessary to focus attention on the group's common interests.

A number of empirical studies of trade policy provide support for the economic self-interest model. For example, in developed countries, protection of an industry tends to be higher the fewer the number of firms and the larger the numbers of workers. Similarly smaller reductions in industry protection during multilateral trade-liberalizing negotiations are associated with low or negative growth rates as well as fewer firms and larger numbers of workers (Anderson and Baldwin 1987). Legislators' voting patterns are also consistent with the economic self-interest model. These officials tend to vote in a protectionist manner the higher the proportion of voters in their district or state who are employed in import-sensitive industries and the higher the campaign contributions they receive from protectionist unions (Tosini and Tower 1987; Baldwin 1976). Still another manifestation of economic self-interest shaping political action is the long record of presidential candidates agreeing during close political campaigns to support calls for protection by allegedly injured industries with large numbers of voters.

But there are also a number of trade-policy actions that do not seem to be consistent with the economic self-interest model. For example, a key result from the Grossman-Helpman model is that industry protection will be lower the lower the ratio of an industry's output to its net trade and the higher the elasticity of its import demand or export supply. The authors do not empirically test these propositions, but other empirical work indicates that high levels of industry protection are generally associated with high rather than low import penetration ratios (Baldwin and Anderson 1987). In a study of over 600 petitions conducted by the U.S. International Trade Commission (ITC) between 1975 and 1984, Hansen (1990) found that industries with relatively low import demand elasticities are not more likely to get protection than those with relatively high import demand elasticities.[3] Furthermore an analysis by the author indicated the lack of a statistically significant relationship between import demand elasticities and pre- and post–Tokyo Round U.S. tariff levels for 275 four-digit I–O sectors.

There is also a strong negative relationship between both the level of protection in an industry and the change in industry protection during liberalizing negotiations and average wages in the industry, even though low-wage, unskilled workers are generally not very effective in lobbying to promote their economic interests (Anderson and Baldwin 1987).[4] This suggests that governments may be influenced by income-distribution considerations in setting trade policy.[5] Other indications of governments' concern for the welfare of economically disadvantaged groups are the findings that industries with high proportions of unskilled workers, workers over 45 years of age, and workers employed in rural areas with few alternative employment opportunities tend to be shielded in general tariff-cutting trade negotiations (Cheh 1974). The insistence by the U.S. Congress that the government procurement code negotiated in the Tokyo Round provide preferential treatment for small and minority domestic firms and the granting of duty-free treatment on many manufactured imports to poor developing countries are other manifestations of this social concern.

Trade policies motivated by broad foreign policy considerations also are not explained very well by the economic self-interest model. Lobbying by groups organized on the basis of some common economic self-interest appears to have had very little to do with such policies as the embargo on exports of U.S. grain to the Soviet Union during the Carter administration, the formation of the U.S.–Israel, U.S.–Canada and North American free-trade agreements, and the granting of most-favored-nations treatment to Eastern European nations and China.[6]

By utilizing the economic self-interest assumption, economists have been highly successful in explaining what and how goods and services are produced in market economies, even though, as North (1984) points out, the reality is that people often do things that are not in their pure economic self-interest. The reason seems to be that most individuals are only willing to sacrifice a small part of their potential real income to promote the welfare of others. It is reasonable to ignore such motivations when considering individuals' decisions about their employment and major purchases for consumption and firms' decisions about levels and methods of production. One does fail to account for why some consumers boycott certain goods or why many firms pulled their investments out of South Africa, but these inadequacies of the self-interest model may be regarded as acceptable in view of the vast amount of economic activity that does seem to be explained satisfactorily on the basis of the self-interest simplification.

When, however, attention is turned to the determinants of public policies, the self-interest assumption looks much less adequate. There are many public policies that significantly benefit a relatively small number of voters at the cost of reducing the economic welfare of a large number of other voters by only a small amount. Such is the case in the trade policy area, when particular industries receive protection. If economic self-interest was all that mattered to these voters, we would expect to see them registering their opposition to such policies, when they voted for elected officials, for example. Those relying entirely on the economic self-interest assumption explain the lack of this opposition on the grounds that voters are "uninformed and unorganized" (Magee, Brock, and Young 1989, 36) or because of the costs of becoming informed. In view of the widespread dissemination of information over time about the price-increasing effects of protection, these explanations are hard to accept.

Some economists have broadened the self-interest model by including a concern on the part of the government for the welfare of certain social and economic groups, such as Corden (1974), Fieleke (1976), Lavergne (1983), and Baldwin (1985). Corden's (1974, 107) conservative welfare function

illustrates this notion. According to this social welfare function, governments try to avoid "any significant absolute reductions in real incomes of
any significant section of the community...." This type of framework is
used to account for government actions aimed at easing the adjustment
burdens on politically and economically weak groups. Proponents of the
social concerns approach have not been very precise as to why governments behave in this manner, but they presumably view this as being a
response to the ethical concerns of individual voters. Some political scientists, notably John Ruggie (1982), also stress the role of the governments in
mitigating the social costs of trade liberalization.

Another major criticism made by political scientists (see the next section
for a more complete discussion) of the political economy approach followed by economists is its comparative neglect of the role of institutions
and ideology in shaping international economic policies. Much of the
analysis by economists implicitly assumes the existence of political and
economic institutions and an economic ideology similar to those currently
prevailing in the United States. Yet it is apparent that the political-economic processes by which trade policy is determined in countries like
Taiwan (Baldwin and Nelson 1991) and South Korea (Yoo 1991) or in the
People's Republic of China are very different than in the United States.
Furthermore, even an understanding of the changes in U.S. trade policy
over the last sixty years requires an appreciation of the changes in U.S.
political and economic institutions and trade laws over this period.

Two conclusions seem warranted from this discussion of the strengths
and drawbacks of economists' approach to analyzing trade policy in political economy terms. First, the self-interest economic model is very helpful
in understanding certain types of trade policy behavior. However, this
framework is inadequate for analyzing the full range of trade policies in
the United States and for undertaking comparative studies across countries and over time.

8.2   The Political Economy Framework of Political Scientists

A variety of approaches are employed by political scientists in analyzing
foreign economic policies such as the regulation of trade in goods and
services. One prominent approach views trade policy as being shaped
through the process of political competition among various domestic

common-interest groups. E. E. Schattschneider's (1935) study of the
1930 Tariff Act is the seminal work employing this "society-centered"
(Ikenberry, Lake, and Mastanduno 1988) framework. The economic self-
interest model discussed in section 8.1 fits this category. This approach is
open to the same criticisms as the economic self-interest model.

Another major approach emphasizes the importance of the distribution
of economic and political power among countries in shaping foreign economic policies. The central actor in this approach is the state, which is
viewed as an autonomous, rational decision maker primarily concerned
with increasing its political and economic power relative to other nations
(Krasner 1976; Keohane 1984; Lake 1988). By putting trade and other
international economic policies in a foreign policy context, political scientists rectify a serious weakness in the approach taken by economists.

One such systemic theory maintains that the existence of a hegemonic
power is a necessary condition for the existence of a liberal international
trade and financial system (see Gilpin 1987, 72–80; Kindleberger 1981).
According to this theory, which has received considerable attention in
recent years, the hegemon's international trading and financial interests
are so large that this country will gain under a system of free trade and
stable exchange rates, compared to a system of worldwide protection and
unstable exchange rates, even if smaller states free ride by pursuing
mercantilist trade and exchange rate policies.[7] When, however, the country loses its dominant political and economic position, as the United
States has in recent years, the costs to it of maintaining a liberal regime,
which is like an international public good, are no longer less than its gains
from such a system. Therefore protectionism and "beggar-thy-neighbor"
exchange-rate and monetary policies emerge on a worldwide basis.

This simple version of the theory of hegemonic stability has been criticized by a number of political scientists. One basis has been the continued
relative openness of the international economy, despite the decline in the
economic influence of the United States relative to the European Community and Japan (e.g., see Webb and Krasner 1989). As Keohane (1984,
ch. 5) points out, for example, repeated game theory and the theory of
collective action both indicate that cooperation among countries is quite
possible in the absence of a hegemon, especially when a few large states
continue to dominate the international scene (also see Lake 1993 on this
point). The international regimes created during the hegemonic period

also have served as facilitators of cooperation in the posthegemonic
period (Keohane 1984, ch. 6).

The theory of hegemonic stability also fails to explain adequately
just why the hegemon wants a liberal international economic order
(Conybeare 1984; Stein 1984; Milner 1988, 293). On the basis of static
trade theory, a hegemon should follow a policy of import protection and
export subsidization, since the dominant state can increase its real income
by taking advantage of its ability to improve its terms of trade. An explanation for the hegemon's choice of liberal trade and financial regimes
based on dynamic externalities, economies of scale, asymmetric information and endogenous R&D might be formulated, but the hegemonic theory does not usually include this type of reasoning (see, however, Gowa
1989).

Regarding the state as a unitary, rational actor is a natural simplification for political scientists approaching political economy from an
international relations background. The chief executive of a country is
invariably given broad power to direct policy relating to national security
matters and, in particular, to initiate major changes in such policies. The
collective nature of national defense policies and the differences in the
information available to a country's political leader and the general public
makes it sensible to provide the chief executive with great power in this
field. There also is usually broad agreement among various political and
economic interest groups on crucial national security interests. Consequently, in analyzing efforts of countries to strengthen their national security relationships, political scientists have often regarded the state as
unitary actor.

Extending the unitary-actor framework to the broad range of international economic relations can be misleading, however (McKeown 1986).
Many international economic policies, such as those in the trade field,
have quite different economic effects on various common interest groups,
who are able to organize and influence the policy-making process through
lobbying activities. Consequently treating the domestic political process
as a black box, as the theory of hegemonic stability has been accused of
doing (Lake 1988; Goldstein 1988; Haggard 1988), can result in incomplete and misleading explanations of international economic policies. In
particular, the trade policies of a chief executive whose actions are constrained by the political power of various domestic interest groups are
likely to be quite different than those of the head of a government who has

the freedom, as postulated in the hegemonic stability theory, to promote the collective interests of the nation.[8]

A third, state-centered (Ikenberry, Lake, and Mastanduno 1988) approach followed by political scientists in analyzing foreign economic policies stresses the significance of a state's institutional and ideological structure in shaping international economic policies. Some critics of simple versions of the theory of hegemonic stability base their arguments on this framework (Lipson 1982; Goldstein 1988; Haggard 1988). According to proponents of this approach, the liberal trading order did not disintegrate after U.S. hegemony ended because institutional arrangements (e.g., the GATT) and ideas (e.g., a liberal trade policy promotes economic growth and international political stability) that evolved during the hegemonic period helped to maintain a liberal trading regime. While those who favor this approach do not try to explain all economic policy behavior on the basis of ideas and institutions, they insist that their independent influence on regimes must be recognized in any comprehensive political economy model. Not only are the systemic and interest group approaches of other political scientists criticized because of their failure to do so but the political economy approach followed by economists is also deemed inadequate for this reason.

The political economy models formulated by political scientists, like those developed by economists, clearly have contributed greatly to our understanding of international economic policy-making. The much broader vision of political scientists provides insights on some policy behavior for which economic models are of little use. But, as noted above, systemic models with the state as the central actor can be misleading, and the domestic interest group approach is, by itself, subject to the same criticisms as the models of economists. The institutionalist framework is valuable, but it is a supplement to the other theories. Furthermore the microfoundations of these various approaches are not spelled out so one cannot be sure that the postulated behavior at the group or state level is consistent with the behavior of the individual decisionmakers.

8.3 An Integrative Framework for Analyzing Trade Policy

As the preceding analysis indicates, the various political economy approaches of economists and political scientists all provide important insights for understanding the formation of countries' policies on trade and

other international economic matters, but no one approach seems sufficient for analyzing these policies across countries and over time. Yet, as
Odell (1990) emphasizes, a framework that can be used for such analyses
is very much needed.

A truly general framework would explain not only how a country's
trade policies change in response to exogenous shocks such as a sudden
increase in import competition but how the institutions, values and ideologies, and distribution of international economic and political power that
shape the country's response to these shocks are themselves determined.
Clearly our present knowledge of the processes by which institutions,
ideologies, and economic structures change is insufficient to formulate
such a general model of behavior. Nevertheless, further progress in understanding countries' trade and other international economic policies can
be made by adopting the less general approach of examining how key
decision-making agents interact under various institutional, ideological,
and structural conditions that are taken as exogenously given. Such an
approach is set forth in this section. A formal model is not presented,
but rather a general framework outlining the major actors in the political
economy of trade policy, their motivations, and the manner in which they
interact. Formal modeling of part of the framework should be encouraged,
but unless it is clearly set within a general framework, such modeling can
be misleading.

An Overview

A major drawback of the economic self-interest model is its difficulty in
accounting for international economic policies where considerations such
as foreign policy or income-distribution play an important determining
role. In contrast, while the models of political scientists deal with such
broad concerns quite well, most lack sufficient microfoundations to ensure
that the behavior of the state is consistent with the behavior of those
domestic interest groups and individual citizens who influence the actions
of the government.

The framework outlined here deals with the first criticism by postulat-
ing that individuals maximize their welfare but, in doing so, are concerned
not only with their own economic interests but with broad collective
activities such the nation's foreign policy interests. It recognizes the validity of the second by stressing the necessity of explaining the actions of a
country's chief executive in terms both of her own ability to act autono-

mously and the constraints placed on her actions by the political influence of domestic interest groups and the population generally. Another criticism of economic models by political scientists is also recognized by emphasizing that the role of institutions, ideologies, and economic structures in shaping international economic policies must be explicitly taken into account.

In setting up the framework, it is useful to identify four majors sets of actors whose interactions determine a country's international economic policies: individual citizens, common interest groups, the domestic government, and foreign governments along with various other foreign groups, such as international organizations and foreign private interest organizations.[9] The domestic government is the key participant in the process, since it makes the final policy decisions and implements the policies. However, the other three actors influence the nature of these decisions by exerting various forms of political pressure on the domestic government.

Behavior of the Major Actors

Home Governments National governments, in particular, the chief executives of these governments and others in the executive branch with significant decision-making power, can be usefully viewed as seeking to maximize social welfare, subject to maintaining their political power and to various legal constraints.[10] Governments, unlike individuals and lobbying groups, possess the power to create money and, thus, their actions are less constrained by budgetary constraints than those of individuals and lobbying groups.

Following Arrow (1963), the chief executive, like all individuals, is assumed to be rational and, if she possesses perfect knowledge, to be able to provide a preferential ordering of all possible social states. A social state is a complete description of the amounts of each type of good and service in the hands of each individual, including collective goods and services.[11] As Arrow (1963, 17) notes, collective goods and services cover such diverse activities as "municipal services, diplomacy and its continuation through other means, and the erection of statutes to famous men."

In democracies, the chief executive's ordering of social states relating to the key issues in the most recent national election tends to reflect the views of a majority of the country's citizens, which in turn are influenced by prevailing ideologies, institution, and socioeconomic conditions. However, quite aside from the formal impossibility of passing from diverse

individual orderings of social states (even among members of the same
political party) to a social ordering without violating such reasonable
conditions as consistency (Arrow's impossibility theorem), we know that
on some issues the views of a chief executive may differ substantially from
those of a majority of voters even in a democracy, due to the different
weights attached by voters to a candidate's position on the issues relevant
for determining their votes and to the lack of relevance of some issues for
the electoral outcome. When totalitarian governments replace democratic
governments, the leader's social welfare function initially may be representative of a significant part of the population on major issues, but over time
can diverge considerably from that of the average citizen. The socioeconomic background of such leaders plays a role in determining their social
preferences—for example, those with a military background may give
greater weight to protection on national defense grounds than those from
other social groups—but unique educational influences and early experiences also seem to be important factors in shaping their views.

Key features of the role of a country's chief executive are her responsibilities to represent voters on a national level and to direct the nation's
foreign policies. Both of these responsibilities tend to make heads of state
less receptive to requests for industry-specific protection than legislators
representing a particular geographic area within a country. Furthermore,
in modern times, pressures from the leaders of other states to promote
harmonious international relations tend to move a chief executive toward
a liberal trade position, since reciprocally opening markets is widely regarded as a politically friendly action. Such policies seem to increase a
leader's influence in dealing with other heads of state on various political
matters. Increasing access to foreign markets is of course also strongly
supported by international business interests.

Like other individuals, a president or prime minister does not possess
perfect knowledge and thus can be influenced by domestic or foreign
groups who are prepared to incur the economic costs of supplying information favorable to their social welfare. In countries where lobbying by
private interest groups takes place, lobbyists gain the opportunity to present their views to the president or influential policy advisers by contributing funds to support the political campaigns of the chief executive. The
chief executive in turn uses the funds to lobby voters, who also do not
possess perfect knowledge, about the merits of her position on various
policy issues.

On some issues only modest political pressure is exerted on the chief executive, due to the difficulties of organizing for collective action on these issues (Gowa 1984). In these cases the president or prime minister selects the course of action that maximizes social welfare, as she views it, using government and private technicians to obtain needed information. However, the political-support constraint is sometimes binding. Political competition from others seeking the chief executive position is so intense that implementing her own social preferences on a policy matter involves an unacceptably high risk of losing political power. Consequently the chief executive accepts a policy that does not represent her own ordering of social states, unless she views the matter as so important that it is worth the loss of political power. The variant of the economic self-interest model that depicts government policymakers as merely carrying out the policies that maximize their chances of (re)election is applicable in these circumstances. However, since political markets, like economic markets, are often imperfectly competitive, heads of governments usually are able to implement at least part of their policy preferences.

Authoritarian leaders have much greater leeway to follow their own ordering of social states, since they are usually less constrained by legal and other institutional conditions. The ideologies that shape their economic and social views tend to play a more important role in shaping economic policies than political pressures from domestic economic interest groups. However, as previously noted, even dictators are not immune from political pressures. Although they do not have to worry about losing political power through the ballot box, such leaders must still be concerned about the possibility of losing political power through military coups, riots, and mass demonstrations touched off by policies unpopular with various economic and social groups. Thus the importance of political pressures from common interest groups in shaping economic policies tends to vary in a continuous manner across various forms of government.

In some countries, such as the United States, legislatures have very different orderings of social states than the chief executive and possess the political power to influence the policies of national governments to a significant extent. Like chief executives, individual members of legislatures can be viewed as maximizing social welfare, but they are constrained to a greater extent by the possibility of losing political power if they follow their own social preferences. In particular, the greater need to obtain campaign funds with which to promote their candidacy makes them more vulnerable to political pressures from common interest groups.[12] Thus the behavior of legislatures generally better fits the self-interest model in which government policies are mainly shaped by the nature of the political competition among special interest groups.

Individual Citizens   Each individual citizen, like the head of state or individual legislator, has a social welfare function and seeks to maximize her social welfare, subject to the constraints imposed by her factor endowments and political power. Given perfect knowledge, this welfare function includes an ordering not just of the goods and services the individual consumes but an ordering of the private and collective goods in the hands of every other individual. Under most ethical ideologies, individuals are, to some extent, concerned about the welfare of others. They may be willing to give up, particularly on a temporary basis, part of their real income to increase the real income of others who, for example, have been injured by substantial increases in imports or by foreign actions they deem unfair.

As in the case of their own consumption of a particular good, the more income individuals forego to promote the welfare of others, the smaller the decrease in real income they are willing to give up to increase further the welfare of these others individuals a given amount. Moreover they are assumed to be willing to forego only a small fraction of their total incomes to assist others and not to support actions that would directly reduce economic activity in the particular industry in which their productive services are used. Economic self-interest determines individuals' views on public policies that significantly affect the economic sector in which they are employed or have invested their capital.

Knowledge is both imperfectly supplied to individuals and costly to acquire and disseminate. Individuals acquire some information about the economic and social welfare of others in the process of consuming goods and services as well as through their income-earning activities as participants in production units, but they normally only learn about the welfare conditions of those who live in the same geographical area in these ways. If they had information about the welfare status of other groups, their ordering of social states involving, for example, different income-redistributing public policies could change. Consequently, under democratic forms of government, it is optimal for some individuals and the firms in which they are employed to join with others who share their economic or social interests in undertaking information-disseminating activities aimed at convincing the chief executive and other government officials as well as other voters of the merits of public policies designed to increase either their economic welfare or that of some other group about whom they are concerned. Under authoritarian governments, such behavior by individuals and firms is less likely, since the views of most domestic common-interest groups usually have much less influence on the government.

Common Interest Groups   Individual citizens or production units acting alone to influence public policies are generally not very effective. A single individual's or firm's economic stake in a particular policy usually is not sufficiently high to justify the large fixed costs required to initiate an effective lobbying effort. An individual's voting impact is also insignificant. However, if many individuals or a number of firms who share some common economic, political, or social interest join together to form a political pressure group, they can take advantage of the considerable economies of scale involved in disseminating information by forming lobbying organizations. These organizations may be concerned only about a single issue, such as an industry association formed to promote import protection for the sector, or about a wide range of economic, political, and social policies, such as a national political party. In addition to providing information favorable to their policy positions, they can promise to deliver significant blocs of votes and provide substantial campaign funding to policymakers supporting these positions. Consequently, under political systems that do not discourage the formations of such organizations, common-interest groups are major sources of political pressure on chief executives and other public officials.

Common-interest groups organized to promote economic policies are assumed to be primarily concerned with maximizing the economic welfare of the individuals they represent, subject to their funding constraints. However, the free-rider problem may cause total contributions to fall short of the level that maximizes the industry's collective benefits. Furthermore, like the individuals they represent, these organizations sometimes are prepared on ethical grounds to support policies that help other groups if the economic costs to their members are minimal.

Since empirical evidence seems to indicate that common-interest groups, like individuals, put considerably greater weight on the short-term welfare effects of such economic policies as tariffs and quantitative import restrictions than on their long-run effects, a specific-factors model, in which capital is sector specific and workers are mobile but possess sector-specific skills, is appropriate for analyzing the lobbying behavior of common-interest groups (see Magee 1980). As previously noted, in this model capitalists and workers employed in an import-competing industry benefit significantly from import restrictions and thus lobby for protection. In contrast, capitalists and workers employed in domestic or export-oriented industries in which the output of the protected industry is a significant intermediate input in production lobby against protection for the import-competing industry, since costs in these industries increase appreciably. Foreign firms exporting the product to the protecting country also may lobby against any protective action if the market in the country is large.

Individuals whose own economic or social welfare is not significantly affected by either protection or liberalization for some industry, namely final consumers of most products, may support or oppose these policies. However, because of their large numbers and the small quantity of the product each consumes, it is assumed that these individuals do not organize into consumer lobbying groups due to the free-rider problem. They express their views about trade policies affecting the industry through their voting behavior and other less organized means of communication with political leaders.

Leaders of authoritarian governments generally view privately organized economic lobbying groups as threats to their political power and tend to discourage or, at least, control such organizations. An outcome more likely under this form of government is the bribing of officials by particular capitalists or entrepreneurs in return for government policies that selectively favor these individuals.

Foreign Governments, International Organizations, and Other Foreign Interests Governments not only make the final decisions about their own country's economic policies but try to influence the economic policies of other countries. As noted earlier, one of the objectives of heads of state is to persuade other chief executives to pursue collective policies aimed at promoting more harmonious international political relations and increasing the economic welfare of all nations. Of course, in doing so, each chief executive attempts to maximize her own country's gains. The success of heads of state in achieving their international objectives depends on the economic and political structure of the world economy, the nature of the dynamic factors bringing about changes in this structure, and the nature of the institutions and ideology in which the structure and forces of change are embedded.

A country's size in terms of national income, population, and geography relative to other countries is the major structural variable affecting a country's international economic influence. For example, large, high-income countries are better able than small low-income countries to provide financial assistance to support economic policies of other governments that have favorable implications for their international objectives. Similarly, due to the attractiveness of their internal markets, such countries tend to be more successful in influencing other countries' international economic policies by inviting them to join free-trade areas or customs unions. Policies of the "stick" rather than "carrot" variety involving threats to close their internal markets to other countries also are more effective for large, high-income countries. In contrast, countries whose income and trade levels are small have little chance of imposing their objectives on others. However, these countries are often able to subsidize exports and restrict imports without facing retaliatory actions because the trade effects of their policies on world trade are small.

Interactions among the Major Actors   Figure 8.1 depicts the various possible interrelationships among the major decision makers. The dotted and

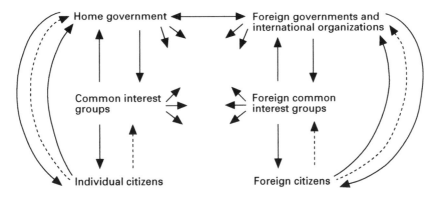

Figure 8.1
Interactions among major decision makers

solid lines running from home-country citizens to the home government
and foreign citizens to foreign governments indicate that in democracies
individual citizens elect their governments and also may exert some pressure on them through direct lobbying. The dotted lines from individual
citizens to common-interest groups indicate that individuals organize
themselves into such groups, either directly or as members of firms, which,
as the solid lines indicate, then lobby their government and other private
citizens. These lobbying organizations also try to influence foreign governments, foreign common-interest groups, and foreign citizens, as the arrows
in the figure show.

As the arrows also indicate, political pressures on the chief executive
come not only from domestic sources but from foreign governments, international organizations, and various private interest groups abroad. Governments do not simply respond in the best manner to these pressures but
(as the arrows show) try to influence the behavior of their citizens and
domestic interest groups by engaging in lobbying themselves. Government lobbying may also be directed at foreign governments, international
organizations, and foreign common-interest groups and citizens. As has
been emphasized, the nature and outcomes of the decision-making process
on international economic issues depend on the characteristics of existing
political and economic institutions, prevailing ideologies, and current political and economic conditions.

Consider the decision-making process of the chief executive of a democratic government who must decide whether to grant a particular industry's request for increased import protection. Suppose that the number of
individuals harmed or helped by the decision and the volume of campaign
funds they contribute to the government are too small to have an appre-
ciable impact on the chief executive's reelection possibilities. Furthermore
assume that retaliation by foreign governments is remote. Under these
circumstances the chief executive can follow her own preferences on social
states in reaching a decision.

The industry's lobbyists will, however, provide information designed to
convince the chief executive that a protectionist decision is consistent with
her ordering of social welfare conditions. By also trying to convince the
general public that such a decision is consistent with their welfare preferences, the lobbyists can go to the chief executive with the argument that a
protectionist response will increase (or, at least, not decrease) her political
support among voters. Industries that are significantly hurt by a protec-

tionist decision will utilize the same channels to lobby for a negative decision by the head of state.

There are many different circumstances that can change the nature of the decision-making process described above, even under the same form of government and basic set of ideologies. For example, if a general election is scheduled for the near future and the race appears to be close, a chief executive is likely to give greater weight in her decision-making process to the views of those significantly affected by the decision, even if their numbers are small. Similarly, if unemployment in the economy is at historically high levels, a protectionist decision is more likely. In contrast, credible threats of foreign retaliation that may significantly reduce exports increase the chance of a negative decision on protection.

An authoritarian leader faced with the same decision is less likely to be constrained in following her own ordering of social states by the short-term views of a small numbers of citizens significantly affected by the decision. However, if domestic political conditions are already somewhat unstable, she may take into account the possibility that the decision could touch off mass demonstrations and rioting. Such a leader may, however, be quite responsive to threats of foreign retaliation if the country is highly dependent on export markets.

Sometimes political support for an elected head of state may be so weak and her views on trade policy so different from a significant part of the population that she must ignore her own social preferences in order to remain in power. Under these circumstances an appropriate model for analysis is one in which the chief executive is portrayed as selecting those trade policies that maximize domestic political support (see Hillman 1982). However, if the chief executive is not forced to react in this manner on all policy issues, she may choose certain policies to increase political support sufficiently so that she can offset the loss in political support associated with following her own preferences on those matters ranked highest in her social welfare function.

In some circumstances it is useful to view the chief executive as being involved in a bargaining game with domestic interest groups, since the best course of action for both the chief executive and the domestic interest groups depends on their assessments of how the other is going to act. One game often utilized for such analyses is the Nash noncooperative bargaining model. In this model each player selects the policy position that maximizes social welfare, given the policy position of other players.

For example, an industry is likely to react to the level of protection set by the chief executive by being willing to contribute more campaign funds, the higher the level of protection granted the industry. (At low protective levels the industry may give funds to opposition candidates.) Similarly the chief executive is likely to react to the level of campaign contributions from common interest groups by being willing to grant higher levels of protection the higher the levels of campaign funding. The Nash equilibrium is the set of policy positions at which it is impossible for any player to raise her social welfare, given the policies of the other players. It can be shown that unique and stable Nash equilibrium exist in games of this type under quite reasonable assumptions. (Friedman 1986).

Another situation where this game-theoretic framework seems appropriate is when a U.S. president tries to get a major trade bill through Congress in order to undertake a GATT-sponsored multilateral trade negotiation. On these occasions common-interest groups put strong political pressures on members of Congress to pass legislation favoring their economic interests. In the bargaining that goes on between the executive and legislative branches of the government, the president knows that a majority of the members of Congress must approve any legislation before she can sign it, while members of Congress know that two-thirds of their number is required to implement legislation that the president vetoes.

The policy interactions between home and foreign governments and between governments and international organizations can also be usefully analyzed in game theoretic terms in some circumstances. Policy-making cases where this analytical framework yields important insights are negotiations on such matters as the tariff-cutting formula in the Tokyo Round (see Baldwin and Clarke 1987), the recent talks between the United States and Japan aimed at reducing Japan's bilateral trade surplus with the United States, U.S.–EC negotiations on agricultural liberalization in the Uruguay Round, and developing countries' negotiations with the International Monetary Fund or World Bank for financial assistance. When a government bargains both with domestic common-interest groups and foreign governments, the final outcome can be viewed as the second level of a two part game.[13] Suppose, for example, that the level of retaliatory tariff imposed by a foreign government, in response to a home government's increase in a tariff protecting one of its industries, depends on the tariff level set by the home government. The lobbying process in the home country between the home government and domestic interest groups, the first level of the two-part game, determines the tariff rate the home government sets for any given level of retaliatory tariff by the foreign country. Given this set of domestic reactions together with the tariff responses of the foreign government for different tariff levels of the tariff for the domestic industry,[14] the Nash equilibrium for the domestic and foreign retaliatory tariffs is determined as the point where the two reaction curves intersect, since at that point neither the domestic or foreign governments can improve their social welfare, given the other's action at that point.

8.5 Conclusions

This chapter has criticized the approaches of both economists and political scientists to international political economy, especially as applied to trade policy. The self-interest model of economists, for example, fails to explain adequately trade policy actions that are influenced by the broad social and national concerns of voters and governments. The assumption that governments merely respond to the political pressures exerted by various groups in a manner that maximizes their reelection chances also is deficient for the many situations where governments take a leadership role in shaping trade policy, quite independent of domestic or international pressure groups. Insufficient attention to the influence of other nations on a country's trade policy and to the role of institutions and ideologies in determining policy are additional drawbacks of economists' approaches to international political economy.

Political scientists have not given sufficient attention to the behavioral micro-foundations of the key actors in their models. The problems that arise in not doing so are evident in such systemic approaches as the model of hegemonic stability, which tends to ignore the process by which domestic pressure groups influence the state's international actions through the domestic political process. Although some political scientists view international economic policies as being shaped by the domestic political process, much as economists do, this society-centered approach has not been well linked backward to the behavior of individual voters nor forward to the influence of other states on these policies.

The integrative framework proposed here tries to avoid these drawbacks of other approaches. It focuses on the maximizing behavior of four major participants in the policy determination process: national governments, in particular their chief executives who seek to maximize social welfare according to their ordering of possible social states, subject to maintaining political power; individual citizens who, subject to their factor endowment and political power constraints, maximize social welfare based on their own social welfare functions, which include an ordering not only of the goods and services these individuals consume personally but also of the private and collective goods in the hands of every other individual; common-interest groups who, if organized for economic purposes, are primarily concerned with maximizing the economic welfare of the interests they represent and are further subject to budgetary and political power constraints; and foreign governments, international organizations and other foreign groups who maximize their social welfare, subject to various constraints as well.

As political scientists have understood much better than economists the nature of the interactions among these actors, and the resulting policy outcomes depend on the nature of existing domestic and international political and economic institutions, prevailing economic and political ideologies, economic and political conditions domestically and abroad, and the economic and political effect of a policy. In a modern democracy like the United States, for example, analytical approaches that stress the importance of lobbying activities by domestic, self-interested pressure groups in shaping international economic policies provide valuable insights in understanding certain policy actions. But some international economic policy decisions are not explained well with this framework, even under the same institutions, ideologies, and world economic and political conditions. To understand the policy-making process on some issues, it is necessary to recognize the importance of such diverse factors as the independent role of the chief executive, the social concerns of citizens, the world distribution of economic power, and the economic impact of the policy being considered.

Such conditions as the magnitude of political support for the chief executive, the political power of the country relative to others, and the economic effects of a policy also influence the nature of the policy determination process. In some combinations of these conditions, analyzing policymaking as a bargaining game between the chief executive and domestic economic interest groups or between the domestic government and foreign governments is appropriate. Under others, it is more appropriate to view the various actors as not taking into consideration the actions of others when determining their own actions.

When international economic policies are being analyzed in places and times with very different political and economic institutions and ideologies than currently exist in the United States, an even broader framework is needed. Under authoritarian governments, for example, policies well explained in the United States by an economic pressure group approach are more likely to be determined by the chief executive with little influence from domestic economic interest groups. Whether or not a country is a member of the GATT, its level of development, its commitment to a free-market ideology, and so on, significantly influence its policy-determination process and policy outcome on any issue.

In analyzing particular international economic policies in political economy terms, it is therefore incumbent on researchers to consider explicitly the extent to which their conclusions about the policy-making process depend on the nature of prevailing institutions, ideologies, and structural conditions. The assumption by economists that behavior is based on economic self-interest has proved to be very useful in explaining activities of consumers and firms across a wide spectrum of institutions and ideologies. However, economists must support generalizations about government policies with explicit analyses of why different institutions and ideologies do not matter for their conclusions. Not only can this help to avoid unwarranted generalizations, but it will begin to build a body of knowledge about how particular institutions, ideologies, and structural condition do influence policy outcomes.

Notes

The author is grateful for the comments of Joanne Gowa, Stephan Haggard, David Lake, Timothy McKeown, and Douglas Nelson on an earlier version of this chapter.

1. Discussions of approaches to international political economy by political scientists are included in Gilpin (1988) and Keohane (1984), while summaries of contributions in this field by economists are presented in Frey (1984) and Hillman (1989).

2. These models represent examples of positive political economy. However, another important part of the field is concerned with the welfare implications of particular policy outcomes, taking into account the resources used in achieving the policy and in competing for the rents created by the policy. The papers by Krueger (1974) and Bhagwati (1980) illustrate this branch of the subject.

3. One would want to test the Grossman-Helpman propositions concerning import penetration ratios and import demand elasticities more formally before reaching a firm conclusion on the matter, but these results cast doubt on their empirical validity.

4. Obviously workers in the textiles and apparel industries are an exception to this generality.

5. It might be argued that the government protects economically disadvantaged workers as part of its objective of maximizing national welfare, taking account of adjustment costs. However, there are various empirical studies indicating that the labor adjustment costs associated with trade liberalization are much lower than the consumer welfare benefits from liberalization (e.g., see Baldwin, Mutti, and Richardson 1980; also see Lawrence and Litan 1986 for a discussion of this argument).

6. Such matters as the length of the phase in period in free-trade agreements for different goods are, however, significantly influenced by self-interested lobbying.

7. As Mansfield (1992) points out, Kindleberger (1981) suggests that hegemons provide a liberal trading system for altruistic reasons. In his paper Mansfield presents empirical evidence indicating that features of the concentration of power in the international system are positively related to the level of global commerce.

8. Lake (1988) is an example of an author who tries to integrate a systemic approach and an approach that recognizes the role of domestic politics.

9. It should be noted that a framework for organizing analyses of the processes by which international economic policies are determined is being proposed rather than a formal model of these processes.

10. This chapter focuses on international economic policies that must be approved by the chief executive before going into effect.

11. It is assumed, for simplicity, that the chief executive and other top officials in the executive branch have identical social welfare functions. Obviously this is not always a reasonable assumption.

12. Individual voters and the communications media tend to make a greater effort to learn about and disseminate the views of presidents and prime ministers than those of legislators, due to the greater political power of chief executives.

13. Putnam (1988) proposes viewing the decision-making process an international economic issues in this manner.

14. The lobbying process in the foreign country determines the foreign government's reaction curve depicting levels of its retaliatory tariff for different levels of the home country's tariff.

References

Anderson, Kym, and Robert E. Baldwin. 1987. The political market for protection in industrial countries. In Ali M. El-Agraa, ed., *Protection Cooperation, Integration and Development: Essays in Honour of Professor Hiroshi Kitamura*. London: Macmillan.

Arrow, Kenneth J. 1963. *Social Choice and Individual Value*. 2d ed. New York: Wiley.

Baldwin, Robert E. 1976. The political economy of postwar U.S. trade policy. *Bulletin*, 1976-4, New York University Graduate School of Business.

Baldwin, Robert E. 1984. Rent seeking and trade policy: An industry approach. *Weltwirtschafliches Archiv* 4:646–77.

Baldwin, Robert E. 1985. *The Political Economy of U.S. Import Policy*. Cambridge: MIT Press.

Baldwin, Robert E., John H. Mutti, and J. David Richardson. 1980. Welfare effects on the United States of a significant multilateral tariff reduction. *Journal of International Economics* 10:405–23.

Baldwin, Robert E., and Richard N. Clarke. 1987. Game-modeling multilateral trade negotiations. *Journal of Political Modeling* 9:257–84.

Baldwin, Robert E., and Douglas Nelson. 1991. The political economy of U.S.–Taiwanese trade and other international economic relations. Presented at Second Annual East Asia Seminar on Economics: Trade and Protectionism, Chung-Hua Institution for Economic Research and National Bureau of Economic Research, Taipei, Taiwan, June 19–21, 1991.

Bhagwati, Jagdish N. 1980. Lobbying and welfare. *Journal of Public Economics* 14: 355–63.

Caves, Richard E. 1976. Economic models of political choice: Canada's tariff structure. *Canadian Journal of Economics* 9:278–300.

Cheh, J. H. 1974. United States concessions in the Kennedy round and short-run labor adjustment costs. *Journal of International Economics* 4:323–40.

Cohen, Benjamin J. 1990. The political economy of international trade. *International Organization* 44:261–81.

Conybeare, John A. 1984. Public goods, prisoners' dilemmas and the international political economy. *International Studies Quarterly* 28:5–22.

Corden, W. Max. 1974. *Trade Policy and Economic Welfare*. Oxford: Clarendon Press.

Das, Satya P. 1986. Foreign lobbying and the political economy of protection. Department of Economics, University of Wisconsin-Milwaukee.

Diebold, William, Jr. 1952. The end of the I.T.O. Essays in International Finance, no. 16 (October). International Finance Section, Department of Economics, Princeton University.

Fieleke, Norman. 1976. The tariff structure for manufacturing industries in the United States: A test of some traditional explanations. *Columbia Journal of World Business* 11: 98–104.

Findlay, Ronald, and Stanislaw Wellisz. 1982. Endogenous Tariffs, the Political Economy of Trade Restrictions, and Welfare. In Jagdish Bhagwati, ed., *Import Competition and Response*. Chicago: University of Chicago Press.

Frey, Bruno S. 1984. *International Political Economy*. Oxford: Basil Blackwell.

Friedman, James W. 1986. *Game Theory with Applications to Economics*. Oxford: Oxford University Press.

Gilpin, Robert. 1987. *The Political Economy of International Relations*. Princeton: Princeton University Press.

Goldstein, Judith. 1988. Ideas, institutions, and American trade policy. *International Organization* 42:180–217.

Gourevitch, Peter. 1986. *Politics of Hard Times: Comparative Responses to International Economic Crisis*. Ithaca: Cornell University Press.

Gowa, Joanne. 1984. Public goods and political institutions: Trade and monetary policy processes in the United States. *International Organization* 38:16–31.

Gowa, Joanne. 1989. *Rational hegemons, excludable goods, and small groups: An epitaph for hegemonic stability theory*. World Politics 41:307–24.

Haggard, Stephan. 1988. The institutional foundations of hegemony: Explaining the Reciprocal Trade Agreements Act of 1934. *International Organization* 42:91–119.

Hansen, Wendy L. 1990. The International Trade Commission and the politics of protectionism. *American Political Science Review* 84:21–46.

Hillman, Arye L. 1982. Declining industries and political support protectionism. *American Economic Review* 72:1180–87.

Hillman, Arye L. 1989. *The Political Economy of Protection*. New York: Harwood.

Hillman, Arye L., and Heinrich W. Ursprung. 1988. Domestic politics, foreign interests, and international trade policy. *American Economic Review* 78:719–45.

Ikenberry, G. John, David A. Lake, and Michael Mastanduno. 1988. Introduction: Approaches to explaining american foreign economy policy. *International Organization* 42:1–14.

Keohane, Robert O. 1984. *After Hegemony: Cooperation or Discord in World Political Economy.* Princeton: Princeton University Press.

Kindleberger, Charles P. 1981. Dominance and leadership in the international economy: Exploitation, public goods, and free rides. *International Studies Quarterly* 25:242–53.

Krasner, Stephen D. 1976. State power and the structure of international trade. *World Politics* 28:317–47.

Lake, David A. 1988. The state and American trade strategy in the pre-hegemonic era. *International Organization* 42:33–58.

Lake, David A. 1988. *Power, Protection, and Free Trade.* Ithaca: Cornell University Press.

Lake, David A. 1993. Leadership, hegemony, and the international economy: Naked emperor or tattered monarch with potential? *International Studies Quarterly* 37:459–89.

Lavergne, R. P. 1983. *The Political Economy of U.S. Tariffs: An Empirical Analysis.* New York: Academic Press.

Lawrence, Robert Z., and Robert E. Litan. 1986. *Saving Free Trade: A Pragmatic Approach.* Washington: Brookings Institution.

Lipson, Charles. 1982. The transformation of trade. *International Organization* 36:417–56.

Magee, Stephen P. 1980. Three simple tests of the Stolpher-Samuelson theorem. In Peter Oppenheimer, ed., *Issues in International Economics.* London: Oriel Press.

Magee, Stephen P, William A. Brock, and Leslie Young. 1989. *Black Hole Tariffs and Endogenous Policy Theory: Political Economy in General Equilibrium.* Cambridge: Cambridge University Press.

Mansfield, Edward D. 1992. The concentration of capitalists and international trade. *International Organization* 46:733–63.

Mayer, Wolfgang. 1984. Endogenous tariff formation. *American Economic Review* 74:970–85.

McKeown, Timothy J. 1986. The limitations of "structural" theories of commercial policy. *International Organization* 40:43–64.

Milner, Helen V. 1988. *Resisting Protectionism.* Princeton: Princeton University Press.

North, Douglas. 1984. Three approaches to the study of institutions. In David C. Colander, ed., *Neoclassical Political Economy: The Analysis of Rent-Seeking and DUP Activities.* Cambridge, MA: Ballanger.

Odell, John S. 1990. Understanding international trade policies: An emerging synthesis. *World Politics* 43:139–67.

Olson, Mancur. 1965. *The Logic of Collective Action.* Cambridge: Harvard University Press.

Olson, Mancur. 1983. The political economy of comparative growth rates. In D. C. Mueller, ed., *The Political Economy of Growth.* New Haven: Yale University Press.

Peltzman, Sam. 1976. Toward a more general theory of regulation. *Journal of Law and Economics* 19:211–40.

Putnam, Robert D. 1988. Diplomacy and domestic politics: The logic of two-level games. *International Organization* 42:428–60.

Rogowski, Ronald. 1989. *Commerce and Coalitions.* Princeton: Princeton University Press.

Ruggie, John G. 1982. International regimes, transactions, and change: Embedded liberalism in the postwar economic order. *International Organization* 36:379–415.

Schattschneider, E. E. 1935. *Politics, Pressures, and the Tariff.* Englewood Cliffs, NJ: Prentice-Hall.

Stein, Arthur A. 1984. The hegemon's dilemma: Great Britain, the United States, and the international economic order. *International Organization*, 38:355–86.

Stern, Robert M., Jonathan Francis, and Bruce Schumacher. 1976. *Price Elasticities in International Trade: An Annotated Bibliography*. Toronto: Macmillan of Canada/Maclean-Hunter Press.

Stigler, George. 1971. The theory of economic regulation. *Bell Journal of Economics* 2:3–21.

Tosini, Suzanne, and Edward Tower. 1987. The textile bill of 1985: The determinants of congressional voting patterns. *Public Choice* 54:19–25.

Webb, M. C., and S. D. Krasner. 1989. Hegemonic stability theory: An empirical assessment. *Review of International Studies* 15:183–98.

Wilkinson, Joe R. 1960. *Politics and Trade Police*. Washington: Public Affairs Press.

Yoo, Jung-Ho. 1991. Political economy of protection structure in Korea. Presented at Second Annual East Asia Seminar on Economics: Trade and Protectionism, Chung-Hua Institution for Economic Research and National Bureau of Economic Research, Taipei, Taiwan, June 19–21, 1991.

9 On the Political Economy of Trade: Notes of a Social Insurance Analyst

Peter Diamond

Since I did not want to miss the opportunity to celebrate Jagdish, I have spent much of my summer and fall reading about trade and its political economy. As I was foolish enough not to have studied with Charlie Kindleberger, I started with little foundation for this crash course. I have enjoyed it and thought that it might be useful to draw out some of the parallels with the political economy of social insurance, particularly the effect of institution design on political outcomes.

This chapter calls for study of the class of circumstances where Congress uses a noncongressional institution to select the details of legislation that is then subjected to a single up or down vote. Such study might identify the conditions that increase the likelihood of continuing fast-track procedures that seem to increase the likelihood of liberal trade outcomes. Second, the chapter identifies the difficulty in having case-by-case congressional response to requests for protection. This difficulty suggests study of the details of institution design to handle such requests in the context of a "general" policy.

Since uncertainty about the future of the economy is an integral part of the political process, I will also discuss the problem of modeling the economy in which the political process is working. In particular, I will object to the methodological strictures laid down by Avinash Dixit (1990) that models with an incomplete set of markets should derive incompleteness, not assume it.

9.1 Politics

Destler (1992) begins *American Trade Politics*, with the apparent contradiction between a history of repeatedly lowered trade barriers and Schattschneider's (1935) observation that the political balance of forces was heavily weighted on the side of protection. Destler writes:

For a politician who must respond to concentrated interests, a vote for lowering trade barriers is therefore, as one former trade official put it, an "unnatural act." [footnote omitted] If he is to vote this way—and if Congress, more generally, is to divert or turn back the pressures for trade protection—counterweights have to be built into our policymaking system. These counterweights can be ideas, such as the view espoused by Cordell Hull, Franklin D. Roosevelt's secretary of state, that liberal trade promotes peace among nations. These can be processes: means of setting tariffs that insulate Congress from direct responsibility. They can be institutions: an executive branch agency that measures its success in terms of how well it copes with trade-restrictive pressures and thus allows international commerce to flourish. (p. 5)

Destler identifies ideas, processes, and institutions as keys to liberal trade outcomes. Jagdish has been a major contributor to the ideas leg of this stool. His writings, such as *Protectionism* (1988) and *The World Trading System at Risk* (1991), have helped make the case for liberal trade to both politicians and the public. For my purpose, I will not be discussing the ideas leg. Rather, starting with the observation that the political system sometimes selects processes and institutions to encourage liberal trade outcomes, I want to note similar outcomes elsewhere, suggesting that liberal trade outcomes are not an anomaly but a part of the way that the political process works some of the time on a variety of issues. I will argue that good policy often calls for protecting representatives from the consequences of their votes, that sometimes it is protection from general interests and not special interests that is needed,[1] and that Congress sometimes chooses to protect itself in this way, a fact calling for modeling such institutional design as a political outcome.[2] In particular, this discussion directs attention to the need to identify circumstances when Congress will select such processes and institutions. This discussion is not meant to deny the observation that the invisibility of some congressional actions contributes to some poor policies.[3]

Formal models of political economy work with (generally a subset of) four differently modeled agents. There are general voters, organized voters (referred to as special interests or lobbying groups), politicians, and civil servants (frequently referred to as bureaucrats). The median voter model, which has only general voters who know the effects of political outcomes on their own utilities, has no room for ideas, processes, and institutions. While it can be useful to know how a majority of voters would evaluate different policies, this would not be a good starting place for building a model for the questions I have identified. Similarly it is hard to start with a model concentrating on power-seeking bureaucrats or contribution-seeking politicians and have room for ideas and the selection of processes and institutions that result in more liberal trade outcomes, although one could probably imagine some contribution extraction technology that results in such outcomes.[4] More promising to my mind is an approach based on more complicated motivations.[5] Thus I like models in which politicians are assumed to care about social welfare as well as contributions, as in Grossman and Helpman (1994).

Political Decision Processes

Governments distribute and redistribute a vast amount of income, using a large variety of mechanisms. Distribution decisions involve such questions as whether to give or sell government goods and assets. Redistribution decisions involve mechanisms that may involve identifiable (or somewhat identifiable) losers as well as gainers. This distinction between distribution and redistribution is arbitrary from an economic point of view since government assets are lost to "all of us" when they are given away. But it may not be arbitrary from a political economy point of view, where the extent of political identification of the losers is important. I want to suggest that redistributional actions happen in two different sorts of settings, one where policy seems to come out better with less visibility and one where policy seems to come out better with more visibility.[6] I will only consider cases that fit in the former category. Visibility is not a satisfactory term. Maybe salience is better, or transparency, or visible political responsibility. I duck the complications in defining good policies in a setting of political economy. Since there are many different outcomes that could happen with alternative democratic institutions, having policy be the result of a democratic process is not a sufficient basis for defining good policies. Yet being a democratic outcome should count for something. Often good policies are like giraffes—we know them when we see them.

The value of lower visibility or responsibility is a commonplace of the discussion of trade policy. The ability to yield power to the administration is felt to be critical in the ability of Congress to support tariff reductions. That is, Congress wants protection from voters and campaign contributors. The form of protection is decreased responsibility over details. While I will refer to this as decreased visibility, it should be remembered that it is not visibility of the vote that approves a tariff reduction as much as visibility of or responsibility for the full process resulting in reduced tariffs. Conversely, some of the popularity of nontariff import restrictions may well be their lack of visibility (of causation) to consumers paying higher prices (as well as their popularity with foreign exporters having their market artificially restricted).

Congress often selects the mechanism that then controls distribution. We academics are very sensitive to the tension between congressionally voted grants to individual universities and appropriations for grant-giving institutions, such as the National Science Foundation. Another example is the auctioning of part of the electromagnetic spectrum that received much press coverage this summer. As a system, this auction replaced giveaways of parts of the spectrum by lottery (a system installed under Reagan) and the previous system of giveaways after extensive hearings, to politically selected individuals and groups. This evolution would be interesting to study since it cuts against a naive view of behavior of both politicians and bureaucrats trying to maximize their power.

Sometimes Congress designs an institution to structure a single Congressional vote, as with fast-track rules. One social insurance example was the 1983 Greenspan commission that recommended a particular package of reforms to Social Security to affect both short-run and long-run fiscal balance. Another example is the use of the base closure commission to recommend a set of military bases to close. Potential closing of a military base is a very visible risk to those in the neighborhood of such a base. Thus it is not surprising that elected politicians work hard to prevent closing of bases in their districts, nor that there has been a considerable history of successful resistance to closure of bases that the military wanted to close. There is no decrease in awareness of the risk by congressional creation of a base-closing commission, whose recommendation Congress voted to accept or reject in whole. Rather, politicians seem willing to accept a process that may result in the closing of their base, even though they would muster sufficient resistance to block a vote for the same closure without the intervening commission process. Backward induction (even with uncertainty about outcomes) suggests a difficulty for a model that derives outcomes purely from preference primitives. Rather, acceptance of losing one's base as part of a "legitimate" process increases protection for politicians, allowing them to begin on a process whose outcome is known to be risky, and possibly, in some cases, very likely to be negative. From the perspective of trade, fast-track procedures play a similar role. Politicians lobby for particular protections as part of the reciprocal trade negotiations, just as they lobby about particular military bases. But then the Congress as a whole has been able to accept the outcome of the process in both cases. This suggests a value in enhancing the image of the information gathering process that leads to the administration's stance in trade negotiations. Having received a fair hearing helps reconcile voters and contributors to not receiving their preferred outcomes. The role of such reconciliation should be seen in light of the fact that individual votes in congressional elections have a vanishingly small probability of affecting outcomes, and so may be a form of self-expression as much as a vote of interests. Indeed Brennan and Buchanan (1984) have likened voting to cheering for one's preferred sports team.[7] Fast-track procedures seem to enhance the likelihood of liberal trade outcomes. Since it is not assured that the fast-track procedures will be approved, it seems useful to place such procedures in a wider set of similar legislative processes to try to understand the circumstances under which their approval is more likely.[8]

Political Implications of Programs

The examples above were examples of processes designed to affect a vote by Congress. In addition the design of operating institutions affects the political debate about how the institutions will evolve. Let me give a few examples from the public provision of pensions. In Poland, before the end of communism, there were separate defined benefit pension rules for different industries. Coal miners, with considerable political power, had particularly favorable terms. These were "justified" in political discussion by the difficulty in mining coal, a justification that was hard to extend to journalists who were similarly favored.

In Chile, after the Pinochet government had replaced the pay-as-you-go system by a mandatory savings plan with individual accounts, the appeal by coal miners for special treatment received considerable verbal support from politicians, but no action. Presumably the apparent need to identify the source of the funds that would be added to the individual accounts affected the outcome, although simply putting government debt into the accounts would be functionally very similar to the increase in implicit debt associated with improved benefits in a pay-as-you-go system. At times such a contribution is acceptable. Indeed, in Chile, the changeover to the new system was accompanied by the allocation of what were called "recognition bonds" to accounts of people who had contributed to the old system that was being phased out. This situation was clearly different from a response to one of a sequence of requests for more benefits.

One of the elements that intrigues me about this comparison is the similar effect in the design of private pensions. That is, companies setting up new defined-benefit systems customarily give some "past service credit"

for work before the system was established. While I have not done extensive searching, repeated inquiries have not turned up similar giveaways to
older workers when defined-contribution systems were set up. The presence of such a difference in privately provided pensions suggests that
something in the thinking process is at work as well as issues of visibility,
although managers are also concerned about visibility to shareholders. In
particular, defined-contribution systems focus on contributions and so
providing more assets is naturally seen as a giveaway or redistribution.
Defined-benefit systems focus on benefits and so distributions of outcomes, not redistributions of resources. One's reactions to many questions
depend on how they are framed, and this framing difference may have
significant implications for the distribution of incomes. Thus political
economy needs to recognize which types of hidden transfers "fit" with the
institutional structure. While it would be wonderful to be able to derive
this from a deeper level, we may not do badly by simply imposing restrictions on the allowable transfers when examining equilibrium in a political
economy game.

In the United States we have a single, uniform, defined-benefit social
security system. There have been no calls for special formulas for particular industry groups, although there is periodically debate on rules
impacting differently single workers, two-earner couples, and one-earner
couples. More at issue are changes that affect people of different ages. The
continued political efforts on behalf of the "notch" generation is an example that fits with the U.S. structure. Again, the institutional structure
affects the range of political discourse and so outcomes.[9]

Risk and Institution Design

When a major earthquake strikes, many people make contributions to aid
the victims. In the presence of such public attitudes and actions, it is
natural for politicians to vote similar contributions from the public coffers.
One might argue that on democratic grounds, this is what a representative
government should do. One might argue that individuals want representatives who will provide them with insurance if they have similar problems,
although I think that what is really at work is an altruistic response to
need, combined with a desire to be part of the provision of help. This is
similar to the "warm glow" that has been used in explanations of charitable donations (Andreoni 1989).

On self-interest grounds, politicians do not want to run the risk of being labeled hard-hearted in upcoming elections. Politicians recognize that repeated disaster relief can be poor policy, since it induces less risk-avoiding behavior. Moreover, politicians can think that some of these risks should have been privately insured, so the cost falls on the people choosing to bear the risks. But it has been hard for the government to design a process that protects politicians from feeling the need to respond so much to disasters. The prime political response has been to encourage, and sometimes coerce, the purchase of insurance to shift the cost of insurance (with the accompanying incentives). To a casual eye this resembles the examples above, which try to change the definition of the vote from a single issue to a general policy.[10]

Stephen Breyer (1993) has recently reviewed the trade-off between costs and lives saved in a range of government responses to health risks. Breyer feels that public perceptions of risk are inaccurate[11] and that Congress is responsive to these public perceptions, resulting in a set of policies that are not good in aggregate. In particular, the cost of the marginal life saved varies enormously over different risks. Breyer calls for an institutional change to increase the role of administrative expertise in designing public policy responses to risks. He argues that increased power for civil servants will result in a more consistent relative treatment of alternative risks. In effect, Breyer has argued for the need to prevent Congress from doing what the public appears to want.[12]

These observations suggest analyses of the potential for improving institutions, along the lines of what Breyer called for with regard to health risks. The first step in such analysis is to judge whether to have such decisions moved away from politicians and to decision makers less sensitive to public response. In trade policy, the International Trade Commission is such a body, but, from my limited reading, it does not seem to work as well as it might. One way of helping such bodies to work well is to have professional standards for their activities. For example, the Office of the Actuary in the Social Security Administration plays a professional role in keeping the costs of social security before the public. Another example is how the FASB responds to professional considerations when setting accounting rules. Along these lines Destler (1992, 253) has called for "an analytic agency, free of short-run dependence on either the White House or the Congress, whose job would be to measure, as objectively as possible, the real impact of present and prospective cases of trade protection."

And Jagdish (1988, 116) has proposed "bilateral or (preferably) multilateral panels [to] investigate the complaints." In the absence of such panels, it might help to have an association of ITCs that work to harmonize measurement techniques and policies across countries, creating a professional counterweight toward general policies and away from individual cases.

It seems that people have a stronger political claim for help when they are in poor circumstances that are not seen to be their own fault. Thus trade shocks create a natural basis for claiming special treatment. General procedures are needed to block responses to claims of this sort. But the institution organizing the general procedure can become a mechanism for continued hidden transfers once they are started up. One can't help but wonder if some of the popularity of protection isn't related to this view. That is, from this perspective free trade with no mechanism for helping those hurt by trade events may not be a viable political outcome. If this is the case, the question becomes the design of an institution that attempts to identify the "appropriate" candidates for help, that selects from a menu of "allowable" devices for help, and that attempts to limit both the extent and duration of help. This is obviously a tall order, but it may be a way to approach the design of trade liberalization. I have rambled through enough examples suggesting the benefits of more complex modeling of institution design without doing such modeling. So let me turn to my second topic.

9.2   Uncertainty

A discussion of the design of institutions to affect later political decisions has an (at least) implicit model that is not equivalent to one where all decisions are made at once. Future legislation both substitutes for incomplete current commitments (governmental or private) and generates risks about future outcomes. Both aspects of future legislation should be parts of the analysis of institution design. That is, legislation is incomplete in the sense that legislation does not fully distinguish all states of nature; legislation is drawn in the expectation that there will be further legislation.[13] Just as discussion of political institutions needs to reflect the repeated nature of political decision making, so too analysis of the surrounding economy needs to recognize the repeated nature of economic decision making and deal making over time. Such repeated decision making is a reflection of the incompleteness of markets at time zero (or whenever the Garden of Eden was abandoned). This leads me into my second discussion—the methodology of good modeling of an economy with incomplete markets.

As with legislation, consumers and firms know that they will be making additional transactions in the future—the set of markets is incomplete. The question I want to explore is a methodological one; What constraints should we impose on ourselves in modeling incompleteness in order to learn the most from our modeling efforts? This question has been addressed by Avinash Dixit in the context of trade models, so I will start with his stance, and then spell out how and why mine differs. Avinash has raised the importance of considering this question in three articles (1987, 1989a, 1989b) that are summarized in his chapter in the Baldwin volume (1990). Avinash begins by naming five trade analyses that simply assume a given incomplete structure of markets.[14] He then writes:

Almost all previous research in this area has a fundamental flaw. It defends the absence of contingent contracts as a *realistic assumption*. While this may be a *feature of reality* in many situations, it has no business being an *assumption* in an economic model. We must search for the underlying reasons for the absence of such contracts. Failure to do so may sometimes be excusable in a positive model, but it is fatal in policy analysis. This is because the underlying reasons for market failure will also affect the feasibility and the desirability of various policy interventions. Neglecting the fundamentals and making ad hoc descriptive assumptions will yield falsely optimistic results about the potential for policy. This point is well known as the Lucas Critique in the context of macroeconomic policy, but is no less important for tax and tariff policies." (1990, 10–11)

Since I have been and continue to be guilty of just such assumption making,[15] I want to defend the practice. I do not intend to denigrate the use of models that start one level deeper and derive incompleteness. Rather, I want to argue for the advantages of both types of modeling. I will proceed in two steps. First I will discuss the methodology of using incomplete market models for policy analysis. Then I will dispute Avinash's implicit assumption that the special place of the complete market model is such that one must justify within the model any deviations from the assumption of complete markets.

Before discussing whether an assumption of a particular incomplete market structure is a "fundamental flaw," it seems useful to consider the role of theoretical analyses in thinking about policy. If one were to take such models literally,[16] then there would be a fundamental flaw in any model containing an inaccurate assumption that significantly affected the results. Since every model has inaccurate assumptions (Why else do we have models?), every model may be presumed to have fundamental flaws until it is shown by a deeper analysis that the same conclusions will hold without this fundamental flaw. Because of the infinite regress that seems possible here, at some point judgment replaces proof. At some point one must answer intuitively whether the shortcuts that made the model tractable in the first place have made the conclusions inappropriate as a direction for policy improvement.[17] That is, at some point one must engage in a back and forth between formal models and less formal thought. As Marshall has put it:

... it [is] necessary for man with his limited powers to go step by step; breaking up a complex question, studying one bit at a time, and at last combining his partial solutions into a more or less complete solution of the whole riddle.... The more the issue is thus narrowed, the more exactly can it be handled: but also the less closely does it correspond to real life. Each exact and firm handling of a narrow issue, however, helps towards treating broader issues, in which that narrow issue is contained, more exactly than would otherwise have been possible. With each step ... exact discussions can be made less abstract, realistic discussions can be made less inexact than was possible at an earlier stage. (1948, p. 366)

I have argued that sooner or later, one must make a judgment call. Why then should that be after one has constructed a model that derives incomplete markets rather than before? Offhand, I see no reason for a general conclusion on the right stage for such a call. The question is whether the model at hand illuminates the policy issue at hand, in the judgment of the reader. A model with an assumed incomplete market structure might pass this test and might fail this test. A model with a derived incomplete market structure might pass this test and might fail this test. I see nothing inappropriate in testing both kinds of models. And I believe that accepting the judgment that we should not derive policy conclusions in models without the additional complexity of a derived market structure would seriously handicap the development of tractable models.

Appeal to authority is inappropriate in academic debate. But Avinash and I would probably agree to an exception for Bob Solow. As Bob has written (1992, 273): "To put the point differently, I think my general maxims for coping are especially compatible with an opportunistic approach to doing economics. I do not mean 'opportunistic' in the sense of 'amoral,' but as shorthand for 'unwilling to sacrifice a potentially useful insight on the altar of methodological purity.'" Indeed Avinash himself is prepared to jettison his prescription in order to gain insights. In his paper with Rafael Rob (1994), he proceeds with a given set of markets. Of course he is self-conscious about it and writes: "Because we have not modelled the reasons for the missing markets explicitly, any suboptimality of equilibria cannot be *automatically* interpreted as justifications for policy intervention.... We use this simplification to secure a toehold on a difficult problem, and hope that future research in this area will include proper policy analyses" (Dixit and Rob, p. 269; emphasis added).

Indeed, Avinash has it just right here. To my taste, this is an example of the aphorism "do as I do, not as I say." I have underlined automatically to make my point that it is never appropriate to use a model automatically. One must always use judgment in deciding what lessons from the model are useful lessons about policy rather than useful lessons about modeling—another valuable exercise, though a different one.

In the passage quoted at the start, Avinash identified two reasons why the direct assumption of missing markets may be misleading. One is that the policy intervention being analyzed may not be feasible; the second is that it may not be desirable. To argue that a policy can accomplish what it can not accomplish is to misuse models that assume such policies are feasible. This seems to me to be an argument about the use of models, not their construction. What one wants is an accurate picture of what is feasible for the market and what is feasible for the government. Accuracy seems to me to be the key element. Doing explicit modeling might help one to get a better judgment of accuracy. But then again, it might not. In contrast, Avinash has written: "To obtain a fair comparison of markets and policies, any informational restrictions should be explicitly and consistently imposed on both institutions" (1989b, 235). I don't think fairness has anything to do with it. Accuracy is the point. And thinking about feasibility can be done within the model and outside it.

For example, in his discussion of equilibrium with moral hazard, Avinash observes that government can improve on equilibrium when the government has policy tools not available to private insurers. As he notes, this is frequently, but not always the case. He does not derive this difference in available tools in a model which is also used to calculate the effects of such policies. He is right in arguing that we should be realistic about the policies available, which are not likely to include detailed observation of individual behavior that is not observable (at a comparable cost) by private industry. And the models he presents are good ways to help people understand this point. In addition they add understanding to the advantage the government does have from the use of anonymous policies, such as the taxation of transactions, a tool that is not available to private industry.

Market Incompleteness

Avinash considers three reasons for market incompleteness: lack of public observability of the contingency to be insured, lack of public observability of actions (moral hazard), private information about innate characteristics (adverse selection). He dismisses administrative costs as an independent source of market failure, asserting that they are really costs of observation and enforcement. For starters, I want to disagree with this claim. In their pioneering analyses of the causes of market incompleteness, Duncan Foley (1970) and Frank Hahn (1971) cite the cost of setting up contracts and markets as a reason for not insuring low probability events, since the cost is paid with certainty, but a transfer is called for only with low probability. Discounting gives a similar result for trades sufficiently far in the future. Of course this argument depends on a limited ability to bundle contract terms, since it is the additional cost of differentiated coverage, not the full cost of a contract, that is at issue.[18]

Another problem with the market solution when there is a significant time lapse comes from the issue of fulfillment of obligations. You do not want to pay for insurance that will not pay benefits. For a future risk, how confident can you be that the insurer will still be there when the time comes? And in an area like health insurance, how confident can you be that the insurer will behave in a way you will like when evaluating claims that cannot be simply related to the rules of coverage. Thus risks calling for long lead times in the design of insurance are hard for the market to deal with well. We see that currently in the issue of insurance for long-term care needs.

Avinash's list occurs within a context of fully rational optimizing agents. Yet deviation from this assumption seems to me both pervasive and central. In general terms, it is not easy for individuals to optimize utility. In a setting of frequent evaluations with feedback, people learn to take good advantage of the opportunities available. However, when there is not such a learning experience, experimental economics finds that people have trouble figuring out optimal strategies. The insurance setting is one where the insurance of infrequently occurring events does not offer the type of feedback that will educate people at a reasonable cost.[19] Moreover insurance is directed at random events. Cognitive psychology has documented the pervasive extent to which people do not comprehend stochastic events. That is, many individuals make sizable and systematic errors when asked to answer questions about stochastic outcomes. Even sophisticated, trained individuals make mistakes once the stochastic environment is subtle and reliance is made on intuition rather than explicit calculation.

More basically, I think that complete markets are an impossibility. I go beyond the view that it would be prohibitively expensive to try to construct a list of all states of nature to the view that it is impossible for humans to list all states of nature. If complete markets are impossible, then one needs to think about how one models incomplete markets, and one needs to think about the applicability of results from models with particular incomplete market structures, but one does not need an underlying reason for incompleteness. Rather, one needs to be careful with the conclusions from complete market analyses.

Recapping, with three different reasons why markets might be incomplete, all of which hold in reality, is it noticeably more legitimate to do policy analyses in models omitting two out of three reasons and deriving the resulting market structure, rather than omitting three out of three and assuming a structure that might reflect all three reasons? This point becomes stronger as the list of reasons grows.

The Lucas Critique

I switch now from Avinash's feasibility point to his desirability point. Avinash invokes the Lucas critique. The Lucas critique refers to the interpretation of empirical estimates of private responses to government actions when the empirical methods used are argued to make measurements that do not reflect how behavior varies with the government policy. Let me contrast my interpretation of the Lucas critique with what I take to be Avinash's interpretation. The Lucas critique says that if there is a behavioral response that varies with policy regime, then one will make a mistake in considering a change in policy using a description of behavior that does not vary with policy regime. In particular, this may happen when behavior depends on predictions of future opportunities, predictions that vary systematically across policy regimes, and the model does not explicitly consider the role of policy in affecting predictions.

In the setting of missing markets, the parallel question is whether the assumed structure of available markets would be altered by a government policy designed to offset the inefficiencies caused by market incompleteness. In many settings it seems to me plausible that the pattern of incompleteness will be robust to a range of interventions. Again one needs to think about whether to use the results of a specific model.

And there is a further parallel argument. Clearly articulated by Joe Farrell (1987) is the argument that nonmarket institutions respond, in part, to the incompleteness of markets.[20] So we also need to worry about the extent to which nonmarket institutions will respond to changes in policy, and whether such changes will undercut the findings of the model. Moreover, in such a setting, the nonmarket institutions may not only undo government actions but convert actions that are good in a particular nonmarket setting into ones that are bad in a different nonmarket setting. This point has been made by Buchanan and Stubblebine (1962), who point out that Pigouvian taxes correcting externalities if there are no negotiations to directly correct the externalities can create inefficiency when the externalities have been internalized through bargaining and the tax structure involves transfers between the set of negotiating parties and others with whom there are no negotiations.

Let me rephrase the issue. Assume that the government provides insurance that has not been provided by the market, or that is only approximately available in complex ways that individuals do not make use of. How wrong is the analysis if it simply assumes a competitive structure with missing markets rather than deriving it. The analysis can be very wrong if the government institution does not provide appropriate insurance, merely duplicating approximate insurance already used. The analysis can be misleading if it matters more that some people were making some form of insurance arrangement than that other people were not. And the model can be misleading if the adaptation of market structure to the presence of government insurance worsens some other problem.

Let me take an example. Exchange rates fluctuate a great deal. This greatly affects importers and exporters, workers in these industries, creditors of these firms, and, to a lesser extent, consumers. Some such firms engage in exchange market hedging activities. A few consumer/workers have part of their wealth invested in assets denominated in foreign currencies, while others hold shares in firms that are themselves partially invested in assets and opportunities dependent on other currencies. While I have no evidence to cite, I would bet that the vast majority of workers subject to both export- and import-generated unemployment do nothing explicitly (beyond a possibly higher level of savings than otherwise) to protect themselves from the unemployment risks associated with changes in exchange rates. Yes, there are both moral hazard and adverse selection complications in trying to insure people against unemployment generally that carry over to trying to insure workers against exchange rate generated risks of unemployment. Thus it seems to me that if one considers government action to smooth exchange rate fluctuations or to temporarily protect import industries, one is probably not going to go far wrong relative to the gain to the workers from simply assuming missing markets. Yet there is a problem that some firms do engage in hedging transactions that affect the risks borne by their workers and the amount of hedging is indeed endogenous to the amount of smoothing that goes on. A central question is the extent to which one can use the simpler models that do not have the additional paraphernalia to derive missing markets without necessarily misleading oneself. (One can always manage to mislead oneself by inappropriate use of any model.)

The Arrow-Debreu Straitjacket

In addition to these specific comments on Avinash's analysis, I want to comment on the general methodological frame that puts the Arrow-Debreu model in a position that I consider inappropriate. Avinash's opening statement is that one must have a reason for incompleteness of markets before one can analyze behavior in a setting of incomplete markets. That suggests that it is acceptable to analyze issues in a context of complete markets even though that is clearly counterfactual. We know people aren't aware of all their economic opportunities over the rest of their lives at its start. We know that people do not make all of their economic decisions at a single time. We know that no one ensures that all markets clear at all times. Thus it seems to me that there is a burden of proof is on people who use a complete market model—a burden to argue that the findings are robust to the incompleteness that we observe. This is part of what seems to me to be the appropriate methodology, the need to argue an empirical belief, hunch, conjecture, that the conclusions from the behavioral structure one employs is robust for the policy variations one is considering.

This empirical belief will rest on a depth of modeling that one needs to have a structure that one thinks is robust to the policy change being considered. The Arrow-Debreu model looms large in the intellectual life of economists in part because it is the device we use, collectively, to organize our research and communication. That is, describing a model and its results in terms of deviations from the Arrow-Debreu model has real advantages. But that does not imply that it is appropriate to press all studies into this mold. Convenience is not a good source of methodological necessity. I agree that understanding the sources of such deviations can well be instructive. But straitjacketing all models into the additional complexity that comes from requiring the inclusion of such factors seems to me to be a large (distorting) tax on doing simple theory.

9.3   Political Economy

Just because a model passes an intuitive test for getting the economics right for a policy question being analyzed doesn't imply that it is a good basis for a policy recommendation. There is a second test for any recommendation, that the political economy of the recommendation makes it likely that the policy will work roughly as advertised. It is good to understand the economics of good policy, even good policy that cannot be implemented. In part, politics can change; in part, understanding good economics is a step in the design of good workable policy. But one should not move from good economics of policy to a policy recommendation without the second step of whether there is workable politics of the recommended good economics.

The politics of policy seems to me to have two important steps. One is whether it is likely that the policy will be implemented close enough to the recommendation to be an improvement. Second is the Lucas emphasis on analyzing policies, not single actions. These two points seem particularly important in the realm of policy to deal with uncertainty. A good response to a temporarily poor outcome often needs to be a temporary policy. But policy in place is hard to remove. This asymmetry seems to me central for political economy.[21] Thus one does not want to end up with long-term protection from a temporary need for help. Also one needs to recognize that there will be repeated occurrences of similar events. Just as it is hard to remove protective policies for individual industries, so it is hard to stop giving disaster relief.

Both circumstances seem to me to call for further analysis of how ideas and institutions shape policy. That is, it may or may not be the case that arguing for free trade in all circumstances gives better political outcomes than arguing for an institution whose job it is to distinguish legitimate cases for temporary support from illegitimate cases and which tries to keep support temporary. Maybe we can design such institutions, and maybe not. But since always favoring free trade does not result in always having free trade, this is an important issue.

Turning to social security again for an example, the 1977 Act adopted a wage index for earnings records, while continuing a price index for benefit increases after retirement. I supported the alternative approach of using price indexing for both purposes. With real wage growth and a progressive benefit formula, price indexing results in a smaller average level of benefits than wage indexing under the assumption of no further legislation. My support for price indexing was based, in part, on the belief that further legislation would raise benefits under price indexing to the level under wage indexing if that level were viable, combined with the belief that the allocation of these additional benefits would improve the distribution of benefits. A second basis for my support was recognition of the problems that might arise if wage indexing were not viable without further legislation, while price indexing was. The current proposals for major reform in social security (such as the means testing of benefits proposed by the Concord Coalition) might not be on the political table if it were not for the need for significant changes in Social Security finances. That is, even someone interested in maximizing the size of social security would not necessarily favor legislation that maximizes the size of social security under the assumption that there would be no further legislation. There is always the possibility of further legislation.

9.4   Conclusions

Recognizing that economist's recommendations and political outcomes have only a loose (and stochastic) relationship is, of course, a central premise of the political economy literature. Once one recognizes this link, not only does economic analysis have to reflect political concerns but also normative analysis of political processes must also recognize this issue. That is, there must be some political decision-making institution. Any institution will have its pluses and minuses. Inevitably we are confined (condemned?) to the complexities of second best analysis. In "Lobbying and Welfare," Jagdish (1980) has made the point that second-best considerations in the economy can reverse the normative conclusions about the costs of lobbying. In his 1982 paper, Jagdish observed that second-best considerations in the political process can well reverse the conclusion that an institutional structure that is open to lobbying is necessarily a bad thing.

As a simple (and unrealistic) example, assume that politicians are target contribution collectors. Assume that they know what level of campaign contributions will guarantee reelection and they seek that level by responding to lobbying efforts, preserving their remaining freedom of action to pursue the public welfare. These preferences are a version of those employed by Grossman and Helpman, without the linearity they assumed between contributions and welfare. Assume also a representative politician, thought of as the entrenched incumbent. Then politicians will accept contributions where the distortions to the economy from acceding are the smallest, they will be individual Ramsey-style optimizers in some bargaining game. But they can only optimize over the policy tools that are up for grabs, not the ones that are locked up by the constitution or by political processes and institutions. Increasing the set of taxes for a Ramsey optimizer decreases the deadweight burden associated with collecting a given level of revenue. Therefore locking up a lobbying opportunity in a new institution will only worsen the economic outcome from the lobbying process. In considering institutions, one must therefore consider general political equilibrium. This point should be considered an extension of the analysis by Jagdish and T. N. Srinivasan (1980) that there will be revenue seeking whether one protects by tariffs or protects by quotas, a point that needs to be kept in mind when comparing institutional approaches.

While my example is farfetched, the basic perspective is not. Democracy is neither a simple nor an inexpensive decision-making process. This should not lead us to implicitly take an idealized nondemocratic alternative to be the comparison point. As Jagdish has written (1982, 990): " . . . lobbying to install a distortionary tariff is undoubtedly directly unproductive from an economic viewpoint, though it may possess a political legitimacy and value as constituting an element of a vigorous, pluralistic democracy!"

Notes

I am grateful to Avinash Dixit, Gene Grossman, Jon Gruber, Jim Poterba, and Bernie Saffran for helpful comments and the National Science Foundation for research support under grant SBR-9307876.

1. I do not try to address the issue of how, if at all, special and general interests can be defined in a useful way. Nor do I explore the tension between the interests of a representative's constituents and the interests of a larger population.

2. It is well known that in many voting settings, agenda design affects voting outcomes. Thus agenda choice is itself in need of explanation.

3. In the area of tax policy, there are many examples. One notorious one is section 1240 of the 1954 Internal Revenue Code, commonly referred to as the "Louis B. Mayer amendment," and believed to apply to only two persons. This amendment provided for capital gains rather than ordinary income treatment for "amounts received from the assignment or release by an employee of over twenty-years employment of his rights to receive, after termination of his employment and for a period of not less than five years, a percentage of future profits or receipts of his employer ... if the employee's contract providing for those rights had been in effect at least twelve years." (Surrey 1957, 1147 n.4). This summer, it was natural to question the inclusion of $10 million for Lamar University in the crime bill, a clause that was eliminated before passage after considerable public exposure. Without examining the role of such giveaways in the overall workings of Congress, one does not have an automatic conclusion about their harm.

4. That exporters like free trade does not seem a comparable source of benefits for politicians or bureaucrats as the desire for protection.

5. A similar view has been expressed by Baldwin (1985, 174): "... one broad conclusion that does seem warranted on the basis of the analyses undertaken is that the models focusing exclusively on short-run, direct self-interest are insufficient for explaining the wide range of behavior patterns observable in the trade policy area."

6. I do not explore a framework for identifying these different cases. Some of the examples seem to fit a description that better policies come when the political forces associated with benefits and costs are brought more closely into balance. This might call for more or less visibility.

7. "Neither the act of voting nor the direction of a vote cast can be explained as a means to achieving a particular political outcome, any more than spectators attend a game as a means of securing the victory of their team." (See Brennan and Buchanan 1984, 187.)

8. One theme of delegation to a commission or the administration is the move to a more "anonymous" or "symmetric" system. An auction is not only formally open to everyone but designed to be genuinely open as part of its intent and logic. Similarly the job of the base-closing commission was to use anonymous criteria to decide which bases were to be closed. Anonymity rules in government decision making are designed to be more "fair" and may sometimes turn out to be more efficient.

9. It is also interesting to note the automatic indexing of social security benefits that removed Congress from the process of periodically increasing benefits for retirees and future retirees.

10. In models with voters and politicians, it is easy to slide into a principal-agent vocabulary to consider the relationship between voters and representatives, for example, to refer to deviations of representative behavior from median voter preferences as "shirking." This discussion suggests that this vocabulary may not be helpful. There is another tradition in the discussion of politics that gives more scope for the political process as a process of reasoning and debate. In contrast with the first literature, which takes voter preferences as given and may have a role for information gathering but not education and reconsideration of

attitudes, the second approach sees debate as part of the shaping of how voters will vote. Similarly it sees voters as delegating to representatives the time-consuming activity of debate, with delegation of the job of finding out what would be good policy, across several dimensions of definitions of good, including narrow self-interest and ethical considerations. In this approach voters may want protection from their initial instincts by having representatives, and those representatives may in turn need protection from the voters who haven't adjusted their initial instincts.

11. Cognitive psychology finds that stochastic outcomes are not intuitive; frequently people do not think consistently about them.

12. Viewing institution design as a problem of combining good judgment and public responsiveness has a starting place near the observation of Schattschneider (1960, 137): "Democracy is like nearly everything else we do; it is a form of collaboration of ignorant people and experts."

13. I have explored this issue in the social insurance context in Diamond (1994) and will not repeat that analysis here.

14. Batra and Russell (1974), Turnovsky (1974), Helpman and Razin (1978), Newbery and Stiglitz (1984), and Eaton and Grossman (1985).

15. Diamond (1967, 1980) and Diamond and Mirrlees (1992).

16. Sometimes the expression "taking a model seriously" is used to mean "taking a model literally." I think that taking a model seriously means trying to use its insights when thinking about the world, a process that is inconsistent with taking a model literally.

17. The size of the role of intuition in the use of economic models reflects limitations on what formal empirical work can learn. In the absence of controlled experiments, data analysis can often estimate parameters reasonably, conditional on the structure of the model, while being unable to distinguish interestingly between sufficiently rich models.

18. Not particularly relevant for trade issues is the limit on market spreading of risk from the inability to transact with the unborn.

19. For example, consider the possibility that someone selecting limited health insurance coverage might not be accurate in projecting utility should he be very sick and needing a treatment not covered by the chosen policy.

20. There are several ways one can use the terms "market" and "nonmarket." One way is that market refers to all quid-pro-quo transactions, whether they happen in organized markets, in regular transactions settings, like stores, or whether they happen after pairwise search for individual transactors. Then nonmarket impacts on resource allocation refer to actions without a clear quid pro quo. These latter would include gifts, to personal contacts, to individual strangers, or through charitable intermediaries. An example of the study of the impact of policy on gifts is Schoeni (1994) who considers the effect of AFDC on family assistance. Similarly the effect of social security on support given to parents was debated earlier. Nonmarket impacts would also include norms that affect how people make use of production and trading opportunities. An alternative use of the words "market" and "nonmarket" refers to transactions mediated through a mechanism that is adequately modeled by demand and supply behaviors with a known array of alternatives, as opposed to transactions requiring substantial organizational effort to arrange, whether search or negotiation of a detailed contract.

21. In the social security setting, the political process has exploited the asymmetry between legislating and repealing, along with the lower level of resistance to future tax increases rather than present ones. For example, the 1977 Act set future payroll tax rates increases by having rates (on employers and employees, each) of 6.05 in 1978, 6.13 in 1979, 6.66 in 1981, 6.7 in 1982, 7.05 in 1985, 7.15 in 1986, and 7.65 in 1990. The 1983 Act increased the 1984 tax to 7.0, and the 1988 tax to 7.51. Proposals to roll back such future increases have been frequently made but never enacted.

References

Andreoni, James. 1989. Giving with impure altruism: Applications to charity and Ricardian equivalence. *Journal of Political Economy* 97:1447–58.

Baldwin, Robert E. 1985. *The Political Economy of U.S. Import Policy*. Cambridge: MIT Press.

Batra, Raveendra N., and William R. Russell. 1974. Gains from trade under uncertainty. *American Economic Review* 64:1040–48.

Bhagwati, Jagdish N. 1980. Lobbying and welfare. *Journal of Public Economics* 14:355–64.

Bhagwati, Jagdish. 1988. *Protectionism*. Cambridge: MIT Press.

Bhagwati, Jagdish N. 1982. Directly unproductive, profit-seeking (DUP) activities. *Journal of Political Economy* 90:988–1002.

Bhagwati, Jagdish. 1991. *The World Trading System at Risk*. Princeton: Princeton University Press.

Bhagwati, Jagdish N., and T. N. Srinivasan. 1980. Revenue seeking: A generalization of the theory of tariffs. *Journal of Political Economy* 88(6):1069–87.

Brennan, Geoffrey, and James Buchanan. 1984. Voter choice: Evaluating political alternatives. *American Behavorial Scientist* 28:185–201.

Breyer, Stephen. 1993. *Breaking the Vicious Circle: Toward Effective Risk Regulation*. Cambridge: Harvard University Press.

Buchanan, James, and William Craig Stubblebine. 1962. Externality. *Economica* NS 29:371–84.

Destler, I. M. 1992. *American Trade Politics*. 2d ed. Washington: Institute for International Economics.

Diamond, Peter. 1967. The Role of a Stock Market in a General Equilibrium Model with Technological Uncertainty. *American Economic Review* 57:759–76.

Diamond, Peter. 1980. Efficiency with uncertain supply. *Review of Economic Studies* 47: 645–51.

Diamond, Peter. 1994. Insulation of pensions from political risk. Paper presented at the conference Mandatory Pensions: Funding, Privatization and Macroeconomic Policy, Santiago, Chile, January 26–27.

Diamond, Peter, and James A. Mirrlees. 1992. Optimal taxation of identical consumers when markets are incomplete. In P. Dasgupta, D. Gale, O. Hart, and E. Maskin, eds., *Essays in Honor of Frank Hahn*. Cambridge: MIT Press.

Dixit, Avinash. 1987. Trade and insurance with moral hazard. *Journal of International Economics* 23:201–20.

Dixit, Avinash. 1989a. Trade and insurance with imperfectly observed outcomes. *Quarterly Journal of Economics* 104:195–203.

Dixit, Avinash. 1989b. Trade and insurance with adverse selection. *Review of Economic Studies* 56:235–47.

Dixit, Avinash. 1990. Trade policy with imperfect information. In R. W. Jones and A. O. Krueger, eds., *The Political Economy of International Trade, Essays in Honor of Robert E. Baldwin*. Oxford: Basil Blackwell.

Dixit, Avinash, and Rafael Rob. 1994. Risk-sharing, adjustment and trade. *Journal of International Economics* 36:263–87.

Eaton, Jonathan, and Gene Grossman. 1985. Tariffs as insurance: Optimal commercial policy when domestic markets are incomplete. *Canadian Journal of Economics* 18:258–72.

Farrell, Joseph. 1987. Information and the Coase theorem. *Journal of Economic Perspectives* 1:113–29.

Foley, Duncan K. 1970. Economic equilibrium with costly marketing. *Journal of Economic Theory* 2:276–91.

Grossman, Gene M., and Elhanan Helpman. 1994. Protection for sale. *American Economic Review* 84:833–50.

Hahn, Frank H. 1971. Equilibrium with transaction costs. *Econometrics* 39:417–40.

Helpman, Elhanan, and Assaf Razin. 1978. *A Theory of International Trade under Uncertainty*. New York: Academic Press.

Marshall, A. 1948. *Principles of Economics*. 8th ed. New York: Macmillan.

Newbery, David, and Joseph Stiglitz. 1984. Pareto inferior trade. *Review of Economic Studies* 51:1–12.

Schattschneider, E. E. 1935. *Politics, Pressures and the Tariff*. Englewood Cliffs, NJ: Prentice-Hall.

Schattschneider, E. E. 1960. *The Semi-sovereign People*. New York: Holt, Rinehart and Winston.

Schoeni, Robert F. 1994. Does aid to families with dependent children displace familial assistance? Unpublished Manuscript. RAND.

Solow, Robert M. 1992. Notes on coping. In M. Szenberg, ed., *Eminent Economists, Their Life Philosophies*. Cambridge: Cambridge University Press.

Surrey, Stanley. 1957. The Congress and the tax lobbyist—How special tax provisions get enacted. *Harvard Law Review* 70:1145–82.

Turnovsky, Stephen J. 1974. Technological and price uncertainty in a Ricardian model of international trade. *Review of Economic Studies* 41:201–17.

IV MODELS OF POLITICAL ECONOMY AND TRADE

10 Foreign Investment with Endogenous Protection

Gene M. Grossman and Elhanan Helpman

10.1 Introduction

Jagdish Bhagwati coined the phrase "quid pro quo foreign investment" to describe investments undertaken in anticipation of trade policy and perhaps with the intention of defusing a protectionist threat. In a series of papers beginning with Bhagwati (1987), he and several colleagues and former students explored the role that such direct foreign investment (DFI) might play in shaping tariffs, quotas, voluntary export restraints, and more.[1] These authors typically assumed that the probability of future protection depends on both the extent of import penetration and the stock of DFI, and they viewed DFI as a transfer of capital from one country to another. In this context, firms move their capital and restrict their exports so as to maximize the expected present value of their profits, taking into account the effects of their investment decisions on subsequent policy formation. The foreign government usually was assumed to coordinate investment decisions, although occasionally it has been supposed that foreign oligopolists independently exploit the intertemporal ramifications of their actions (e.g., Dinopoulos 1989). This literature—motivated in large part by the behavior of Japanese firms in the early and mid 1980s—has produced many interesting insights and has enriched our understanding of the link between foreign investment and the formation of trade policies.

Our aim in this paper is to extend Bhagwati's concept of anticipatory investment to situations where (1) DFI is best seen as the opening of a subsidiary by a multinational corporation and (2) trade policy represents an optimal response by politicians to the pressures applied by special interest groups. We follow Markusen (1984) and Helpman (1984) in modeling multinational investment as the *costly* establishment of a branch plant by a firm that has the exclusive right or the exclusive ability to manufacture a particular product. The foreign owners of such an intangible asset face a choice between bearing the cost of opening a new subsidiary and producing in an existing parent facility. In making this choice, they recognize that their attempts to export may be impeded by subsequent home-country trade barriers. We combine this view of DFI with the approach to policy formation that we developed in Grossman and

Helpman (1994a). We suppose that an incumbent government receives offers of campaign contributions that are (at least implicitly) tied to its ultimate policy actions. In setting policy, the government trades off the extra contributions that may be associated with protectionist interventions and the loss of voter goodwill that may be a consequence thereof. At first we assume that there is only one organized interest group attempting to influence policy, namely a lobby representing domestic firms in the industry with DFI. Later we allow for contributions by a lobby that represents domestic workers with skills specific to the industry.

Prospective multinationals anticipate the mechanism by which policy will be set when they make their foreign investment decisions. We treat DFI as a decentralized process wherein each foreign company takes the investment decisions of the others as beyond its control. Given the extent of DFI by other companies, each firm forms an expectation about the host country's eventual trade policy and evaluates the profitability of its own potential foreign investment accordingly. A firm establishes a subsidiary if by doing so it can earn greater profits net of investment costs than it can by exporting from its parent facility. It recognizes that the cost of opening a foreign subsidiary cannot be recovered once the investment has been made. Finally, an equilibrium entails a level of DFI and a rate of protection such that the political process supports the particular rate of protection as an outcome in the stage game, and the expectations about protection that foreign firms hold when they make their investment decisions are fulfilled.[2]

We develop the basic model in section 10.2. This is followed in section 10.3 by an analysis of the determinants of equilibrium tariffs and levels of DFI. We show that, if the cost of opening a subsidiary is small and politicians happen to place great weight on the welfare of the average voter, then two stable equilibria may coexist. In one of these equilibria no multinational investments are made, while in the other all foreign firms establish offshore production facilities. For all other parameter configurations there exists a unique stable equilibrium. In this equilibrium typically some foreign firms choose to build plants in the home country. In the event, an increase in the fixed cost of foreign investment reduces the number of multinationals while a decrease in the home government's concern for the plight of the average voter expands the multinational presence. We find also that when the politicians' concern for the average voter is great and the cost of DFI is low, an increase in the weight attached to average welfare results in a higher rate of protection.

In section 10.4 we examine whether direct foreign investment serves the interests of the average voter in the home country. This issue is particularly interesting when manufacturing costs in the home country happen to be higher than those abroad. Then the entry of foreign multinationals diverts production from the lower-cost location to the higher-cost location, and this would reduce home welfare if trade policy were fixed. But here the presence of multinationals also changes the political environment, so that special interests find it more difficult to lobby for protection. When the political response is factored in, DFI may in fact benefit the average voter.

In section 10.5 we extend the model to account for the interests of workers with skills specific to the sector with DFI. We show that the interests of these workers are closely aligned with the interests of the domestic manufacturers on the issue of trade protection. Given the level of DFI, both wage earners and profit recipients gain from an increase in the tariff. However, on the issue of policy toward foreign multinationals, the two interest groups are bound to conflict. Domestic manufacturers stand to gain from restrictions on DFI, whereas the workers with specific human capital are harmed by such impediments. If elected officials can regulate entry by multinationals, the extent of DFI in equilibrium depends on the relative political strengths of the two competing interest groups. We examine the determinants of "political strength" in this context.

10.2 Basic Model

The home country produces a numeraire good with unskilled labor alone. One unit of labor is required per unit of output. Thus the equilibrium wage equals 1. The home country also manufactures various brands of a differentiated product. Each brand requires a fixed amount of unskilled labor per unit of output. For the time being, we assume that no other inputs are needed. The number and types of the domestic products are treated as given throughout.

The domestic manufacturers of differentiated products compete with a fixed set of foreign brands. Each foreign supplier faces a choice. It can assemble its product in an already-existing plant in its native country or it can build (or purchase) a new, production facility in the home country. The choice between exporting and foreign investment is made based on a comparison of expected profits, where profits from a potential subsidiary are calculated net of the fixed costs of acquiring the facility. These costs, which must be borne before the home country finally sets its trade policy, cannot be recouped in the event that the plant is not used. Thus each foreign company must form some expectations about the likely outcome of the home country's political process.[3] We focus on equilibria with self-fulfilling expectations.

After the foreign investment takes place, the home government sets a tariff on imported varieties of the differentiated product. The height of the tariff reflects the conflicting political pressures it faces. On the one hand, the government is concerned with the welfare of the average voter, because its prospects for reelection depend on the standard of living it provides. On the other hand, it values the campaign contributions that it collects from special interest groups. We assume that the domestic lobbies—which, to begin with, comprise only a single group representing the domestic manufacturers of brands of the differentiated product—offer donations that are contingent on the tariff imposed by the government. Presumably a higher tariff will elicit a larger contribution from the domestic industry, although the interest group is free to design its contribution schedule in any way it chooses. Faced with the contribution schedule, the government sets the policy that maximizes its own political objective function. We take the latter to be a simple weighted sum of total campaign gifts and average welfare.[4] All of this is well understood by the foreign companies at the time that they make their entry decisions.

We now describe the domestic economy in more detail.

Consumption and Production

The home country is populated by a continuum of individuals with measure 1. The utility function of each individual is given by

$$U = x_0 + \frac{\theta}{\theta - 1} x^{(\theta-1)/\theta}, \qquad \theta > 1, \tag{10.1}$$

where x_0 represents consumption of the numeraire good and x is an index of consumption of the differentiated products. The consumption index takes the form

$$x = \left[\int_{j \in N_h} x(j)^{(\varepsilon-1)/\varepsilon} \, dj + \int_{j \in N_f} x(j)^{(\varepsilon-1)/\varepsilon} \, dj \right]^{\varepsilon/(\varepsilon-1)}, \qquad \varepsilon > 1,$$

where $x(j)$ denotes consumption of brand j, and N_h and N_f are the sets of brands manufactured by home and foreign firms, respectively (the latter either in a native plant or in a subsidiary located in the home country).

As is well known, this structure of preferences yields constant-elasticity demand functions for each brand, with ε being the elasticity of demand. In fact, given the two-tier structure of preferences, the demand for any brand j can be represented by

$$x(j) = p(j)^{-\varepsilon} q^{\varepsilon-\theta},$$

where $p(j)$ is the price of brand j and q is a price index for all differentiated products. We assume that $\varepsilon > \theta$, which implies that the different brands substitute more closely for one another than they do for the numéraire good. This assumption ensures a positive cross-elasticity of demand.[5]

Each manufacturer of a brand of the differentiated product maximizes profits by equating marginal revenue to marginal cost. In doing so, the firm treats the price index q as beyond its control. A foreign firm manufacturing in its native facility faces the constant marginal cost c_f. In the home country, c_h units of labor are needed to produce a unit of any brand of the differentiated product. This means that the marginal cost for home firms and foreign subsidiaries is also c_h, since the wage rate equals 1. The mark-up pricing rule then implies

$$p(j) = \begin{cases} p_h \equiv \dfrac{\varepsilon}{\varepsilon - 1} c_h & \text{for } j \text{ manufactured in the home country,} \\[2em] p_f \equiv \dfrac{\varepsilon}{\varepsilon - 1} c_f \tau & \text{for } j \text{ manufactured in the foreign country,} \end{cases}$$

(10.2)

where p_i, $i = h, f$, denotes the consumer price of a variety manufactured in country i and τ represents one plus the *ad ualorem* tariff rate. We denote by n_h the number of brands owned by home-country firms (the measure of the set N_h) and by n_f the number of brands owned by foreign firms (the measure of the set N_f). In addition we let m denote the number of brands controlled by foreign firms that have established production facilities in the home country. Then the price index for x can be written as

$$q = [(n_h + m)p_h^{1-\varepsilon} + (n_f - m)p_f^{1-\varepsilon}]^{1/(1-\varepsilon)}, \tag{10.3}$$

assuming that all foreign firms with subsidiaries in the home country actually use these facilities to produce their output.[6] Finally we calculate output levels and operating profits (i.e., revenue minus manufacturing costs) for firms producing in each location, which gives

$$x_i = p_i^{-\varepsilon}q^{\varepsilon-\theta} \quad \text{for } i = h, f, \tag{10.4}$$

$$\pi_i = \frac{1}{\varepsilon\tau_i}p_i^{1-\varepsilon}q^{\varepsilon-\theta} \quad \text{for } i = h, f. \tag{10.5}$$

Here π_i represents the operating profits derived from a single brand, and we use the notational convention that $\tau_h = 1$ and $\tau_f = \tau$.

For the time being we assume that the tariff is the only policy instrument available to the government. The government redistributes any tariff proceeds to the voters on an equal, per capita basis. We can now use (10.1) to express the average (gross) welfare of a citizen in the home country as a function of the tariff rate and the number of products supplied by subsidiaries of multinational corporations. We have

$$W(\tau;m) = L + n_h\pi_h + \frac{\tau - 1}{\tau}(n_f - m)p_f x_f + \frac{1}{\theta - 1}q^{-(\theta-1)}, \tag{10.6}$$

where L is average labor income in view of an assumed inelastic supply and the fact that the wage rate is equal to 1. The remaining terms on the right-hand side represent average profit income, the average tariff rebate, and the average surplus derived from the consumption of differentiated products, respectively. The complete functional dependence of W on τ and m is obtained by substituting equations (10.2)–(10.5) into (10.6).

The Special Interest Group and the Government

The government chooses the rate of protection τ to maximize its political objective function, which we take to be a linear combination of political contributions and the average welfare of voters. In selecting a trade policy, the government faces a contribution schedule $C(\tau) \geq 0$ that has been proposed by the domestic lobby group. We write the governments' objective function as

$$G = C(\tau) + aW(\tau;m), \tag{10.7}$$

where $a > 0$ is the weight that the government attaches to (gross) voter welfare relative to political contributions.

The lobby represents all of the home-country manufacturers of differentiated products. Somehow they overcome Mancur Olson's "collective-action" problem (see Olson 1965) and coordinate their efforts to influence policy. Multinational corporations with subsidiaries in the home country do not participate in lobbying for protection. We assume for simplicity that the set of voters who own shares in companies that produce brands of the differentiated product is of measure zero. In the event, owners of home firms instruct their lobby to design a contribution schedule that maximizes their joint profits net of campaign contributions. In short, we take the lobby's objective to be the maximization of $n_h \pi_h - C$.[7]

The lobby's leaders know that once a contribution schedule has been proposed to the politicians, the latter will set policy to maximize (10.7). Moreover they know that they cannot drive the politicians' welfare below the level that the latter could attain by declining all contribution offers. The government's reservation welfare level is given by $aW^*(m)$, where

$$W^*(m) = \max_\tau W(\tau; m).$$ (10.8)

The curve G^*G^* in figure 10.1 depicts the combinations of contributions and tariff levels that yield the government a value of G equal to $aW^*(m)$. Curves above G^*G^* represent government indifference curves with higher welfare levels. If the lobby designs a contribution schedule that is located everywhere below G^*G^*, the government will choose τ^*, which secures its reservation welfare. In view of this, the best the lobby can do is to induce the government to choose point A, where the lobby's own indifference curve L^*L^* is tangent to the government's indifference curve. Clearly there are many contribution schedules that will generate this outcome; one example is a contribution schedule that coincides with the horizontal axis to the left of the lowermost point of L^*L^* and coincides with L^*L^* to the right of that point.

Our argument suggests that the lobby implicitly solves the problem

$$\max_{\tau, C} n_h \pi_h - C$$

$$s.t. \ C + aW(\tau; m) \geq aW^*(m) \quad \text{and} \quad C \geq 0.$$

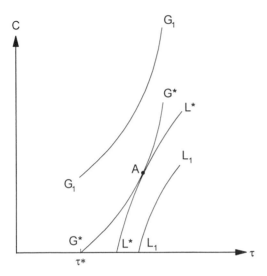

Figure 10.1
Equilibrium lobbying

Thus the political equilibrium is characterized by a tariff that maxi-mizes the joint welfare of the lobby and the government (i.e., $\tau^P = \arg\max_\tau [n_h \pi_h + aW\{\tau; m\}]$) and a level of contributions that satisfies the participation constraint with equality (i.e., $C^P = a[W^*\{m\} - W\{\tau^P; m\}]$). Using (10.6), we can express the equilibrium tariff as

$$\tau^P = \arg\max\left[(1 + a)n_h\pi_h + a\frac{\tau - 1}{\tau}(n_f - m)p_f x_f + a\frac{1}{\theta - 1}q^{-(\theta-1)}\right].$$
(10.9)

When written in this way, we see that the political tariff maximizes a weighted sum of profits, tariff revenue, and consumer surplus. Whereas these components would receive equal weight from a benevolent social planner, the political process gives greater weight to the profits, which accrue to an organized interest group, and relatively less to the tariff revenue and consumer surplus, which go to the general public. Next we can use the first-order condition for (10.9) together with (10.2)–(10.5), to derive an implicit formula for the equilibrium tariff, namely

$$\frac{\tau^P - 1}{\tau^P} = \frac{1 + a}{a\varepsilon}\frac{(\varepsilon - \theta)n_h}{\varepsilon(n_h + m) + \theta(n_f - m)(\tau^P c_f/c_h)^{1-\varepsilon}}.$$
(10.10)

This formula applies provided that $m < n_f$ and so long as the equation has a solution with $\tau^p > (c_h/c_f)^{(\varepsilon-1)/\varepsilon}$. The latter condition ensures that foreign multinationals who have invested in subsidiaries will use these facilities to serve the home market. Otherwise, the multinationals leave their subsidiaries idle and the home government sets the tariff $\tau^p = (c_h/c_f)^{(\varepsilon-1)/\varepsilon}$. Finally, when all foreign companies establish subsidiaries in the home country (i.e., $m = n_f$) any tariff level $\tau^p \geq (c_h/c_f)^{(\varepsilon-1)/\varepsilon}$ solves the maximization problem, because variations in the tariff rate have no real effects as long as the tariff is high enough to induce the multinationals to make use of their offshore production facilities.[8]

Multinationals

We turn now to the first stage of the game, when each foreign firm must decide whether to establish a foreign subsidiary. We will assume that the entry process is decentralized; that is, each firm makes its own decision, taking those of all of the other companies as given. Given its beliefs about aggregate DFI, each firm forms expectations about the tariff rate using (10.9).[9] Then it calculates the difference between expected profits from operating a subsidiary and expected profits from exporting. Finally, it compares this difference to the fixed cost, ϕ, of establishing an offshore facility.

Using (10.2)–(10.5), we can calculate the difference in operating profits as a function of the tariff level and the number of subsidiaries. The result is

$$\pi_h - \pi_f \equiv \delta(\tau;m) = \frac{B(c_h^{1-\varepsilon} - \tau^{-\varepsilon}c_f^{1-\varepsilon})}{[(n_h + m)c_h^{1-\varepsilon} + (n_f - m)(\tau c_f)^{1-\varepsilon}]^{(\varepsilon-\theta)/(\varepsilon-1)}}, \qquad (10.11)$$

where $B = \varepsilon^{-\theta}(\varepsilon - 1)^{\theta-1} > 0$. A foreign company expecting the tariff rate to be τ, and observing a measure m of foreign firms establishing subsidiaries in the home country, will itself invest if $\delta(\tau;m) > \phi$. If $\delta(\tau;m) < \phi$, the company will certainly not open a branch plant, while if the two are equal, it is indifferent between the two options.

An alternative to our specification would allow coordinated entry by foreign multinationals. This would be appropriate if foreign companies could collude in making their investment decisions or if the foreign government were inclined to regulate DFI. In either of these cases, m would be chosen to maximize $(\delta - \phi)m + n_f\pi_f$, recognizing the dependence of the endogenous tariff rate on the choice of m—via (10.9). This alternative setup would be closer in spirit to the formulation suggested by Bhagwati (1987) and explicitly analyzed in Bhagwati et al. (1987). We will not pursue it any further here.

10.3   DFI and Protection

We seek to characterize perfect-foresight equilibria. In what follows we assume that manufacturing costs are higher in the home country; that is, $c_h > c_f$.

Tariff Response Curves

Figure 10.2 depicts two *tariff response curves*, each describing the political tariff as a function of m for a particular set of parameter values. These curves are derived from (10.9).[10] It is easy to verify that all curves above the horizontal line at $\hat{\tau} = (c_h/c_f)(\theta/\varepsilon)^{1/(\varepsilon-1)}$ slope downward and that all curves below this line but above the horizontal line at $\underline{\tau} = (c_h/c_f)^{(\varepsilon-1)/\varepsilon}$ slope upward.[11] Tariff response curves below $\underline{\tau}$ are horizontal because, with such low tariffs, any multinational that happened to own a subsidiary

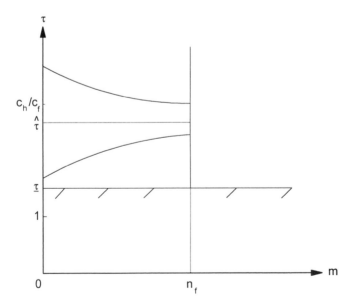

Figure 10.2
Political tariff response curves

in the home country would not use its local plant to supply the home market in any case. We restrict our attention to parameters that give a political tariff at least as high as $\underline{\tau}$. Notice that the figure is drawn under the assumption that $\hat{t} > \underline{\tau}$, but this need not be the case. If $\hat{t} < \underline{\tau}$, then all tariff response curves slope downward. Finally, recall the discussion following equation (10.10), where we argued that in the limiting case where $m = n_f$ (i.e., when all foreign companies establish subsidiaries in the home country), the political tariff can take any value at least as large as $\underline{\tau}$ because all of these tariffs solve (10.9) and all result in the same allocation of resources.

We note for later reference that, when the parameter a rises, the tariff response curve shifts down. In other words, were the political climate to change in such a way as to make the government place relatively greater weight on per capita welfare, the equilibrium tariff would be lower for every (given) degree of multinational presence.

Profit Differential Curves

We show in figure 10.3 five *profit differential curves*, each one representing a given difference between the operating profits of a firm manufacturing in

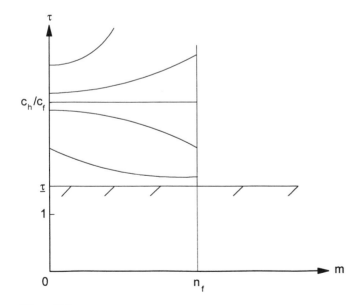

Figure 10.3
Profit differential curves

the home country and one manufacturing in the foreign country, as described by (10.11). A higher curve corresponds to a greater profit differential. When one plus the tariff rate equals the cost ratio c_h/c_f, the profit
differential does not depend on the number of multinational firms m (i.e.,
the curve is a horizontal line). For higher tariffs than this, the curves
slope upward whereas for lower rates they slope downward. A very large
differential that might arise when $m = 0$ may not be possible even with an
infinite tariff for some positive values of m. This is reflected in our depic-
tion of the uppermost curve in the figure.

Entry

Each foreign company compares the profit differential with the fixed cost
ϕ, after forming some expectation about the eventual tariff. Let $\tau^e(m)$
describe (one plus) the tariff rate that a foreign firm expects when the
number of multinationals equals m. Then there are three possible equilibrium configurations:

- $m = 0$ and $\delta[\tau^e(0), 0] \leq \phi$;
- $0 < m < n_f$ and $\delta[\tau^e(m), m] = \phi$;
- $m = n_f$ and $\delta[\tau^e(n_f), n_f] \geq \phi$.

In the first case, no DFI occurs and no firm finds it profitable to enter on
its own. In the second case, some multinationals form and net profits for
firms that establish subsidiaries are the same as for ones that do not. In the
third case, all foreign firms form subsidiaries and net profits are at least as
high as the profits that a single firm would attain if it refrained from
investing in the home country.

   As we will see in a moment, occasionally more than one of these types
of equilibria can exist for given parameter values. When this happens we
will select among them on the basis of a stability criterion. We adopt the
following (ad hoc, but intuitive) adjustment process:

$$\dot{m} = M(\delta[\tau^e(m), m] - \phi) \qquad \text{for } 0 < m < n_f, \qquad (10.12)$$

where $M(0) = 0$ and $M(\cdot)$ is everywhere an increasing function. This
process presumes that whenever the existing number of subsidiaries is
such that it would be profitable for a single firm to invest, the number
of subsidiaries rises, and that whenever it would be profitable for a
single firm to refrain from investing, the number of subsidiaries falls. Of
course this "adjustment" does not take place in real time; recall that

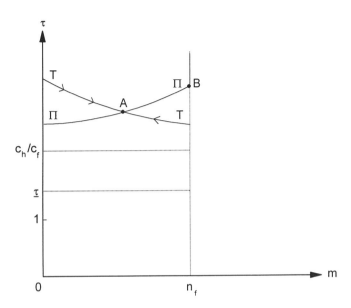

Figure 10.4
Equilibrium DFI and protection

the fixed costs of purchasing a subsidiary are assumed to be sunk, once incurred.

Equilibrium DFI and Protection

We now combine these elements in order to characterize the stable, perfect-foresight equilibria. Figure 10.4 depicts a case with a high fixed cost of entry ϕ and a low value of a. The latter means that the government is primarily concerned with amassing campaign contributions. As a consequence of these parameter restrictions, the tariff response curve and the profit differential curve corresponding to a difference of ϕ both lie everywhere above the cost ratio c_h/c_f for all relevant values of m. This means that the tariff response curve TT slopes downward while the relevant profit differential curve $\Pi\Pi$ slopes upward.

The point A in the figure represents a perfect-foresight equilibrium. So do all points on the vertical line above point B. In the former case, penetration of foreign multinationals is partial, and a firm that invests in the home country enjoys the same net profit as one that serves the home market with exports. In the latter case(s), all foreign firms establish subsidiaries, and the ensuing political tariff causes none of them to regret its decision. Note, however, that these latter equilibria are all unstable. If, for example, the number of multinationals were slightly less than n_f, then the expected tariff would be on the tariff response curve below B, causing a reduction in the number of multinationals, an increase in the expected tariff, and so on, until the economy converged (following the arrows) to the equilibrium at point A.

To clarify the source of the instability, it may help to think as follows. Each foreign firm knows that if all others establish subsidiaries, the home government will be indifferent among all tariffs above $\underline{\tau}$. In consequence the government would indeed be willing to choose a tariff above the one at point B, which would sustain an equilibrium there. But the firm also knows that if a single other foreign firm were to refrain from investing in the home country, the political tariff would be well below that at point B. If this were to happen, the firm would very much regret any decision to invest. So it might decide not to take the risk. If all firms think in this way, they will all be led to expect the tariff at A and to make their investment decisions accordingly.

We now can examine the effects of varying the underlying parameters slightly. We focus on the cost of entry and the degree to which the government cares about the average voter. First consider the parameter a. The less weight the government attaches to per capita welfare (lower a) the higher is the tariff response curve and the higher is point A on the profit differential curve. The result is a higher rate of protection and a greater presence of foreign multinationals. Now consider the cost of entry. When ϕ is lower, so too is the relevant profit differential curve and the location of point A along the tariff response curve. It follows that DFI is greater and protection lower the lower are the costs of foreign entry.

Figure 10.5 depicts another possible situation, which can arise when the government cares significantly about welfare, entry costs are low, and $\hat{\tau} < \underline{\tau}$.[12] In this case, point A again represents the unique, stable equilibrium (as before, the arrows indicate the adjustment path). Here again lower entry costs imply a greater number of foreign subsidiaries and a lower rate of protection. But, unlike in the previous case, now if the government were to concern itself more with contributions and less with per capita welfare, the tariff rate would *fall*.

A comparison of the two cases depicted in figures 10.4 and 10.5 shows that there is no clear-cut relationship between a government's willingness

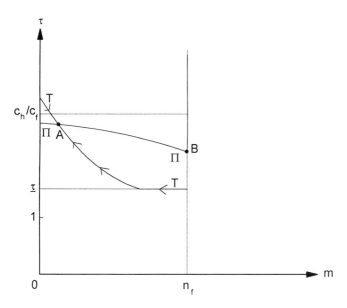

Figure 10.5
Alternative equilibrium configurations

to cater to special interests and the degree of protection that ultimately obtains. The reason is that foreign firms make their investment decisions in anticipation of policy formation and their decisions can alter the political climate in which the tariffs are eventually determined. In both cases the direct effect of a decrease in a (given m) is to generate an incipient increase in the expected tariff; in both cases this induces more foreign firms to enter; and in both cases recognition of this entry causes expectations of the tariff increase to moderate. In the case depicted by figure 10.4, the entry of multinationals does not cause the tariff to fall below its initial level. But in the case depicted in figure 10.5, the assumed adjustment process indeed causes this to happen.

Figure 10.6 depicts still another possibility. This situation can arise when the politicians place a great weight on voter welfare and when fixed costs of forming a subsidiary are low. It also requires $\hat{\tau} > \underline{\tau}$. Here there are two stable perfect-foresight equilibria, at points A and C (whereas the equilibrium at point B is unstable). If all foreign firms were to refrain from investing, as at point A, the political tariff would be reasonably low. Then the firms that had expected this low tariff would be happy that they had chosen to export from their home plants. On the other hand, if all foreign

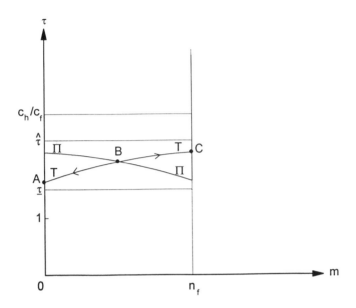

Figure 10.6
Multiple stable equilibria

firms were to form subsidiaries, as at point C, then the political tariff would be high, and the firms would be glad to have their production facilities inside the protected market.

The comparative statics are simple in this case. Neither a small change in the government's utility weights nor a small change in the fixed cost of entry has any effect on the existence of the two extreme equilibria. If a were dramatically lower, however, the TT curve would lie everywhere above the $\Pi\Pi$ curve, and then the unique equilibrium for firms expecting very high tariffs (at all m) has entry by all. Similarly, if ϕ were dramatically lower, the $\Pi\Pi$ curve would lie below TT, and again all would enter. Finally, if either a or ϕ were much higher than the values depicted by the figure, the unique equilibrium would have low tariffs or prohibitive entry costs, and no MNC's in either case.

10.4   Does DFI Benefit the Average Voter?

Our analysis has focused on the joint determination of direct foreign investment and the rate of protection when domestic companies lobby for protection. The resulting equilibrium has of course implications for the well being of the general electorate. There are many welfare questions that one could address with our model. In this section we concentrate on one that may be particularly interesting. Namely we examine whether foreign investment serves the interests of the average voter.

In our model there is no efficiency rationale for such investment. After all, foreign firms must bear an extra (fixed) cost to open a plant in the home country and, moreover, manufacturing costs are higher at home than abroad. The foreign firms' motivation for DFI comes entirely from the anticipated protection of the home market; by opening a subsidiary in the home country, these firms can "jump" the eventual tariff barriers. When Brecher and Díaz-Alejandro (1977) studied the implications of DFI (viewed as international capital flows) that is induced by a *fixed* tariff, they found that such investments always reduce aggregate host-country welfare. Thus restrictions on foreign investment into protected markets would be desirable in their context. But the same need not be true here because the rate of protection may vary endogenously with the extent of multinational presence.

To demonstrate the possibility that impediments to DFI may harm the average voter, we consider a situation where the government attaches very little weight to the public interest and the fixed cost of establishing a subsidiary is relatively low. In the event the unique stable equilibrium when DFI is tolerated has entry by all foreign firms ($m = n_f$) and a tariff high enough to ensure that all these firms actively use their subsidiaries. Moreover, once all foreign firms have built their plants in the home country, gross welfare of the average voter does not depend on the tariff rate (provided that $\tau > c_h/c_f$). This means that the government would be happy to provide the equilibrium protection without contributions from the interest group. Then net welfare (which is gross welfare less any political contributions) would equal gross welfare, which in turn could be expressed, using (10.2)–(10.6), as

$$\tilde{W}(q) \equiv L + \frac{n_h}{\varepsilon} p_h^{1-\varepsilon} q^{\varepsilon-\theta} + \frac{1}{\theta-1} q^{-(\theta-1)} \tag{10.13}$$

for $q = (n_h + n_f)^{1/(1-\varepsilon)} p_h$.

Now compare this outcome to the one that would obtain if foreign investment were prohibited. A government that cared little about average welfare would cater readily to the interest group. It would be induced by the group to choose the tariff that maximized domestic profits, which in this case is a prohibitive one. Moreover it would require only a minuscule contribution in order to provide such protection. It follows that net welfare again would equal gross welfare and that the latter would again be given by (10.13), but this time with $q = n_h^{1/(1-\varepsilon)} p_h$. Our comparison thus hinges on whether $\tilde{W}[(n_h + n_f)^{1/(1-\varepsilon)} p_h]$ exceeds $\tilde{W}(n_h^{1/(1-\varepsilon)} p_h)$ or *vice versa*. It is easy to show that the function $\tilde{W}(q)$ is everywhere decreasing in q.[13] Then, since the price index q is decreasing in n_f, it follows that a prohibition on foreign investment must harm the average voter when the government is highly receptive to interest group pressures. The source of the welfare loss is in the political economy of the situation. Whereas the anticipatory foreign investment allows domestic consumers to enjoy some surplus from foreign varieties, they would realize no such surplus in an equilibrium without DFI in which the government would be induced to erect very high trade barriers.

10.5   Workers versus Capitalists

The fact that DFI might yield benefits to the average voter does not of course mean that foreign firms will be able to enter freely in a political equilibrium. The domestic industry has the same incentive to lobby for barriers to investment as it has to lobby for impediments to trade. So we might expect politics to stand in the way of quid pro quo foreign investment just as it restricts potentially gainful trade. However, our basic specification misses an important distinction between the politics of protectionism and the politics of investment barriers. Because we have modeled an economy where skills are general and labor freely mobile, workers' interests have not been tied to their sector of employment. In reality workers often acquire skills that are specific to an industry. Then these workers gain a stake in the policies that affect their industry. Often we see organized labor as a distinct interest group lobbying the government. And, whereas the interests of wage earners align closely with those of profit earners on issues of protection, this may not be the case where policy toward DFI is concerned.

To explore this point in more detail, we propose a simple modification to our model. We suppose now that differentiated products are manufactured with both "skilled" (or specific) and "unskilled" (or general) labor and that the skills are not useful for production of the numéraire good. In the numéraire sector, output is still produced by unskilled labor alone, and a choice of units again makes the equilibrium wage of these workers equal to 1. In the other sector, differentiated products are produced by a combination of unskilled and skilled labor, with a constant-returns-to-scale technology. There is a fixed supply S of skilled labor. And similar factor proportions are used in manufacturing the differentiated varieties as are used in establishing the plants needed to produce these goods. Accordingly we denote the marginal cost of producing a unit of some brand of differentiated product in the home country by $c_h(w)$ and the fixed cost associated with DFI by $\phi c_h(w)$, where w is the wage paid to skilled workers.

Before turning to the political economy, let us note the requirements for equilibrium in the market for skilled labor. Each firm manufacturing differentiated products in the home country employs $s(w)$ units of skilled labor per unit of output, where $s(w) \equiv dc_h(w)/dw$. Each foreign multinational also employs $\phi s(w)$ units of skilled labor to establish its subsidiary. Total demand for skilled labor is the sum of demand by manufacturers and demand by foreign firms for use in building their plants. Finally, market clearing requires that aggregate demand be equal to the inelastic supply, or

$$(n_h + m)x_h s(w) + m\phi s(w) = S. \tag{10.14}$$

Now we can replace c_h in (10.2) by $c_h(w)$ and combine (10.2)–(10.4) with (10.14) to express the equilibrium wage as a function of the number of foreign subsidiaries and the rate of protection; we denote this relationship by $w(\tau; m)$. Note that w increases with τ, because a higher tariff means greater demand for locally produced varieties, and so a greater derived demand for the sector-specific labor.[14] As for the relationship between the number of multinationals and the skilled wage, we see from (10.14) that there is a direct effect that is positive: Each additional multinational demands some skilled labor to build its plant and produce its output. There is also an indirect effect that works through the induced change in x_h. If the consumer price of domestically produced goods exceeds the price of imports (as will be the case if $\tau c_f < c_h$), then an increase in m raises the price index for differentiated products and so raises the demand for each locally produced good. In this case the indirect effect on the wage also is positive, and the wage rate must rise as the number of multinationals expands. On the other hand, if domestic goods are cheaper than imports,

q falls with m and so does x_h. Then DFI has an adverse, indirect effect on the demand for skilled labor. But the direct effect always dominates, and so the skilled wage always rises when the number of foreign subsidiaries increases.[15]

Now let us return to the politics of the situation. Given the number of foreign multinationals m, both π_h and w increase with τ. So, if both the capitalists and workers are politically organized, both will have an incentive to lobby for protection. In contrast, while domestic profits certainly fall with an increase in m, the skilled wage rises in response to an inflow of foreign firms. So domestic firms and industry workers will find themselves in conflict concerning policy toward multinationals.

How will such a conflict be resolved? To gain some insight into this issue, we focus on the extreme case where a is close to zero. In the event the government puts no weight on consumer surplus or tariff revenue and so is willing to accede to workers' and firms' demands for a prohibitive tariff. Indeed home interest groups need pay only a tiny political contribution in order to secure a fully protected market. Foreign firms should expect an infinite tariff no matter what the degree of multinational presence.[16] Accordingly we know that some foreign firms will wish to establish subsidiaries provided $\pi_h > \phi c_h(w)$ when $m = 0$. It remains to be seen only whether a government that can set investment barriers will choose to impede this foreign investment.

Suppose that the lobbies compete to influence the government's policy toward multinationals. Let each propose a contribution schedule linking the political gift to the number of foreign firms allowed to enter. We focus on Nash equilibria—in which each group's contribution schedule is optimal given the schedule of the other—and, among these, on equilibria that are not Pareto dominated for the two lobby groups. There is in fact a unique, Pareto-undominated Nash equilibrium in the situation we have described; namely the lobby groups induce the government to choose m so as to maximize the sum of the skilled wage bill and domestic profits.[17]

What does this tell us about investment restrictions in the ensuing political equilibrium? To answer this question, we define $J \equiv n_h \pi_h + wS$, and calculate that

$$J = \varepsilon^{-\theta}(\varepsilon - 1)^{\theta-1}n_h(n_h + m)^{(\varepsilon-\theta)/(1-\varepsilon)}c_h(w)^{1-\theta} + wS,$$

when the tariff is prohibitive. Also (10.14) reduces to

$$s(w)\left[\varepsilon^{-\theta}(\varepsilon-1)^{\theta}(n_h+m)^{(\theta-1)/(\varepsilon-1)}c_h(w)^{-\theta}+m\phi\right]=S$$

as $\tau \to \infty$. From these two equations we can evaluate how the joint (gross) welfare of the interest groups is affected by the entry of foreign firms. We find that

$$
\frac{dJ}{dm}\frac{m}{J} = -\frac{(1-\omega)m(\varepsilon-\theta)}{(n_h+m)(\varepsilon-1)} + \left[\omega-(1-\omega)(\theta-1)\beta_s\right]
$$

$$
\times \frac{(1-l_x)+l_x[m(\theta-1)/(n_h+m)(\varepsilon-1)]}{\sigma_s+\theta\beta_s l_x}, \tag{10.15}
$$

where $\omega = wS/J$ is the share of skilled wages in the aggregate income of members of the two interest groups.

Inspection of (10.15) reveals that joint income falls with m when ω is close to zero. In the event the political equilibrium entails a complete ban on all foreign investment. Intuitively, when $\omega \cong 0$, the sector-specific factor has only a (relatively) modest stake in the policy toward multinationals. Meanwhile the owners of domestic firms are more seriously affected by DFI. So the firms' lobby outbids the workers' lobby in the competition for the government's favor. Of course the situation is just the reverse when ω is close to 1. Then an inflow of multinationals boosts the income of skilled workers, and these workers have the most at stake in the outcome of the policy. In this case the workers win the political battle and all foreign firms are free to enter. Finally, if ω is not so extreme, the political contest may give rise to compromise. The political limit to foreign entry can be found by maximizing J with respect to m. This number will be greater, the larger are skilled wages in comparison to the profits of the domestic industry (large ω), the less elastic are firms' demands for the skilled labor (small σ_s), and the larger are the fixed costs of establishing a facility (large ϕ, which implies a small l_x for a given m).

10.6 Conclusions

We have developed a model of anticipatory foreign investment that resembles in some respects the quid pro quo foreign investment described by Bhagwati (1987). In the model, foreign investment is assumed to be irreversible, while trade policies can be more readily changed. Therefore foreign firms must base their investment decisions on their expectations about subsequent policy formation. The firms bear the extra cost of establishing subsidiaries because they fear the eventual imposition of import barriers by the home country.

In our model there is no simple relationship between the number of multinationals and the politically determined tariff rate. In an equilibrium with endogenous trade policy but no impediments to DFI, the stock of foreign investment increases with the home government's taste for campaign contributions and decreases with the fixed cost of entry. But a government that is willing to cater more to special interests does not necessarily provide a higher rate of protection in equilibrium; this depends on how many foreign firms respond to the anticipation of a government with more protectionist proclivities by relocating their production to the home country.

We have shown that DFI can be welfare improving, even if domestic manufacturing costs exceed foreign costs, so that "tariff-jumping" is the sole motivation for the investment. This conclusion is somewhat at odds with prevailing wisdom in the literature (e.g., see Brecher and Díaz-Alejandro 1977). Our result can be reconciled with the earlier literature in view of the assumed endogeneity of protection; that is, DFI may be harmful for a given tariff rate but still beneficial if it induces a more liberal trade-policy outcome.

Finally, we have examined the possibility that the home government might regulate inward foreign investment. When policy toward DFI is endogenous, the politics may generate a conflict between domestic firms wanting investment restrictions and domestic workers with industry-specific skills wanting free entry by multinationals. The resolution of this conflict depends on the elasticity of the industry demand for the skilled labor, the ratio of the skilled wage bill to industry profits, and the size of the fixed cost of establishing a multinational facility.

Notes

We thank Rob Feenstra and Kar-yiu Wong for valuable comments and the National Science Foundation and the U.S.-Israel Binational Science Foundation for financial support. Grossman also thanks the John S. Guggenheim Memorial Foundation, the Sumitomo Bank Fund, the Daiwa Bank Fund, and the Center of International Studies at Princeton University. Part of this work was carried out when the authors were visiting IGIER in Milan and when Grossman was at LEQAM in Aix-en-Provence. Needless to say, these were very hospitable environments.

1. See, for example, Bhagwati et al. (1987), Dinopoulos (1989, 1992), Wong (1989), and Bhagwati et al. (1992).

2. Horstmann and Markusen (1992) have studied how protection affects the equilibrium level of DFI under the assumption that home-country trade policy is exogenously given. Hillman and Ursprung (1993) examined how the extent of multinational investment influences the determination of trade policy, given the numbers of national and multinational firms. Our analysis is distinguished by the fact that we treat both multinational investment and trade policy as endogenously (and jointly) determined.

3. We choose this order of play in order to emphasize that investments in plant and equipment are often irreversible, whereas policy can be changed by the government at will. In these circumstances foreign firms must realize that long-run trade policy will reflect political conditions prevailing after all decisions regarding DFI are made.

4. This political objective function can be derived as a reduced form of a game in which the incumbent government competes in an election with an opposition party. See Grossman and Helpman (1994b).

5. An increase in the price of competing brands always causes substitution from these brands to variety j. At the same time it raises the price index q, which causes consumers to substitute the numéraire good for the entire group of differentiated products. When $\varepsilon > \theta$, the former effect dominates and the demand for good j increases.

6. If this is not the case, then m in (10.3) should be replaced by the number of multinationals that supply the home market with output produced in their subsidiaries. Of course, in an equilibrium with fulfilled expectations, all firms that make costly investments in foreign plants will use these plants for production.

7. If the set of shareholders were nonnegligible in the voting population, then the lobby's members would receive a nonnegligible share of any redistributed tariff revenue and would enjoy a nonnegligible share of aggregate consumer surplus. In the event they would share in any deadweight loss caused by the tariff policy. In Grossman and Helpman (1994a) we show how these considerations (slightly) affect the formula for the equilibrium tariff.

8. Our discussion in the text ignores one last possibility. It may happen that, given m, a choice of $\tau^p < (c_h/c_f)^{(\varepsilon-1)/\varepsilon}$, which is low enough to make the multinationals export to the home market, provides higher joint welfare to the lobby and the government than any policy with $\tau^p > (c_h/c_f)^{(\varepsilon-1)/\varepsilon}$. This case cannot arise in equilibrium, however, because foreign firms would not bear the positive cost of DFI if they expected such a low tariff.

9. With a continuum of firms, the aggregate amount of DFI is independent of the decision of any one firm.

10. Equation (10.10) does not always provide a unique solution for τ^p as a function of m. Two solutions exist, for example, when $m = 0$, $a = 0.217$, $\varepsilon = 2$, $\theta = 1.1$, $c_h = 5$, $c_f = 1$, $n_h = 1$, and $n_f = 1$. In this case neither one of them solves (10.9); the solution to (10.9) instead is an infinite tariff. Equation (10.10) can be inverted, however, to express m as a function of τ^p.

11. We should emphasize the ambiguity in the slope of the tariff response function. Most of the literature that follows Bhagwati assumes a priori that an increase in the number of multinationals reduces the expected rate of protection.

12. This requires that $c_h/c_f < (\varepsilon/\theta)^{\varepsilon/(\varepsilon-1)}$.

13. We calculate that $\tilde{W}'(q)$ has the same sign as the expression

$$\left[\left(\frac{\varepsilon - \theta}{\varepsilon}\right)\left(\frac{n_h}{n_h + n_f}\right) - 1\right],$$

which implies that $\tilde{W}'(q) < 0$.

14. Simple comparative statics reveal that the partial derivative of $w(\cdot)$ with respect to τ is

$$w_\tau = \frac{w}{\tau} \frac{(1-\eta)(\varepsilon - \theta)l_x}{\sigma_s + \beta_s l_x[\eta\theta + (1-\eta)\varepsilon]} > 0,$$

where $\eta \equiv (n_h + m)p_h^{1-\varepsilon}/[(n_h + m)p_h^{1-\varepsilon} + (n_f - m)p_f^{1-\varepsilon}]$ and $l_x \equiv (n_h + m)x_h/[(n_h + m)x_h + m\phi]$ are between zero and one, $\sigma_s \equiv -s'w/s > 0$ is the elasticity of demand for skilled labor in each of its uses, and $\beta_s \equiv sw/c_h$ is the share of skilled wages in the total cost of manufacturing differentiated products or establishing subsidiaries.

15. We calculate that

$$w_m = \frac{w}{m} \frac{\left(1 - \dfrac{n_h}{n_h + m}l_x\right) + \eta\dfrac{\varepsilon - \theta}{\varepsilon - 1}\dfrac{m}{n_h + m}\left(\dfrac{p_f^{1-\varepsilon} - p_h^{1-\varepsilon}}{p_h^{1-\varepsilon}}\right)l_x}{\sigma_s + \beta_s l_x[\eta\theta + (1-\eta)\varepsilon]}$$

which is nonnegative, because $l_x \leq 1$ and the terms multiplying l_x in the numerator of the second fraction sum to something less than or equal to one.

16. An infinite tariff with an infinitessimal contribution is the unique Nash equilibrium when both interest groups independently set their contribution schedules. It is also the outcome if only one of the groups lobbies for protection.

17. This conclusion follows from theorem 2 of Bernheim and Winston (1986). They have shown that all coalition-proof equilibria in menu-auction games maximize the joint welfare of the principals and the agent. Here the government is the agent and its welfare is just a transfer from the principals when $a = 0$. So m must maximize $n_h\pi_h + wS$ in any coalition-proof equilibrium. Finally, the set of coalition-proof equilibria coincides with the set of equilibria that are Pareto undominated for the principals, when there are only two principals bidding for influence.

References

Bernheim, Douglas B., and Michael D. Whinston. 1986. Menu auctions, resource allocation, and economic influence. *Quarterly Journal of Economics* 101:1–31.

Bhagwati, Jagdish N. 1987, Quid pro quo DFI and VIEs: A political-economy-theoretic analysis. *International Economic Journal* 1:1–14.

Bhagwati, Jagdish N., Richard A. Brecher, Elias Dinopoulos, and T. N. Srinivasan. 1987. Quid pro quo foreign investment and welfare: A political-economy-theoretic model. *Journal of Development Economics* 27:127–38.

Bhagwati, Jagdish N., Elias Dinopoulos, and Kar-yiu Wong. 1992. Quid pro quo foreign investment. *American Economic Review* 82:186–90.

Brecher, Richard A., and Carlos F. Díaz-Alejandro. 1977. Tariffs, foreign capital, and immiserizing growth. *Journal of International Economics* 7:317–22.

Dinopoulos, Elias. 1989. Quid pro quo foreign investment. *Economics and Politics* 1:145–60.

Dinopoulos, Elias. 1992. Quid pro quo foreign investment and VERs: A Nash bargaining approach. *Economics and Politics* 4:43–60.

Grossman, Gene M., and Elhanan Helpman. 1994a. Protection for sale. *American Economic Review* 84:833–50.

Grossman, Gene M., and Elhanan Helpman. 1994b. Electoral competition and special interest politics. Woodrow Wilson School discussion paper in economics 174. Princeton University.

Helpman, Elhanan 1984. A simple theory of multinational corporations. *Journal of Political Economy* 92:451–71.

Hillman, Arye L., and Heinrich W. Ursprung. 1993. Multinational firms, political competition, and international trade policy. *International Economic Review* 34:347–63.

Horstmann, Ignatius, and James R. Markusen. 1992. Endogenous market structures in international trade. *Journal of International Economics* 32:109–29.

Markusen, James R. 1984. Multinationals, multi-plant economies, and the gains from trade. *Journal of International Economics* 16:205–26.

Olson, Mancur. 1965. *The Logic of Collective Action.* Cambridge: Harvard University Press.

Wong, Kar-yiu. 1989. Optimal threat of trade restriction and quid pro quo foreign investment. *Economics and Politics* 1:277–300.

11 The Tax Treatment of Imperfectly Mobile Firms: Rent-Seeking, Rent-Protection, and Rent-Destruction

John Douglas Wilson

11.1 Introduction

An important theme running through Jagdish Bhagwati's work on directly unproductive profit-seeking (DUP) activities is the possibility that such activities may be "indirectly" beneficial. For example, the expenditures of real resources to obtain the rents or revenues generated by trade restrictions may alter the economy's output vector in a way that lessens the distorting effects of these restrictions. See Bhagwati's (1982) overview and unified treatment of a wide variety of DUP activities.

While the expenditure of real resources on DUP activities may be beneficial in some cases, any resulting lump-sum transfer of rents or revenue typically does not itself have additional efficiency implications. Under the usual assumption of homothetic demand functions, this transfer simply alters the distribution of purchasing power among different agents in the economy without affecting total purchasing power or the equilibrium prices and quantities. In contrast, this chapter considers a situation in which the transfer of economic rent from the initial "rent-holders" to the "rent-seekers" results in the "destruction" of part of this rent. Specifically, some rent-holders seek to avoid either surrendering or protecting their rents, choosing instead to destroy them. The decision to engage in "rent-destruction" occurs because the rent-seekers are forced by imperfect information to collect the same tax payments from all rent-holders, although their rents differ. As a result some rent-holders are asked to pay a tax that exceeds their rents, causing them to abandon the rent-generating activities. The destroyed rents represent a real welfare loss for the economy. Consequently costly activities designed to "protect" or "defend" these rents are potentially welfare improving, simply because they help preserve the level of valuable rents in the economy.

The specific situation that I have in mind is one in which a region (representing a country or jurisdiction within a country) seeks to attract mobile firms by offering subsidies. The residents of this region supply a factor to these firms (labor) and therefore benefit from the entry of additional firms into the region. After these firms locate in the region, however, they become partially immobile in the sense that they will suffer lost profits if they move. In other words, they face "moving costs." As a result of these costs, the earnings these firms obtain in the absence of taxes or subsidies now exceed those available elsewhere; they represent "economic rents." The residents therefore have an incentive to obtain these rents through government tax policies. Doing so leads those firms with low moving costs to exit the region, thereby effectively destroying their rents. Since firms contemplating a move to the region anticipate the future rent-seeking activities of residents and their possible rent-destruction responses, they demand higher initial subsidies or lower wages. Residents respond by providing positive subsidies to new firms, which are financed by the future taxes. Moreover the costs of destroyed rent opportunities for firms are shifted to residents through the lower wages. For this reason, the expenditures of existing firms on rent-protection activities (i.e., "lobbying") may benefit residents. I will identify circumstances under which such welfare improvements do occur.

This argument involves a "time-consistency" problem. If the residents could commit not to seek rents in the future, then new firms would be willing to enter the region without the need for subsidies or lower wages. Given that such commitments are not possible (perhaps in part because government decision makers change over time), rent-protection activities represent a means for achieving a limited form of commitment. Consequently residents may benefit from rent-protection activities, even in cases where their short-run interests lead them to expend lobbying effort to combat these activities.

The common practice of granting "tax holidays" to new firms suggests that governments typically encounter difficulties in committing to future tax policies.[1] Bond (1981) uses data from the Puerto Rican experience with tax holidays to provide some interesting empirical evidence that tax holidays encourage rapid firm turnover, as in this chapter. Mintz (1990) analyzes the effectiveness of tax holidays in several developing countries and reports that the effective tax rates on capital invested during a tax holiday can be surprisingly high. The problem is that some countries do not allow depreciation allowances for investments made during the holiday to be deferred until after the holiday, when they could be used to lower tax payments. This evidence of high tax rates roughly accords with my finding that the negative tax burdens confronting new firms serve only as a means of offsetting relatively high future taxes.[2] The common use of economic development incentives also corresponds to the subsidies in my model. Ó hUallacháin and Satterthwaite (1992) report mixed evidence on the effectiveness of these incentives as a means of affecting firm location decisions, but this mixed evidence is consistent with the use of subsidies to offset future taxes.

The plan of this chapter is as follows: In section 11.2 I present the model of a single region for the case where there are no expenditures on rent-seeking or rent-protection activities. In the absence of rent-protection, it is assumed that residents control government tax and subsidy policies. Section 11.3 shows that they use this power to subsidize firms that have recently entered the region and to tax the rents earned by established firms. Section 11.4 adds rent-seeking and rent-protection to the model in the form of lobbying efforts by both firms and residents. The equilibrium levels of these activities are derived, and it is found that firms always manage to protect some of their rents. Section 11.5 examines the welfare consequences of these activities, for both the case of a single region and for a system of regions. Circumstances are identified under which the lobbying activities within a single region are welfare improving for residents. For a system of regions, however, it is shown that the firms are the potential beneficiaries of lobbying, not the residents. The reason for this difference is that a single small region receives the benefits of rent protection in the form of the higher wages that mobile firms are willing to pay workers. In contrast, the (assumed) inelastic supply of firms for the system of regions as a whole implies that rent-protection has no effect on equilibrium wages; the benefits remain with the firms. The concluding remarks in section 11.6 contain some implications of this last finding.

11.2 The Model without Rent Protection

Consider a single region containing a fixed number of residents, each of whom supplies one unit of a single input, labor, to competitive firms operating within the region. These firms combine labor with firm-specific inputs to produce a single output. These other inputs may be interpreted as "capital" or "entrepreneurial talent." In any case they are fixed in supply for each firm and therefore omitted as explicit arguments in a firm's production function, denoted $f(l)$ for l representing units of labor. This function exhibits decreasing returns to scale, implying that firms earn positive profits, or, equivalently, positive returns on their fixed factors. A firm's profits before any taxes are paid depend on the wage rate, w, as follows:

$$\pi(w) = \max_{l} f(l) - wl. \tag{11.1}$$

The region is small in the sense that it faces an infinitely elastic supply of interregionally mobile firms. However, once a firm locates in the region, it becomes partially immobile, in the sense that it can only move at a cost, which is not publicly known.[3] This cost is defined quite generally as the decline in the present value of profits relative to the present value of profits available to a new firm in the region. To conduct a steady-state analysis, I assume that this cost is identically and independently distributed in each time period, with each firm learning a given period's cost only at the start of that period. Consequently a new firm occupying the region in period t does not know whether it will move in period $t + 1$ until it learns the cost of moving at the start of period $t + 1$. Thus all potential new firms are ex ante identical, and their only ex post difference is the cost of moving. The cumulative distribution function for moving costs is assumed to be continuous, and this distribution is public information and identical across all firms. I also assume that there exists a positive measure of firms that possess moving costs arbitrarily close to zero, implying that some firms always move in response to the imposition of taxes.

The existence of costly exit opportunities implies that the residents as a group possess some degree of market power over old firms, these being firms that have been located in the region for at least one period. I assume that these residents are free to exercise this power by levying different taxes or subsidies on old firms and new firms. Commitment to taxes beyond the next period is ruled out, so firms contemplating entry into the region must solve the residents' optimization problem to predict the taxes and wages they will face after their first period of operation in the region. I assume perfect foresight so that predicted values equal the actual values. In the equilibria considered below, each firm has "static expectations," in the sense that it views future wages, taxes, and subsidies as being fixed at their steady-state values even if current policy choices deviate from the steady state. These expectations will be shown to be valid if these initial deviations are not too large.[4]

To summarize, the timing of events is as follows: At the start of period $t - 1$, old firms learn their moving costs. Based on these costs, some of these firms exit the region and new firms enter. Entry occurs until the wage equates the discounted profits available to new firms in the region to those available elsewhere. Next production and consumption occur, taxes are collected, subsidies are received, and the government chooses taxes and subsidies for period t. This choice problem is next analyzed.

The control variables in the government's problem are a tax payment by old firms, T_t, a subsidy paid to new firms, S_t, and the total number of firms producing within the region, N_t (which can be indirectly controlled via the choice of the subsidy). This number of firms determines the labor per firm, which then determines the marginal product of labor and therefore the wage rate: $w_t = w(N_t)$, where $dw/dN_t > 0$. The government's objective function is the present value of resident income, which depends on both wages and net transfers of income to residents via the system of firm subsidies and taxes.[5] To state this function, let β_t denote the percentage of period $t - 1$ firms that choose to exit the region in period t (which is endogenously determined below), let ρ denote a fixed discount factor that lies between zero and one, and normalize the region's labor supply to equal one. Then the government's objective function is

$$w(N_t) - S_t[N_t - (1 - \beta_t)N_{t-1}] + T_t[(1 - \beta_t)N_{t-1}]$$

$$+ \rho\{w(N_{t+1}) - S_{t+1}[N_{t+1} - (1 - \beta_{t+1})N_t]$$

$$+ T_{t+1}[(1 - \beta_{t+1})N_t]\} + \rho^2\{\ldots \tag{11.2}$$

An important feature of the taxes and subsidies is that they do not distort production decisions, which here consist only in the choice of how much labor to supply. They could be levied as a percentage of profits, for example, since all firms possess identical production functions.

In setting up the maximization problem, I limit consideration to the interesting case where the government does want to attract new firms into the region. In symbols, I assume that N_t exceeds $(1 - \beta_t)N_{t-1}$ at the optimum. This assumption will necessarily hold in the steady state, where $N_t = N_{t-1}$, since some firms will always choose to exit the region ($\beta_t > 0$) under my assumptions about moving costs. But with a sufficiently high exit rate for firms, the region will want to attract new firms even in cases where it wishes to lower N_t below N_{t-1}.

Given its desire to attract new firms, the government faces a "migration constraint," which requires that S_t and $w(N_t)$ be set so that potential new firms in period t receive the expected present value of profits that is available to them in other regions. Let Π^n represent this value, and assume that it is constant across time. To determine the profits available within the region, note that a potential new firm contemplating entry in period t knows with certainty that it will receive single-period profits of $\pi(w_t) + S_t$ in that period. However, it then faces uncertainty about how long it will remain in the region after period t, given its uncertainty about moving costs. If it does remain in period $t + 1$, then its expected present value of profits will equal that for a new firm Π^n minus the subsidy provided to a new firm S_{t+1}, minus the tax imposed on an old firm T_{t+1}: $\Pi^n - S_{t+1} - T_{t+1}$. If a firm with moving costs m_{t+1} exits the region in period $t + 1$, then the definition of these costs implies that the firm will receive an expected present value of profits equal to $\Pi^n - m_{t+1}$, inclusive of any costs associated with transferring operations to another region. Thus the "marginal firm" in period $t + 1$, which is indifferent between staying and moving, has moving costs equal to $S_{t+1} + T_{t+1}$, which I denote by D_{t+1}:

$$D_{t+1} = S_{t+1} + T_{t+1}; \tag{11.3}$$

in words, D_{t+1} is the excess of the old-firm tax (T_{t+1}) over the new-firm tax $(-S_{t+1})$. Thus the percentage of old firms that exit the region is an increasing function of D_{t+1}:

$$\beta_{t+1} = \beta(D_{t+1}), \quad \beta'(D_{t+1}) > 0. \tag{11.4}$$

Given the distribution function for moving costs, (11.4) says that the expected moving costs for the set of firms that leave in period $t + 1$ is an increasing function of D_{t+1}:

$$E_t(m_{t+1}) = m^e(D_{t+1}), \quad m^{e\prime}(D_{t+1}) > 0. \tag{11.5}$$

Using (11.3)–(11.5), I can write the migration constraint as follows:

$$\Pi^n = \pi(w(N_t)) + S_t + \rho\{\Pi^n - D_{t+1}[1 - \beta(D_{t+1})] - m^e(D_{t+1}) \cdot \beta(D_{t+1})\}, \tag{11.6}$$

where the right side is the expected present value of profits for a firm entering the region in period t, given the information available at the start of period t.

With the migration constraint now fully specified, it is convenient to rearrange the objective function given by (11.2) so that the maximization problem may be stated as

(P.1) $\displaystyle\max_{S_t, D_t, N_t}$ $w_t(N_t) - S_t N_t + D_t[1 - \beta(D_t)]N_{t-1}$

$\qquad + \rho\{w(N_{t+1}) - S_{t+1}N_{t+1} + D_{t+1}[1 - \beta(D_{t+1})]N_t\}$

$\qquad + \rho^2\{\ldots,$

subject to the migration constraint (11.6).

It is clear from this setup that no variable chosen prior to period $t - 1$ will affect the solution. Although N_{t-1} appears in the objective function, it does so in a multiplicative fashion that has no effect on the optimal value of D_t or the other two control variables. Thus (P.1) will yield the steady-state solution, even if the values of the control variables in the previous period $(S_{t-1}, D_{t-1},$ and $N_{t-1})$ depart from their steady-state values. This immediate convergence to a steady state is consistent with the assumption of static expectations that underlies the setup of (P.1): Potential new firms recognize that a deviation by the government from its steady-state solution in period t will not alter the government's incentive to return to the steady state in period $t + 1$.[6]

11.3   Rent Destruction

I now describe the government's optimal tax policy toward new and old firms and demonstrate that it leads to the costly turnover of firms, as some old firms abandon the region in order to escape high taxes. In other words, they "destroy" their economic rents within the region.

Consider first the optimal tax on old firms. It is clear from the objective function that this tax is set to maximize the "excess taxes" collected from old firms. In symbols, the D_t that solves (P.1) also solves

$$\max_{D_t} D_t[1 - \beta(D_t)]. \qquad (11.7)$$

The first-order condition is

$$1 - \beta(D_t) - D_t \frac{\partial\beta}{\partial D_t} = 0. \qquad (11.8)$$

This condition can be solved to obtain the steady-state value of D_t. It is clear from the setup of the problem that this D_t is positive:

$$D_t = S_t + T_t > 0. \qquad (11.9)$$

Thus old firms face positive excess taxes. This D_t then determines the steady-state value of β_t, $\beta(D_t)$. I will omit time subscripts when referring to these values.

Consider now the relation between S_t and T_t. This can be found by perturbing N_t and S_t from their optimal values for (P.1). In particular, increase N_t by dN_t, thereby raising the marginal product of labor by $dw_t = w'(N_t) \cdot dN_t > 0$. Accompany this rise in w_t with a reduction in S_t that keeps the migration constraint (11.6) satisfied, and raise T_t to keep D_t fixed. In symbols, the change in S_t satisfies

$$dS_t = -\pi'(w_t) \cdot dw_t = N_t^{-1} \cdot dw_t, \tag{11.10}$$

where the second equality follows from the envelope theorem, since N_t^{-1} represents the amount of labor employed by a single firm, given our normalization of the region's labor supply to equal one. Given that the policy perturbation takes place from the optimum, it must have a zero first-order impact on the objective function. Using (11.10), this condition may be written as

$$\{-S_t + \rho \cdot D_{t+1} \cdot (1 - \beta)\} \cdot dN_t = 0. \tag{11.11}$$

By substituting the previously determined excess tax D into (11.9) and (11.11), these two equations may be solved for the steady-state values of S_t and T_t. I will omit time subscripts when referring to this equilibrium tax system. Equation (11.11) then yields

$$S = T \frac{\rho(1 - \beta)}{1 - \rho(1 - \beta)}. \tag{11.12}$$

Finally, it is instructive to rewrite the right side of (11.12) as an infinite sum:

$$S = \sum_{i>t} T \cdot [\rho(1 - \beta)]^{i-t}. \tag{11.13}$$

Thus the subsidy awarded to a new firm equals the expected present value of all future taxes paid by that firm, taking into account the increasing probability over time that the firm will be faced with favorable "outside opportunities" and therefore exit the region. In this sense the region has no long-run ability to exploit imperfectly mobile old firms. This finding is explained by the perfect mobility of new firms. These firms anticipate future taxes, forcing the government to offset the distorting effects of these taxes on firm turnover through higher initial subsidies or lower wages.

11.4   Rent Protection

To demonstrate the value of the "rent-protection" activities of old firms, I now introduce a political model that allows both the old and new firms occupying the region in period t to increase the expected present value of their profits by engaging in lobbying activities. These activities give rise to lobbying by organizations representing the welfare of the residents, and the size of the rent transfer from old firms to residents depends on the relative amounts of lobbying expenditures by the two groups.

The timing of events builds on the no-lobbying model discussed above. At the start of period $t - 1$, new firms enter the region and old firms exit, given the previously determined values of S_{t-1}, T_{t-1}, and w_{t-1}. Production and consumption then occur, taxes and subsidies are exchanged, and next period's policy variables are chosen. It is here that the analysis departs from the no-lobbying case. Following Findlay and Wellisz (1982), Wellisz and Wilson (1986), and many subsequent contributors to the literature on endogenous trade policy,[7] I posit a function that maps relative lobbying efforts into policy choices. The relevant policy choice in this instance can be ascertained from (11.6), by replacing t with $t - 1$, to show that the firms remaining in the region after entry and exit have occurred at the start of period $t - 1$ should be concerned only with reducing D_t, this being the excess of their tax payments (T_t) over those of new firms ($-S_t$). Thus I treat these excess tax payments as the object of lobbying activities and specify a "transfer formation function," $D_t = D(C_{r,t-1}, C_{f,t-1})$, where $C_{r,t-1}$ is lobbying expenditures by residents and $C_{f,t-1}$ is lobbying expenditures by firms. I also follow the common practice of assuming homogeneity of degree zero, in which case the transfer formation function may be written

$$D_t = D\left(\frac{C_{f,t-1}}{C_{r,t-1}}\right), \tag{11.14}$$

where a rise in the relative lobbying effort of firms (i.e., more rent protection) leads to a decline in the excess tax, D_t.[8] It is natural to assume that firms will be successful in reducing D_t below its optimal value for residents, now denoted D^r, at least in those cases where they expend more resources on lobbying than do residents. Thus I assume that

$$D\left(\frac{C_{f,t-1}}{C_{r,t-1}}\right) < D^r \qquad \text{if } C_{f,t-1} > C_{r,t-1}. \tag{11.15}$$

Residents and firms play a Nash game in lobbying expenditures. To determine the equilibrium D_t, consider the maximization problems solved by the firms and residents. By adding lobbying expenditures to the expression for a firm's profits given by (11.6), the problem confronting the firms may be stated as

(P.2) $\max_{C_{f,t-1}} - C_{f,t-1} + \rho\{\Pi^n - D_t \cdot [1 - \beta(D_t)] - m^e(D_t) \cdot \beta(D_t)\}N_{t-1},$

$$\tag{11.16}$$

where D_t is determined by lobbying expenditures as specified by (11.14). Free-rider problems are ignored here by assuming that the (ex ante identical) firms maximize discounted profits. Similarly I assume that residents lobby to maximize their discounted income, but the model could easily be generalized by assuming, for example, that free-rider problems cause each interest group to obtain only a fixed fraction of their optimal lobbying expenditures. Using (P.1), the problem for the residents may be stated as

(P.3) $\max_{C_{r,t-1}} - C_{r,t-1} + \rho D_t(1 - \beta(D_t))N_{t-1}.$ $\tag{11.17}$

It turns out that the equilibrium lobbying levels satisfy a surprisingly simple rule. To state this rule, let E_t denote the negative elasticity of the supply of old firms with respect to the excess tax:

$$E_t = -\beta'(D_t)\frac{D_t}{1 - \beta(D_t)} < 0. \tag{11.18}$$

The following proposition demonstrates that this elasticity alone determines relative lobbying expenditures.

PROPOSITION 11.1   In the Nash equilibrium for lobbying, $C_{r,t-1}/C_{f,t-1} = 1 + E_t < 1$. Thus lobbying reduces the transfer of rents from old firms to residents ($D_t < D^r$). Moreover both firm and resident lobbying per firm, $C_{f,t-1}/N_{t-1}$ and $C_{r,t-1}/N_{t-1}$, are independent of N_{t-1}, implying that $C_{f,t-1}/C_{r,t-1}$ and D_t are also independent of N_{t-1}.

Proof Omitting time subscripts for brevity, the first-order condition for the firm's problem, (P.2), may be stated as

$$-1 - \rho D' \cdot C_r^{-1} \cdot (1 - \beta)N = 0, \tag{11.19}$$

where use is made of the envelope theorem; that is, since marginal firms are indifferent between staying and leaving, any change in β (and the resulting change in m^e) induced by a marginal change in C_f will have no impact on the objective function. For residents the first-order condition is

$$-1 - \rho D' \cdot \frac{C_f}{C_r^2} \cdot (1 - \beta) \cdot N + \rho D \cdot \beta' \cdot D' \cdot \frac{C_f}{C_r^2} \cdot N = 0. \qquad (11.20)$$

Multiplying (11.20) by C_r/C_f and then subtracting (11.19) from the resulting equality yields

$$1 - \frac{C_r}{C_f} = -\rho D \cdot \beta' \cdot D' \cdot C_r^{-1} \cdot N. \qquad (11.21)$$

Solving (11.19) for $\rho D' \cdot C_r^{-1} \cdot N = -(1 - \beta)^{-1}$ and then substituting this equality into (11.21) gives

$$1 - \frac{C_r}{C_f} = \frac{D \cdot \beta'(D)}{1 - \beta(D)}, \qquad (11.22)$$

where $D = D(C_f/C_r)$. This equality may be rewritten as the equality in the proposition, and it determines values of C_f/C_r and D that are constant across time.[9] Note also that C_r/C_f is independent of N, implying that D is independent of N. It follows immediately from (11.19) that C_f/N and C_r/N are also independent of N. □

The assumption given by (11.15) certainly plays a role in this proposition, but it cannot fully explain the result because it requires only that firms would be no worse off than they would be in the absence of lobbying if they at least matched the lobbying expenditures of residents. That firms expend more resources than residents follows from the residents' indifference to a marginal reduction in old-firm rents from the no-lobbying level, that is, a small fall in D_t from D^r. The firms gain from this increase, whereas the residents experience no first-order gain or loss, since D^r has been chosen to maximize their welfare. For residents to possess an incentive to lobby in equilibrium, the equilibrium D_t must lie below D^r by some discrete amount.

There remains the issue of how the new-firm subsidy S_t and number of firms N_t are chosen in a given period $t - 1$. These variables are not contested through lobbying because they are a matter of indifference to the firms operating in the region in period t. However, S_t and N_t are not a matter of indifference to residents. They are chosen to solve problem (P.1), amended to include lobbying activities.

There are two ways in which lobbying affects (P.1). First, D_t is now a parameter determined through lobbying, rather than a control variable. Second, the costs of lobbying must now be added to both the objective function and the migration constraint. In particular, proposition 11.1 implies that period $(t-1)$ residents must now anticipate that a rise in the number of firms operating in the region in period t (N_t) will raise the total resources that they will spend on lobbying in period t. This consideration is accounted for by introducing into the problem the per firm lobbying expenditures, $c_{rt} = C_{rt}/N_t$ and $c_{ft} = C_{ft}/N_t$. I may consider steady-state values of both these variables and D_t, since proposition 11.1 shows that they are independent of N_t and N_{t-1}. Omitting time subscripts to describe these values, the amended problem is stated as follows:[10]

(P.1*) $\quad \max_{S_t, N_t} w_t(N_t) - S_t N_t + D(1-\beta)N_{t-1} - c_r N_t + \rho \cdot \{w(N_{t+1})$

$$- S_{t+1}N_{t+1} + D(1-\beta)N_t - c_r N_{t+1}\} + \rho^2\{\ldots,$$

$$\text{s.t. } \Pi^n = \pi(w(N_t)) + S_t - c_f + \rho\{\Pi^n - D(1-\beta) - m^e(D)\cdot\beta\}.$$
$$(11.23)$$

Given the addition of future lobbying costs $c_{rt} N_t$ to the problem, it is easy to see that the first-order condition for N_t, previously given by (11.11), must now be amended to read

$$\{-(S_t + c_r) + \rho D(1-\beta)\}\cdot dN_t = 0. \qquad (11.24)$$

As before, combining (11.24) with the equality $D = S_t + T_t$ enables us to solve for the steady-state values of S_t and T_t. Substituting $T + S$ for D in (11.24) then gives

$$S + c_r = (T - c_r)\frac{\rho(1-\beta)}{1 - \rho(1-\beta)}. \qquad (11.25)$$

By writing the right side of (11.25) as an infinite sum, I then find that the existence of lobbying modifies the previous relation between the subsidy and future taxes, (11.13), as follows:

PROPOSITION 11.2   In the equilibrium with lobbying activities,

$$S + c_r = \sum_{i>t} [T - c_r]\cdot[\rho(1-\beta)]^{i-t}. \qquad (11.26)$$

Thus the expected present value of taxes confronting new firms now exceeds the value of their current subsidies. This excess equals the expected present value of the additional lobbying expenditures residents incur when a new firm enters the jurisdiction. In other words, the expenditures devoted to a new firm, consisting of both a subsidy and lobbying expenditures, equal the expected present value of future taxes *net* of future lobbying expenditures.

11.5 Welfare

Lobbying in this model enhances efficiency by reducing the taxation of old firms, thereby lowering costly firm turnover. In this section I first identify conditions under which the residents of a single region benefit from the lobbying game played there. Then I demonstrate that the welfare effects of lobbying are quite different when lobbying takes place throughout a closed system of regions, instead of in only a single small region. Section 11.6 addresses some implications of this result.

Single-Region Lobbying

The impact of lobbying on resident welfare depends on whether the commencement of lobbying activities starting in some period J is anticipated by firms that entered the region prior to J, or whether only those firms arriving after period J anticipate future lobbying activities. I consider both cases.

The first case may be constructed by assuming that lobbying starts in the "initial time period," or period 0, when firms have not yet occupied the region. Then there can be no firms that entered the region prior to the period in which lobbying activities first occur, and I may assume that all firms choosing whether to enter take into account future lobbying activities. To isolate the welfare implications of the lower excess tax obtained through lobbying, I first reduce the excess tax without the use of lobbying expenditure. Assuming that the government continues to choose subsidies and the number of firms in each period to maximize resident welfare (P.1*), tax payments net of subsidies will equal resident lobbying expenditures (proposition 11.2) regardless of how much the excess tax is reduced. However, this reduction does lower wasteful firm turnover, which by itself raises expected discounted profits. It follows that wages must rise to keep these profits equal to Π''. This increase in wages shifts the benefits of the reduced firm turnover from the firms to the residents. As a result, the following proposition holds:

PROPOSITION 11.3   Keeping lobbying expenditures fixed at zero, consider a reduction in the excess tax from its no-lobbying level (D') in each time period after the initial time period. Assume that S and N continue to be chosen in each period to maximize resident welfare (P.1*). Then the reduction in the excess tax will raise the present value of resident income.

I now bring lobbying expenditures into the comparison. The system of taxes and subsidies forces firms to effectively pay for the expenditures residents devote to lobbying. Thus residents will benefit from lobbying activities if the wage rises. The problem is that the wage will fall if the efficiency gains from lower firm turnover are more than offset by the burdens that lobbying activities impose on firms, either directly through the firms' own lobbying expenditures or indirectly through the use of the tax and subsidy system to finance resident lobbying expenditures. Examples can easily be constructed where this does not happen. In particular, consider an infinite sequence of regions that are identical in every respect except for the transfer formation function, $D_i(C_f/C_r)$ for region i. Assume that these regions possess identical equilibrium values of the migration elasticity E and, by proposition 11.1, therefore possess identical equilibrium values of the lobbying ratio, denoted R. Assume also that $D_i(R)$ is identical for all i but that its derivative goes to zero as i goes to infinity.[11] Then first-order condition (11.19) implies that the equilibrium levels of c_r and, hence, c_f for a region i go to zero as $D_i'(R)$ goes to zero. Thus lobbying costs also go to zero. On the other hand, D changes by the same amount in all regions. I can then conclude that the benefits of the lower D will dominate lobbying costs in regions indexed by a sufficiently high i, so residents benefit from lobbying activities in these regions.

Consider now an unanticipated commencement of lobbying activities in some future period J, while the economy is in a steady state. These activities then take place in every period after J and are anticipated by firms entering after J. Until $J + 1$, S_t, T_t, and the period t wage are unaffected by the future lobbying activities. But then the economy moves to a new steady state, which includes a lower excess tax.[12] To investigate the change in proposition 11.3, I consider the welfare effect of this reduction in the excess tax, while again keeping lobbying expenditures fixed at zero.

This welfare effect is measured by the change in the present value of resident income calculated in period J.

As before, the fall in the excess tax will lower wasteful firm turnover, thereby increasing the real wage from period $J + 1$ onward. But this is not the only source of the residents' income change. Firms that entered the region prior to period $J + 1$ have received subsidies that did not reflect future lobbying activities, given that these activities were unanticipated. Hence the fall in the excess tax represents a transfer of income from residents to these firms, and this transfer may more than offset the rise in the wage. I next investigate the magnitude of the transfer.

Since we are comparing two steady states, the transfer of income from residents to old firms must take the form of a uniform fall in the tax revenue net of subsidy payments and lobbying expenses from period $J + 1$ onward. I refer to the steady-state flow of net tax revenue to residents as the "net cash flow." The following proposition relates its magnitude to the excess tax:

PROPOSITION 11.4   In the steady-state equilibrium with or without lobbying, if D is the excess tax, then the net cash flow per firm (NCF) is

$$NCF = (1 - \rho)(1 - \beta(D))D. \tag{11.27}$$

Proof   Again let T, S, and c_r denote the equilibrium old-firm tax, new-firm subsidy, and resident lobbying per firm ($c_r = 0$ in the no-lobbying case). The net cash flow per firm is

$$NCF = (1 - \beta)T - \beta S - c_r, \tag{11.28}$$

or

$$NCF = T - \beta D - c_r. \tag{11.29}$$

Equation (11.27) is obtained by substituting from (11.24) into (11.29) and using the equality $D = T + S$.   □

Note first that this net cash flow is positive whenever the excess tax is positive. The reason is that, in any period t along the steady state, there always exist firms that received their subsidy prior to t and will therefore generate a positive expected present value of net tax revenue from period t onward; only for new firms will this value be zero (proposition 11.2). This positive revenue yield from old firms at each point on the steady state translates into the positive NCF identified in proposition 11.4.

Observe next that the D that maximizes the net cash flow in (11.27) also solves the residents' maximization problem in the absence of lobbying (P.1). Thus a reduction in the excess tax reduces the net cash flow per firm. As noted above, this drop in the NCF represents an income transfer from residents to old firms, which may offset the higher wages that firms are willing to pay when the excess tax declines. The next proposition shows that the wage change dominates the fall in the NCF if the discount factor is sufficiently close to one.

PROPOSITION 11.5   Assume that the economy is initially in a steady-state equilibrium without lobbying. Keeping lobbying expenditures fixed at zero, consider an unanticipated fall in the excess tax from D^r from period $J + 1$ onward. Assume that S and N continue to be chosen in each period to maximize resident welfare (P.1*). Then the reduction in the excess tax will raise the present value of resident income as of period J if the discount factor is sufficiently close to one.

Proof   We have seen that the reduction in D reduces the expected future moving costs confronting new firms and thereby increases the wage to keep their discounted expected profits equal to Π^n. Since a firm incurs these moving costs only after it has been operating in the region for at least one period, the benefit that the lower moving costs provides a new firm rises with the discount factor. Hence the reduction in D raises the equilibrium wage by an amount that is positively related to the discount factor.

In contrast, proposition 11.4 shows that a reduction in D from D^r changes the net cash flow by an amount that goes to zero as the discount factor approaches one. Putting these two observations together, we can conclude that the present value of resident income rises if the discount factor is sufficiently close to one.   ∎

Neither D^r nor the lobbying-induced decline in D depend on the discount factor [see (11.8) and proposition 11.1], but proposition 11.5 tells us that this fixed decline in D benefits residents if the discount factor is sufficiently close to one. One way to interpret this dependence is to observe that the discount factor goes to one as the length of a period goes to zero. Consequently residents will benefit from a reduction in D in cases where they can commit to providing an initial subsidy for only a short length of time. As already argued above, it is easy to construct examples in which the costs of lobbying do not fully offset this direct benefit from the lobbying-induced decline in D.

To conclude, the unanticipated commencement of lobbying activities is more likely to harm residents, since these activities effectively transfer income to firms that entered the region in periods before these activities began. In both cases, however, examples can be found where residents benefit from the lobbying.

Systemwide Lobbying

The welfare implications of lobbying throughout a system of identical regions are quite different from those for a single region. Whereas a single region faces an infinitely elastic supply of new firms, the supply elasticity for the entire system should be significantly lower. As a result new firms will no longer obtain an exogenously determined discounted profit level. This creates the possibility that firms may benefit from the effficiency gains that lobbying generates in the form of lower costly firm turnover.

Consider the case where the supply of firms is fixed for the entire system of regions. Under this assumption lobbying cannot alter the equilibrium wage: With the total supply of firms fixed, lobbying in all regions will leave unchanged the number of firms in each region, and therefore the marginal product of labor. But the wage change from lobbying was the only reason for the resident welfare gains identified in proposition 11.3. With the wage now fixed, none of the efficiency gains from lower firm turnover are transferred to residents; firms receive them all. In the case where lobbying is unanticipated before it begins, residents not only fail to benefit from a wage change, but they are harmed by the drop in the net cash flow identified in proposition 11.4.

Reversing the comparison, I can say that the system of regions as a whole actually benefits from the rise in the excess tax that would result from an unexpected cessation of lobbying activities. In this sense there is an incentive for the system of regions as a whole to eliminate lobbying, although the unilateral elimination of lobbying by a single region may not be welfare improving.

11.6 Concluding Remarks

This chapter has shown that rent-protection activities by partially immobile firms may actually benefit the residents trying to obtain the rents, even though these residents possess short-run incentives to engage in their own costly rent-seeking activities. This possibility has been demonstrated for a small open economy with no market power over the discounted profits that new firms must receive. In the absence of lobbying, residents subsidize new firms but tax old firms, creating inefficient firm turnover. Lobbying reduces these taxes and subsidies, thereby lowering this costly turnover, and the increased attractiveness of the region to potential new firms raises the equilibrium wage. But lobbying throughout a system of regions produces quite different welfare implications for residents. Assuming a fixed supply of firms, the wage will not rise as a result of lobbying.

These different results suggest a form of welfare-worsening, political-system competition in a system of regions, whereby it is possible for the residents of individual regions to support unfettered lobbying between residents and firms, although it is advantageous to eliminate lobbying in all regions. This possibility points to a new dimension in the study of the welfare implications of decentralized government decision making. The local public economics literature has identified many cases where governments choose inefficient tax and expenditure policies, although they act in the best interests of their residents. In contrast, we see here that there may exist inefficiencies in the choice of the political systems that determine these policy instruments. It would be useful to explore the efficiency of political-system choices by independent governments in other contexts, and to examine what devices might be employed by a central authority to improve these choices.

Notes

I am grateful for the comments from Elias Dinopoulos and other participants at the conference on "Political Economy of Trade Policy," in honor of Jagdish Bhagwati, and from seminar participants at Tulane University, the University of Colorado, and the University of Illinois. Funding for this research was provided by the National Science Foundation, grant number SES-9209168.

1. For some previous theoretical modeling of tax holidays, see Doyle and van Wijnbergen (1994) and Bond and Samuelson (1986, 1989). My approach has parallels to the two-period models that they use to examine bargaining over tax holidays between a single firm and government. But those models assume that the firm's outside profit opportunities in the second period are public knowledge, in contrast to the heterogeneous firm setup in this chapter.

2. The existence of subsidies in my first model relies on the assumption that firms impose no external costs on jurisdictions, such as infrastructure requirements or environmental costs. If such costs do exist, then the new firms may face positive taxes, but these taxes do not

compensate for these external costs. Instead future taxes are increased to finance these costs. In my model with lobbying, one such cost is the lobbying expenditures undertaken by residents to counteract the lobbying activities of firms.

3. This specification of moving costs is similar to that used by Wildasin and Wilson (1996) to investigate the tax and subsidy policies local governments employ in response to imperfect labor mobility. They work with an overlapping-generations model, whereas firms last forever in the current setup, and they do not develop a political model.

4. There will usually exist equilibria that differ from the steady-state equilibrium described below, corresponding to different expectations. For example, I do not consider the possibility that regions can build "reputations" for not being exploiters of old firms. Such reputational equilibria are ruled out so that I can better focus on lobbying as a commitment device.

5. Note that residents are assumed not to have an equity interest in the firms operating within the region. In other words, "absentee ownership" of firms is assumed.

6. A sufficiently large increase in N_t would move the period $t + 1$ solution out of the steady state by creating the "excess firm problem" discussed previously, where the constraint $N_{t+1} \geq (1 - \beta_t)N_t$ binds and no new firms enter the region. But for purposes of calculating the first-order conditions for problem (P.1), we need only consider small deviations from the steady state.

7. For recent reviews of this literature, see Riezman and Wilson (1995) and Rodrik (1995).

8. The case of lobbying by mobile firms is related to the phenomenon of "foreign lobbying" in the trade protection literature. Hillman and Ursprung (1988) and Das (1990) also use homogeneous policy formation functions to tackle this problem, and Hillman and Ursprung (1993) use the same setup to investigate the liberalizing influence that multinational firms exercise on trade policy. For some recent attempts in the trade literature to endogenize the manner in which given amounts of expenditures by special-interest groups affect policy choices, see Grossman and Helpman (1994) and Riezman and Wilson (1996).

9. Depending on the distribution of moving costs across firms (which determines how the derivative, $\beta'(D)$, varies with D), (11.22) may have multiple solutions. In this case we may assume that the same solution describes the equilibrium D in each time period.

10. Since profits Π'' take into account firm lobbying costs, c_f, no such cost term multiplies ρ in (11.23).

11. The second-order conditions for problems (P.2) and (P.3) can be maintained by choosing a sufficiently high second derivative for $D_i(R)$.

12. As discussed in section 11.2, I assume that the constraint $N_{J+1} \geq (1 - \beta_J)N_J$ does not bind. But this will definitely be the case if lobbying does lead to a higher wage (see the previous discussion), since N_{J+1} is then greater than N_J.

References

Bhagwati, J. 1982. Directly unproductive, profit-seeking (DUP) activities. *Journal of Political Economy* 90:988–1002.

Bond, E. W. 1981. Tax holidays and industry behavior. *Review of Economics and Statistics* 63:88–95.

Bond, E. W., and L. Samuelson. 1986. Tax holidays as signals. *American Economic Review* 76:820–26.

Bond, E. W., and L. Samuelson. 1989. Bargaining with commitment, choice of techniques, and direct foreign investment. *Journal of International Economics* 26:77–98.

Das, S. P. 1990. Foreign lobbying and the political economy of protection. *Japan and the World Economy* 2:169–79.

Doyle, C., and S. van Wijnbergen. 1994. Taxation of foreign multinationals: A sequential bargaining approach to tax holidays. *International Tax and Public Finance* 1:211–26.

Findlay, R., and S. Wellisz. 1982. Endogenous tariffs, the political economy of trade restrictions, and welfare. In J. Bhagwati, ed., *Import Competition and Response*. Chicago: University of Chicago Press.

Grossman, G., and E. Helpman. 1994. Protection for sale. *American Economic Review* 84: 833–50.

Hillman, A. L., and H. W. Ursprung. 1988. Domestic politics, foreign interests, and international trade policy. *American Economic Review* 78:729–45.

Hillman, A. L., and H. W. Ursprung. 1993. Multinational firms, political competition, and international trade policy. *International Economic Review* 34:347–63.

Mintz, J. M. 1990. Corporate tax holidays and investment. *World Bank Review* 4:81–102.

Ó hUallacháin, B., and M. A. Satterthwaite. 1992 Sectoral growth patterns at the metropolitan level: An evaluation of economic development incentives. *Journal of Urban Economics* 31:25–58.

Reizman, R., and J. D. Wilson. 1995. Politics and trade policy. in J. S. Banks and E. A. Hanushek, eds., *Modern Political Economy: Old Topics, New Directions*. Cambridge: Cambridge University Press.

Reizman, R., and J. D. Wilson. 1996. Political reform and trade policy. *Journal of International Economics*, forthcoming.

Rodrik, D. 1995. What does the political economy literature on trade policy (not) tell us that we ought to know? In G. M. Grossman and K. Rogoff, eds., *Handbook of International Economics*, vol. 3. Amsterdam: North Holland.

Wellisz, S., and J. D. Wilson. 1986. Lobbying and tariff formation: A deadweight loss consideration. *Journal of International Economics* 20:386–75.

Wildasin, D. E., and J. D. Wilson. 1996. Imperfect mobility and local government behavior in an overlapping-generations model. *Journal of Public Economics*, forthcoming.

12 Endogenous Trade Restrictions and Domestic Political Pressure

B. Peter Rosendorff

12.1 Introduction

Since the mid 1970s we have seen the growth of bilaterally negotiated nontariff barriers such as voluntary export restraints (VERs), especially in oligopolistic markets, such as cars, steel, and TVs, and elsewhere. Moreover these VERs relinquish the revenues that would otherwise accrue to the domestic government under a tariff.[1] Why then would a self-interested government choose to use tariffs at times, and restrain trade by using VERs at others? This chapter investigates the choice of instruments by a government motivated by political concerns. Such a politically motivated government may choose to adopt a VER over a tariff when the marginal electoral return from protecting profits of the domestic industry is higher than that from tariff revenue and consumer surplus. Moreover the foreign industry is not harmed by the switch from a tariff to a VER.

While domestic political pressure has been pointed to as an underlying cause of trade restrictions generally,[2] electoral concerns also determine the optimal choice of policy instrument. In a representative democracy, government is not viewed as a benevolent social welfare maximizer; it is rather composed of politicians pursuing political interests: reelection perhaps. Constituents vote for those politicians that will enact policies that distribute income toward them, and politicians have to balance the competing claims of a variety of constituents. As in Magee, Brock, and Young (1989), Findlay (1982), or Grossman and Helpman (1994), the decision to restrain trade must be viewed in the light of (1) the pressures that domestic interest groups bring to bear on the trade regulating authorities or (2) the voting behavior of individuals whose incomes differ according to their ownership of labor and shares in profits.

In this chapter, I establish that the relative sizes of the various competing constituencies determine both the choice of instrument and its size. First, I consider a game where two firms (one in each country) Cournot-compete in the domestic market once the local government has established the optimal tariff. The government, of course, sets the optimal tariff anticipating correctly the behavior of the firms, bearing in mind its income distribution objectives (a distribution which maximizes electoral returns). I then establish the first result: The size of the optimal tariff depends on the relative size of the electoral support of those receiving the profits from the protected industry. The greater the electoral pressure that the industry places on the government, the larger is the protective tariff.

Free trade is restored as an optimal policy choice even under imperfect competition under appropriate political conditions. Bhagwati (1971) establishes that protection is second best in the presence of a domestic distortion (e.g., imperfect competition in production); here if the consumers' losses from tariffs are electorally costly relative to the electoral gains from protecting the industry, free trade may nevertheless be optimal.

The second stage is to consider if any further electoral gains are possible using a nontariff restriction (Bhagwati 1987). A take-it-or-leave-it bargaining game between the local government and the foreign firm is studied. In this game the local government offers a tariff reduction in exchange for a voluntary restraint of the firm's exports. The foreign firm accepts such an offer only if the profits exceed those gained in the tariff game equilibrium (this is the "voluntary" part of VER). An equilibrium exists with the foreign firm accepting the offer and the local government making it when the relative size of the electoral support of those receiving the profits from the protected industry is larger than some threshold. With government giving greater weight to domestic profits than to tariff revenue and consumer surplus combined, a switch from a tariff to a VER can improve the government's political chances without harming the foreign firm. Hence the major result a VER is preferred (to the optimal tariff) by the local government and the foreign firm if the weight on the profits of the protected industry in the government's objective function is large enough.

Finally, I compare the effects of the optimal tariff with the optimal VER and establish the role political factors play in the lack of equivalence between the two. I also establish that the results are robust to alternative distribution schemes for the tariff revenue.

12.2 Levels of Protection versus Choice of Instruments

Much progress of late has been made establishing the determinants of the levels of protection. Positive tariffs, subsidies, or quantitative restraints have been shown to be welfare maximizing in the presence of domestic market power. These restraints may simply shift the terms of trade in favor of the protecting country (Johnson 1954), they may shift rents from one monopolist to another across international boundaries (Brander and Spencer 1984), or they may facilitate collusion that otherwise is not possible (Krishna 1989; Harris 1985). Tariff protection is a second-best policy in the presence of some domestic distortion (Bhagwati 1971). Political explanations such as Mayer (1984), Magee, Brock, and Young (1989), Magee (1995), and Hillman (1989) provide explanations for the levels of protection based on the relative electoral strength or campaign contributions of consumers and producers. Consistent with this approach, this chapter establishes that the optimal degree of rent-shifting depends on the level of political pressure that is brought to bear on the policy-making authority. Moreover free trade is optimal even in the presence of the domestic distortion under certain political configurations.

The approach has traditionally been to compare the effects of a tariff and an "equivalent" quantitative restriction: a VER or quota that when applied leads to the same level of imports as the tariff. If the effects were similar, the two were considered equivalent. Work by Bhagwati (1965, 1968, 1987), Rodriguez (1974), Takacs (1978), Itoh and Ono (1982), Dinopolous and Kreinin (1989), and Copeland (1989) establish the non-equivalence of these tools along a variety of dimensions. Once equivalence breaks down, there is clearly a choice across these instruments for the policy-maker. As a result a literature on the endogenous choice of policy instruments emerged, and it has focused largely on explaining why non-tariff policies are chosen. Explanations have usually been political-economic in foundation: Mayer and Riezman (1987) for example, establish in a direct democracy context (where voters choose policies directly via the voting booth) that voters will choose away from tariffs in favor of a production tax cum subsidy on efficiency grounds. The optimality of a tariff-quota combination is restored in Feenstra and Lewis (1991a, b) when government is incompletely informed as to the effect of a terms-of-trade shift on the utilities of the agents in the economy or when the foreign country is imperfectly informed as to the political pressure the domestic government faces. Cassing and Hillman (1985) show that profits for the domestic firm are higher under a tariff than under a quota, and hence the efficient instrument to achieve a given level of protection is the tariff. This recognizes Bhagwati's (1965) observation that with domestic market power, the implicit tariff under a quota must exceed the explicit tariff that would produce the same volume of imports.

There has been little work that provides an explanation for the choice of VERs over other instruments. It has been suggested that a VER allows domestic governments to compensate foreign firms for acquiescing to domestic protectionist sentiment; foreign governments seem to agree to VERs in an attempt to preempt more costly protectionist measures (Rosendorff 1996). A VER is the policy that maximizes campaign contributions (Hillman and Ursprung 1988) and hence the probability of election when foreign interests can contribute to the campaign funds of the politicians. The tariff-quota combination (with a transfer to the exporting industry) of Feenstra and Lewis (1991a) closely resembles a VER, and it is obtained as a cooperative agreement. This chapter addresses the question of the endogeneity of a VER based solely on domestic political conditions in an imperfectly competitive market and a noncooperative international environment.

The purpose of this chapter is not to argue that VERs are preferable to tariffs—rather merely to suggest an explanation founded in political-economy elements for the observed existence of VERs, and their coming into existence at the expense of tariffs. The political pressures that policymakers face may steer them in the direction of the VER when sufficient pressure is brought to bear.

12.3 The Model

There are two identical countries, each with its own firm producing an identical good for sale in the home market only. This follows Brander and Spencer (1984).

Demand

Utility $U = u(X) + m$, where X is the consumption of the good in question, and m is consumption of a competitively produced numéraire good in the world market with price 1. The subutility functions $u(\cdot)$ are differentiable, increasing, and concave. Then $p = u'(X)$, where p is price.

Profits

Variables without asterisks are associated with the domestic country; output of the foreign firm is x, and of the domestic firm y. Total domestic consumption $X = x + y$. Profits of the domestic firm are

$$\pi = yp(X) - cy - F, \tag{12.1}$$

where c denotes marginal cost and F a fixed cost of production. For the foreign firm (which pays a per unit tariff t),

$$\pi^* = xp(X) - cx - tx - F^*. \tag{12.2}$$

There are no transportation costs, and marginal costs are constant and equal.[3]

Welfare

Governments maximize a weighted sum of the consumer surplus, the profits of the firm, and the tariff revenue. Political pressure is brought to bear to restrict imports, at times by campaign contributions and lobbying (representative democracy as in Baldwin 1987) and at others by voting preferences of the citizens (direct democracy as in Mayer 1984). I use an objective function for government that is a reduced form of either of these models. Hence I weight the firm profit term by a factor s that indicates the political pressure that firms can bring to bear (relative to the pressure of consumers):

$$G^s(t) = u(X) - pX + s\pi + tx. \tag{12.3}$$

The term $s \geq 0$ weights the profits of the firm relative to the welfare of consumers and the tariff revenue. The variable s measures the government's weighting of a dollar of firm profit to its weighting of consumer welfare (the sum of the consumer surplus and the tariff revenue) in its reelection calculus.[4] Baldwin (1987) establishes that the politically realistic objective function[5] in (12.3) can be derived from a standard lobbying pressure group model, while Feenstra and Lewis (1991a) do the same based on the median voter model of Mayer (1984) in a competitive, constant returns economy. Here, unfortunately, we have some increasing returns. Nevertheless, I show elsewhere that a similar function can be derived from a median voter model, where the voters differ according to their ownership of stock in the domestic firm.[6] Under majority voting the government's objectives reflect that of the median voter. If the sum of the consumer surplus and the tariff revenue relative to the income from ownership of stock in the import competing firm is s for the median voter, then that is exactly how the government will weight the terms in its objective function. If the distribution of stock is highly skewed in the economy, then income from profits makes up a small part of most individuals' income. The median voter will care more about the consumer welfare elements than firm profit in her utility function and so the median voter will have a very low s. If, on the other hand, ownership of stock is widely dispersed across individuals, s is likely to be large, and government will put greater weight on the profits of firms in its policy calculus.

The foreign government has no domestic politics and does not apply a tariff,[7] and so it seeks to maximize the foreign firm's profits: $G^* = \pi^*$.

12.4 The Tariff Game

The structure of this game is similar to that of Brander and Spencer (1984) with the addition of the politically determined government objective function. The firms will Cournot-compete, taking the tariff level as given. The government will choose a tariff that maximizes its objective function (12.3). An equilibrium to the tariff game is a triple $(\hat{t}, \hat{x}, \hat{y})$, and given $\hat{t}$, $\hat{x}$ and $\hat{y}$ are given by the intersection of the best response functions to the Cournot competition: $\pi_y = 0$ yields a best response function $y = y(x, t)$; $\pi_x^* = 0$ yields $x = x(y, t)$. Government chooses a tariff level that maximizes its objective function (12.3) given this behavior of the firms:

PROPOSITION 12.1 The optimal tariff given the best response functions of the firms is

$$\hat{t} = \frac{x(1 - p_t) + sy_t(p - c) + yp_t(s - 1)}{-x_t}. \tag{12.4}$$

Proof Setting $G_t^s = 0$, we get

$$G_t^s = -Xp_t + s(y_t p + yp_t - cy_t) + x + tx_t = 0, \tag{12.5}$$

where subscripts denote derivatives. Solving for the optimal tariff $\hat{t}$ yields (12.4). ∎

Stability conditions[8] for the Cournot competition between the firms imply that $x_t < 0$, $y_t > 0$, and $X_t = x_t + y_t < 0$ (a tariff reduces domestic consumption relative to free trade). As the tariff rises, the foreign firm's reaction function shifts inward, raising local production and shrinking the level of exports by the foreign firm to the local market. Moreover, as the foreign firm withdraws from the market, only some of the slack is taken up by the local firm. The local firm produces more but does not raise production by as much as the imports have fallen. Hence local consumption falls with a rise in the tariff, local prices rise, and local profits increase. A sufficient condition for a positive optimal tariff is $p_t < 1$ and $s \geq 1$. The derivative p_t can be interpreted as a "passthrough" elasticity, that is, the amount of tariff passed through to domestic prices. The restriction that $p_t < 1$ implies that domestic prices rise by less than the full amount of the tariff. This depends both on the properties of demand and the market conduct of the firms. The condition is equivalent to the requirement that demand not be too convex[9] in order for a positive tariff to maximize the politically weighted objective function. That is the optimal tariff will be positive if $r > -2$ where $r = p''X/p'$, the appropriate measure of the convexity of demand.

Notice that once $\hat{t}$ and $\hat{x}$ are determined, $\hat{y} = y(\hat{x}, \hat{t})$ is implied. Hence we can consider the equilibrium to the tariff game merely as the pair $(\hat{x}, \hat{t})$. It will be useful to state the domestic firm's best response function:
$\pi_y = p - c + yp' = 0 \Rightarrow$

$$y = -\frac{p - c}{p'}. \tag{12.6}$$

12.5 Comparative Statics on s in the Tariff Game

The politically optimal tariff rises as the political pressure of firms rises (or the pressure of consumers falls):

PROPOSITION 12.2 An increase in the political pressure of firms relative to consumers implies a higher politically optimal tariff. That is, $d\hat{t}(s)/ds > 0$.

Proof Totally differentiating (12.5) with respect to t and s yields $0 = (\partial G_t^s/\partial t)\,dt + (\partial G_t^s/\partial s)\,ds$. Then $dt/ds = -(\partial G_t^s/\partial s)/(\partial G_t^s/\partial t)$. Now $\partial G_t^s/\partial t < 0$ is the required second-order condition for the government's maximization problem and follows from the sum of concave functions. Then sign $t_s = \text{sign}\,\partial G_t^s/\partial s = \text{sign}[yp_t + y_t(p - c)]$, which is positive since $p_t = p'X_t > 0$ and $y_t > 0$. That is, $\partial G_t^s/\partial s > 0$, and so $t_s > 0$. ∎

We see immediately that $x_s < 0$ (since $x_s = x_t t_s$ and $x_t < 0$), $y_s > 0$ (since $y_s = y_t t_s$ and $y_t > 0$), $X_s < 0$ (since $X_s = X_t t_s$ and $X_t < 0$), and $p_s > 0$. That is, as political pressure on behalf of firms rises local production rises and foreign exports are curtailed by a higher tariff. Since any withdrawal by the foreign firm is only partially made up by the added local production, domestic consumption falls with increased political pressure and the price rises.

What are the impacts of changing political conditions in the domestic country on the profit generated by both the foreign firms and the local firm? Since local production and the price rise, the local firm experiences an increase in the level of profit. The foreign firm, however, experiences a lower level of exports but at a higher price. If we take the sufficient condition for the positivity of the electorally optimal tariff ($p_t < 1$) as binding, then the rise in price due to the tariff will not be large, and hence the foreign profit will fall.

PROPOSITION 12.3   An increase in the political pressure of firms relative to consumers implies higher profits at home and lower profits abroad.

Proof   Domestic profits (12.1) imply that $\pi_s = y_s(p - c) + yp_s > 0$, since $y_s > 0$ and $p_s > 0$. Foreign profits (12.2) imply that $\pi_s^* = x_s(p - c - t) + xt_s(p_t - 1)$. Now $x_s < 0$ by the previous proposition, and $p_t < 1$ by the sufficient condition for the positivity of the electorally optimum tariff. Then $t_s > 0 \Rightarrow \pi_s^* < 0$. ∎

The tariff rises in the strength of the firm's political influence, as does output and profit. Also the level of rent shifting that the tariff achieves is a function of the variable s, the weight of the firm's electoral importance.

Note the role of domestic politics: When $s > 1$, domestic politics alters the government's objective function to put more weight on the firm's profits than in the case where politics plays no role (or the political factors are very evenly distributed), and all the terms are weighted evenly. Hence we can expect a higher tariff when domestic politics intrudes in favor of the import competing firms, a lower tariff when domestic politics tilts governments objectives in favor of consumers. Or, if s is lower, we see lower tariffs than if s is higher. A more skewed distribution of the ownership of stock in the economy, or lower campaign contributions to the protectionist lobby, would both act to lower s and hence lower the electorally optimal tariff.

Can free trade be an electorally optimal policy? From theory of trade policy in the presence of distortions, a tariff is usually optimal in the presence of monopoly power. The tariff both shifts rents and improves the terms of trade for the economy. But, if the local government cares little for the profits of the domestic industry, and receives much electoral benefit from ensuring a large consumer surplus, a rational government may forgo the rent shifted from abroad to local producers in favor of greater consumer surplus instead. Free trade may be electorally optimal if s is low enough and $1 > p_t > x/(x + y)$:

COROLLARY 12.4   If $1 > p_t > x/(x + y)$, $\exists s \in (0, 1)$ such that $\hat{t}(s) = 0$. That is, for s low enough, free trade is the policy that maximizes government's objective function.

Proof $p_t > x/(x + y) \Rightarrow \hat{t}(0) = [x(1 - p_t) - yp_t]/(-x_t) < 0$. From (12.4), $\hat{t}(s) > 0$ if $1 > p_t$ and $s \geq 1$. By the intermediate value theorem, $\exists s \in (0, 1)$ such that $\hat{t}(s) = 0$.   ∎

12.6   The VER Game

Let the outcome of the noncooperative tariff game be the status quo, and allow the local government to make the following offer to the foreign firm: "Lower your exports (let x fall); in return, we will lower our tariff t." The deal will be offered and accepted if s is large enough (in a manner to be made precise below). No such deal will be offered if s is not large enough.

If exports fall, say, by 1 unit, but the tariff falls sufficiently, then the tax paid on all exported units falls. If the tax saving exceeds the loss of revenue from the single unit now not sold then the foreign firm's profit rises above the level obtained in the tariff game, and the foreign firm will accept the deal.

Such a deal will be offered by the domestic government if s is large enough. If t and x fall, tariff revenue shrinks. But as x falls, π rises (since the domestic firm continues to act like a Cournot competitor and the foreign firm has withdrawn somewhat from the market), meaning larger profits for the domestic firm.[10] If a \$1 fall in tariff revenue generates \$$\Delta$ increase in domestic firm profits, then the domestic government will offer such a deal, since it weights firm profits at a higher value than it does tariff revenue (when s is large enough). That is, $s\Delta > 1$ for s large enough.[11]

Take the Cournot equilibrium with a positive tariff $(\hat{t}, \hat{x}, \hat{y})$ (which is a function of s) to the tariff game as given. The local government makes the offer of a VER to the foreign firm (as well as an offer of a lower tariff simultaneously). The local government offers to lower the tariff if, in return, the foreign firm restrains its exports to the local market. The local firm will accept any such offer that assures it of at least as much utility as it can gain in the tariff game [i.e., $\pi^* \geq \widehat{\pi^*}$ where $\widehat{\pi^*} = \pi^*(\hat{x}, \hat{t})$, the profits available in the tariff game]. This is what makes a VER "voluntary"; the tariff game serves the function of the "status quo" and the condition that $\pi^* \geq \widehat{\pi^*}$ is a requirement of individual rationality (IR) on the part of the foreign firm.[12] Similarly the local government makes such an offer if its returns are at least as high as in the tariff game as well. Hence, if $G^s(t, x) = u(X) - pX + s\pi + tx$, the government's problem is to

$$\max_{(x,t) \geq 0} G^s(t, x) \quad \text{subject to} \quad \pi^* \geq \widehat{\pi^*}.$$

Now the government and the foreign firm agree on a pair (x, t). The local firm then acts as a Stackelberg follower to this agreement, responding to it along its best response curve (12.6). Notice that the local firm's choice of output depends entirely then on the choice of x, and once x is determined, so is y. That is, $y = y(x)$—the best response function for the local firm is independent of the tariff. Hence we can restate the local government's maximization problem as

$$\max_{(x,t) \geq 0} u(x + y(x)) - p(x + y(x))(x + y(x))$$

$$+ s(y(x)p(x + y(x)) - cy(x) - F) + tx$$

$$\text{s.t.} \quad x(p(x + y(x)) - c - t) - F^* \geq \hat{x}(p(\hat{X}) - c - \hat{t}) - F^*.$$

Let any solution to this problem be $(\bar{x}, \bar{t})$ and $\bar{y} = y(\bar{x})$. If the constraint binds, we can write $x(p(x + y(x)) - c - t) - F^* = \text{constant}$. Totally differentiating with respect to the variables t and x we get

$$dx(p - c - t + xp'(1 + y_x)) = xdt. \tag{12.7}$$

PROPOSITION 12.5   There exists some $\bar{s} \in \mathfrak{R}$ such that $G^s(\bar{x}, \bar{t}) > G^s(\hat{x}, \hat{t})$ for all $s > \bar{s}$.

Proof I plan to show that starting from the tariff game equilibrium, the local government can do better if both x and t fall, all the time ensuring that the IR constraint is satisfied. If the IR constraint is not binding (and the foreign firm is doing strictly better), then the government need drop t slightly at a given x to increase government utility. Then t will fall until

(12.7) is restored; the IR constraint always binds. All one needs prove is that $dG|_{(\hat{x},\hat{i}),dx(p-c-t+xp'(1+y_x))=xdt} < 0$. Now

$$dG = -p'(x + y(x))(1 + y_x)\,dx + s[y_x(p - c)\,dx$$

$$+ yp'(1 + y_x)\,dx] + tdx + xdt,$$

$$dG|_{(\hat{x},\hat{i})} = -p'(\hat{x} + y(\hat{x}))(1 + y_x)\,dx + s[y_x(\hat{p} - c)\,dx$$

$$+ \hat{y}p'(1 + y_x)\,dx] + \hat{i}dx + \hat{x}dt,$$

$$\frac{dG}{dx}\Bigg|_{(\hat{x},\hat{i}),dx(p-c-t+xp'(1+y_x))=xdt} = -p'\hat{y}(1 + y_x) + sy_x(\hat{p} - c)$$

$$+ s\hat{y}p'(1 + y_x) + (\hat{p} - c)$$

from (12.7). Recognizing that (12.6) means that $p - c = -yp'$, we have

$$\frac{dG}{dx}\Bigg|_{(\hat{x},\hat{i}),dx(p-c-t+xp'(1+y_x))=xdt} = -p'\hat{y}(1 + y_x) - sy_x\hat{y}p' + s\hat{y}p'(1 + y_x) - \hat{y}p'$$

$$= -2\hat{y}p' + s\hat{y}p' - \hat{y}p'y_x < 0$$

if and only if $s\hat{y}p' < 2\hat{y}p' + \hat{y}p'y_x$. Recalling that $p' < 0$, we have

$$dG|_{(\hat{x},\hat{i}),dx(p-c-t+xp'(1+y_x))=xdt} < 0 \qquad \text{iff } s > 2 + \frac{dy}{dx}\Bigg|_{(\hat{x},\hat{i})}. \quad \blacksquare$$

I have established that in the case with a general utility function and constant marginal cost functions, there is an equilibrium to the VER game in which the local government offers a VER (and a tariff reduction) that is accepted as long as the weight on the profits of the firm in the government's objective function is large enough. If the foreign firm is rewarded for a smaller export volume with a lower tariff on those items it does export, the gain in revenue from the lower tax bill will exceed the loss associated with a smaller market share. The local government also gains: As imports fall, local profits rise (due to increased prices associated with the cutback in foreign exports). If the weight on profits is large enough, the improvement in the weighted social welfare function due to the rise in profits exceeds the losses due to lower tariff revenue and lower consumer surplus. The local government is happy.

The IR constraint is binding at $(\hat{x}, \hat{t})$; in the movement to a VER from this point, foreign profits are constrained not to fall. They don't rise either, and hence no transfer of revenue has taken place.

Local consumers of course bear the burden—but what is the nature of this burden? Clearly consumers lose due to the fall in the tariff revenue that is redistributed to them. But what has happened to domestic consumption in the move from the tariff equilibrium to the VER? That is, as x falls, what happens to y?

PROPOSITION 12.6   Domestic consumption falls as the VER replaces the tariff, while local production rises. That is, $dX/dx > 0$, while $dy/dx < 0$.

Proof   Recall that $dX/dx = 1 + y_x$. From (12.6), $y_x = -(1 + y_x) + (p - c)p''(1 + y_x)/(p')^2$. Then $1 + y_x = 1/(2 + y(p''/p'))$. From the stability conditions of the Cournot competition (see note 8), $\pi_{yx} = p' + yp'' < 0$. Hence $1 + y(p''/p') > 0$ (since $p' < 0$). Therefore $2 + y(p''/p') > 1$ and $0 < 1 + y_x < 1$. Hence $dX/dx > 0$ and $dy/dx < 0$.   ∎

Consumers' losses are additive: Not only are they consuming less under the VER than they were under the tariff, but the redistributed tariff revenue has shrunk. The local firm is taking up some of the slack induced by the withdrawal of the foreign firm from the local market, but not all of it. The local firm is expanding output as the foreign firm contracts, but the expansion is smaller than the contraction. Hence the total production is lower than before, resulting in higher prices and higher profits.

Using the proof of proposition 12.6, we see that the slope of the domestic firm's reaction function must lie between zero and one (this follows from the stability conditions of the Cournot game). This together with the statement of proposition 12.5 imply:

COROLLARY 12.7 $s \geq 2$ is sufficient for proposition 12.5 to hold.

Proof   Proposition 12.6 implies that $0 > y_x > -1$; then $s \geq 2$ is sufficient to ensure that $s > 2 + y_x$, since $2 + y_x \in (1, 2)$.   ∎

12.7   On the Redistribution of Tariff Revenues

The government agrees to the VER when the losses to consumers (from both reduced tariff revenues and lower consumer surplus) are outweighed by the gains in the profits of the firms, suitably weighted by the parameter

s. This result assumed that the tariff revenue was redistributed back to consumers in a lump sum. An alternative specification would require the tariff revenue to be distributed back to the firms instead. The firms are then compensated directly: they receive protection, and they receive the revenues from protection.

If the government uses a tariff (as in the tariff game above), it can protect the industry at a lower cost, with a smaller price rise and hence a smaller loss in consumer surplus. Of course consumers lose the benefits of the tariff revenue that is now allocated to the firms.

Government's objective function takes on the form

$$G^s(t) = u(X) - pX + s(\pi + tx), \tag{12.8}$$

and as before, we can compute the politically optimal tariff in the tariff game:

$$\tilde{t} = \frac{x(s - p_t) + sy_t(p - c) + yp_t(s - 1)}{- sx_t}. \tag{12.9}$$

Comparing the optimal tariffs under the two redistribution regimes I find that the tariff is lower (when it is positive) when government redistributes the tariff revenue to firms rather than consumers.

PROPOSITION 12.8   If the politically optimal tariff is positive, it is higher (lower) when consumers receive the tariff revenue than when firms receive the tariff revenue, whenever $s > (<) 1$. That is, $\hat{t} > (<) \tilde{t} \; \forall s > (<) 1$ and $\hat{t} > 0$.

Proof $\tilde{t} - \hat{t} = [(1 - s)/s][\hat{t} + (x/(-x_t))] < (>) 0$ for all $s > (<) 1$ and $\hat{t} > 0$.   ∎

Whenever firms are influential ($s > 1$), the government is able to bribe the firms into accepting a lower tariff than they would otherwise by redistributing the tariff revenues to them.

If the government is able to offer a VER, it can, as before, improve its situation if s is large enough. The VER reduces tariff revenue and consumer surplus but raises firm profits. If the increase in firm profits outweighs the fall in tariff revenue, then the effect on firms is to improve their welfare; if this improvement in firm welfare weighted by s is large enough, it may outweigh the losses in consumer surplus. That is, if s (rise in profits + rise in tariff revenue) > loss in consumer surplus, then the government's weighted social welfare function improves under a VER relative to the tariff.

The local government's maximization problem, now that revenues go to firms is

$$\max_{(x,t)\geq 0} u(x + y(x)) - p(x + y(x))(x + y(x))$$

$$+ s(y(x)p(x + y(x)) - cy(x) - F + tx)$$

$$\text{s.t.} \quad x(p(x + y(x)) - c - t) - F^* \geq \tilde{x}(p(\tilde{X}) - c - \tilde{t}) - F^*,$$

where $(\tilde{x}, \tilde{t})$ is the politically optimal tariff and level of exports under the new redistribution scheme. Let any solution to this problem be $(\mathring{x}, \mathring{t})$. Then corresponding to proposition 12.5, we have

PROPOSITION 12.9   There exists some $\mathring{s} \in \Re$ such that $G^s(\mathring{x}, \mathring{t}) > G^s(\tilde{x}, \tilde{t})$ for all $s > \mathring{s}$.

Proof   As before, we need to prove that $dG|_{(\tilde{x},\tilde{t}),dx(p-c-t+xp'(1+y_x))=xdt} < 0$. Now $dG = -p'(x + y(x))(1 + y_x)dx + s[y_x(p - c)dx + yp'(1 + y_x)dx + tdx + xdt]$. Then

$$\left.\frac{dG}{dx}\right|_{(\tilde{x},\tilde{t}),dx(p-c-t+xp'(1+y_x))=xdt} = (1 + y_x)[s(\tilde{p} - c) + (\tilde{x} + \tilde{y})p'(s - 1)]$$

$$= (1 + y_x)p'[s\tilde{x} - \tilde{x} - \tilde{y}]$$

$$< 0 \quad \text{if and only if } s > \frac{\tilde{x} + \tilde{y}}{\tilde{x}}. \quad \blacksquare$$

As before, there is an equilibrium in which a VER is offered and accepted, even though all the tariff revenues are redistributed back to the firms, rather than to the consumers. Notice, however, that $s \geq 2$ is no longer sufficient, since $\tilde{y}$ is likely to be larger than $\tilde{x}$. The influence of firms relative to consumers in government's objective function has to be higher to extract a VER when revenues are redistributed to firms rather than to consumers.

This section has established that the results are robust to changes in the distribution scheme for the tariff revenues. In particular, a VER is offered and accepted whenever s is large enough. If all revenues are distributed to consumers, s must be larger than $1 + y_x$; if revenues are distributed to firms, s must be larger than $1 + \tilde{y}/\tilde{x}$. For any other distribution scheme (part to firms and part to consumers), a VER remains optimal as long as s is larger than some threshold that lies inside the interval $(1 + y_x, 1 + \tilde{y}/\tilde{x})$.

12.8   Facilitating Practices?

In a famous paper Krishna (1989) establishes that a VER acts to commit the foreign firm to a lower export level, allowing the domestic firm to cut back output and exploit the movement toward the monopoly level of output and profit. Hence both firms can gain from the VER—it has facilitated collusion at a point closer to the monopoly level of output and profit.

There are a number of differences with respect to Krishna's facilitating practices. First, this is a Cournot game in a single market where the firms produce an identical good; the Krishna set up is a Bertrand game in two markets where the firms produce different goods.[13] In the Krishna paper, if the goods in the two markets are substitutes, then an imposition of a VER close to the free-trade equilibrium raises both firms' prices and profits and shrinks output. Here a VER close to the tariff equilibrium associated with a small decrease in the tariff itself yields profits at least as high as the tariff equilibrium profits for both firms. Foreign output falls, and local output rises.

Moreover I have added the political dimension to focus on the determinants of the choice of policy instruments by the regulating authorities. Hence the policy to be chosen depends on the parameters of the government's objective function. Proposition 12.6 implies that $dy/dx > -1$ and therefore that $s > 1$ for any specification of utility and demand. That is, the quantitative restriction is not electorally optimal when the elements of the government's objective function are weighted equally, unlike the Krishna result which is always possible. I am able therefore to obtain a VER in an environment where the domestic firm is a Stackelberg follower, while the local government leads; in the Krishna paper, the local firm is the leader.

12.9   Conclusions

This chapter has established an ordering of trade policies, the choice across which will depend on the domestic political conditions. If the improvements in the weighted social welfare function from protecting the import competing industry are low, free trade (or a low tariff for rent-shifting purposes) is the policy of choice. As the pressure by the import competing industry rises, a rise occurs in the optimal tariff until a critical point is reached. For all levels of political pressure that rise above this critical point, a VER is the policy of choice.

The chapter offers first an explanation of when free trade, a VER, or a tariff will be used, and an explanation of the oft-observed movement from tariffs to VERs. For instance, the election of a protectionist legislature can enhance the power of import-competing interests, increasing the size of s in the objective function of the local government. The effect of this election is to increase the size of the protective tariff or encourage the switch to a VER.

It has been suggested by some authors (Baldwin 1985), (Feenstra and Lewis 1991b) that the occurrence of VERs is associated with the existence of asymmetric information and, in particular, that the negotiations over these VERs occurs behind closed doors. This allows "undesirable" political influences to appear. Suggested policy has been to open up this process to public scrutiny (either by forcing negotiations over VERs into the GATT or by requiring notice of an impending VER to be published), and then such "undesirable" influences will be checked. The model presented here takes issue with this policy prescription. The public knows that the policy-makers must balance consumer and producer demands, and a rational policy-maker will find the point that just balances those interests in equilibrium, even if this is done behind closed doors. A VER will appear irrespective of whether the negotiations are public or private as long as all participants recognize that political consequences determine the policy-makers' actions and enough political pressure has been brought to bear.

What determines the level of this parameter s? How might we operationalize the notion of political "clout" needed to win protection from imports?[14]

• In a model where campaign contributions increase the probability of election, an industry with large PACs or which contributes heavily and widely to political campaign funds is likely to have a larger s (the Magee, Brock, and Young 1989 and Grossman and Helpman 1994 approach).
• The electoral model suggests that the wider a stock is held (the larger is s), the greater will be the electoral interest in protection that shifts rents

to that firm. The ownership of stock by trade unions or mutual funds acts to increase the dispersion of ownership of stock across individuals and thereby increase s.
• The size of the industry is a measure of the political power that it can bring to bear. Following Finger et al. (1982), total employment, the value of the physical capital stock, and the value added in the industry are all positively related to the level of political influence.
• It is often suggested that industrial concentration enlarges the possibility of political influence. This notion is rooted in the theory of collective action: Transaction costs of political organization and decision-making costs are low if the industries are concentrated around a few dominant actors (Finger et al. 1982).

No doubt other appropriate determinants of political clout are relevant. Empirical verification of the model would investigate the relationship between the political clout of an industry and the type and size of the protection that it receives.

Notes

Support from The James H. Zumberge Faculty Research and Innovation Fund at the University of Southern California is gratefully acknowledged. Thanks to Rob Feenstra, Susanne Lohmann, and seminar participants at USC, UCLA, UC-Irvine; none are responsible for any remaining errors.

1. A voluntary export restraint is a quantitative restriction levied by the exporting country that allows the exporters to capture the rent from higher export prices. Brecher and Bhagwati (1987) and Dinopolous and Kreinen (1989) investigate whether foreigners actually gain from this transfer. Over 100 VERs govern almost 10 percent of world trade, including most trade in textiles and apparel (Bhagwati 1986; Ethier 1991).

2. See Magee (1995) for an excellent survey of the endogenous protection literature, or Hillman (1989).

3. The results are not altered by insisting on different marginal costs across the firms.

4. Baldwin (1987) and Feenstra and Lewis (1991a) give extra weight to the profits of the local firms in government's objective function to factor in the lobbying pressure firms apply. In this context they are assuming that $s > 1$. While they assume that consumers do not lobby effectively due to the diffuse nature of their losses, here consumers can in fact lobby; all that is relevant is their relative lobbying strength captured in s. It is assumed (in this section) that consumer surplus and tariff revenue have the same weight—perhaps the tariff revenue is distributed back to consumers as a lump sum.

5. The phrase is Baldwin's (1987).

6. Embed the import competing firm in a general equilibrium setting, and apply a median voter model: Government's objective becomes that of the median voter. All individuals are endowed with labor l (total labor supply is 1) and stock S_i in the import competing firm. Individuals have identical utility functions $U = u(X) + m^c$, where m^c denotes the consumption

of the numéraire good (its price is one and its marginal product of labor is constant at one, so the wage is one). Individuals earn income from wages l, from stock ownership $s_i \pi$ and from their share of tariff revenue determined by their share of labor endowment ltx. Normalizing by dividing through by l, we have that income is $1 + s_i \pi + tx$, where s_i is individual i's stock/labor endowment ratio. Consumption of the numéraire good m^c must equal total income minus expenditure on good $X : m^c = 1 + s_i \pi + tx - p(X)X$. Then $U = u(X) - p(X)X + tx + s_i \pi + 1$. Since government policy is to be decided by majority rule, the government's effective objective function is that of the median voter (there are no costs to voting and this utility function possesses the necessary "single-peakedness" to apply Black's 1948 theorem) whose stock/labor ratio is s. Hence the government's objective function can be written as in (12.3). See Rosendorff (1995) for more details.

7. Domestic politics is easily added to the foreign country with no gain in insight. If the firms produce for both markets, there will be intraindustry trade and electorally optimal tariffs in both countries. Each country's tariff would be independent of the other's.

8. Stability is ensured by requiring that each firm's marginal revenue declines when the output of its rival rises. That is, $\pi_{yx} < 0$ and $\pi_{xy}^* < 0$. Notice that constant marginal costs in production imply that $\pi_{yy} < \pi_{yx}$ and $\pi_{xx}^* < \pi_{xy}^*$. Then $D = \pi_{yy}\pi_{xx}^* - \pi_{yx}\pi_{xy}^* > 0$. Together these imply that $y_t = -\pi_{yx}/D > 0$, $x_t = \pi_{yy}/D < 0$ and that $x_t + y_t = (\pi_{yy} - \pi_{yx})/D < 0$. For more details, see Brander and Spencer (1985).

9. Define $r_x = (p''/p')x$ and $r_y = (p''/p')y$; then $r = r_x + r_y$. From the domestic firm's first-order condition $\pi_y = 0$, we have $\pi_{yy} = p''y + 2p'$ and $\pi_{yt} = y_t\pi_{yy} + x_t(p''y + p') = 0$. Then $y_t = -[x_t(p''y + p')]/\pi_{yy}$, and from the foreign firm we similarly obtain $x_t = [1 - y_t(p''x + p')]/\pi_{xx}^*$. Together these imply that $x_t + y_t = x_t - x_t(p''y + p')/\pi_{yy} = x_t/(r_y + 2)$ and that $p_t = p'[x_t/(r_y + 2)]$. Alternatively, $x_t + y_t = [1 - y_t(p''x + p')]/\pi_{xx}^* + y_t = 1/(p''x + 2p') + y_t/(r_x + 2)$. Hence $p_t = 1/(r_x + 2) + [y_t/(r_x + 2)]p'$. Now $p_t = p'[x_t/(r_y + 2)]$ implies that $p'x_t = p_t(r_y + 2)$, and $p_t = [1/(r_x + 2)] + [y_t/(r_x + 2)]p'$ implies that $p'y_t = p_t(r_x + 2) - 1$. Then

$$p_t = p'x_t + p'y_t = p_t(r_y + 2) + p_t(r_x + 2) - 1.$$

Solving, we have

$$p_t = \frac{1}{r_x + r_y + 3} = \frac{1}{r + 3}.$$

Then the condition that $p_t < 1$ is equivalent to the requirement that $1/(r + 3) < 1$ or $r > -2$; that is, demand is not highly convex. For instance, for the constant elasticity of demand function, $r = -1 - 1/\varepsilon$, and $r > -2$ if and only if $\varepsilon > 1$; that is, the demand curve is elastic. Then the optimal tariff is positive for constant elasticities of demand greater than 1. If the demand curve is linear, $r = 0$, and the optimal tariff is positive. If demand is not too convex, a positive tariff maximizes the politically weighted objective function when both a foreign and a domestic firm produce for the domestic market.

10. It is possible that the profit-maximizing response for the domestic firm after observing a cutback in exports by the foreign firm is to reduce its output as well. This is the case where the restriction, here a VER, facilitates tacit collusion at a point closer to the monopoly level of output for the industry, as in Krishna (1987). However, under the stability conditions for the Cournot competition assumed above, no such tacit collusion is possible. See proposition 12.6 below.

11. This intuition should be qualified. As x falls, the local firm raises output but by less than the fall in x; local prices go up, and consumer surplus shrinks. If a \$$\delta$ fall in tariff revenue and consumer surplus generates \$$\Delta$ of added firm profits, the government will gain if $s\Delta > \delta$. Note that δ and Δ are not independent of s, however, and so the existence of s large enough is not trivial.

12. The profits available in the tariff game determine the IR constraint; since those profits are also a function of the political parameter, the "status quo" is endogenous to the political process.

13. See Markusen and Venables (1988) for a discussion of the consequences of these differing assumptions.

14. A number of authors have tried with varying success. See Ray (1981), Finger, Hall, and Nelson (1982), and Baldwin (1985).

References

Baldwin, R. 1987. Politically realistic objective functions and trade policy. *Economics Letters* 24:287–90.

Baldwin, R. E. 1985. *The Political Economy of U.S. Trade Policy*. Cambridge: MIT Press.

Bhagwati, J. 1965. On the equivalence of tariffs and quotas. In R. Baldwin, ed., *Trade, Growth and the Balance of Payments*. Chicago: Rand McNally.

Bhagwati, J. 1968. More on the equivalence of tariffs and quotas. *American Economic Review* 58:142–46.

Bhagwati, J. 1971. The generalized theory of distortions and welfare. In J. N. Bhagwati, R. W. Jones, R. A. Mundell, and J. Vanek, eds., *Trade, Balance of Payments and Growth: Papers in International Economics in Honor of Charles P. Kindelberger*. Amsterdam: North Holland.

Bhagwati, J. 1986. *Protectionism*. Oxford: Basil Blackwell.

Bhagwati, J. 1987. VERs, quid pro quo DFI and VIEs: Political-economy-theoretic analysis. *International Economic Review* 1:1–14.

Black, D. 1948. On the rationale of group decision making. *Journal of Political Economy* 56.

Brander, J. A., and B. J. Spencer. 1984. Tariff protection and imperfect competition. In H. Kierzkowski, ed., *Monopolistic Competition and International Trade*. Oxford: Oxford University Press.

Brander, J. A., and B. J. Spencer. 1985. Export subsidies and international market share. *Journal of International Economics* 18:83–100.

Cassing, J. H., and A. L. Hillman. 1985. Political influence motives and the choice between tariffs and quotas. *Journal of International Economics* 19:279–90.

Copeland, B. R. 1989. Tariffs and quotas: retaliation and negotiation with two instruments. *Journal of International Economics* 26:179–88.

Dinopoulos, E., and M. Kreinin. 1989. Import quotas and VERs: A comparative analysis in a three country framework. *Journal of International Economics* 24:169–79.

Ethier, W. J. 1991. Voluntary export restraints. In A. Takayama, M. Ohyama, and H. Ohta, eds., *Trade, Policy and International Adjustments*. San Diego: Academic Press.

Feenstra, R. C., and T. R. Lewis. 1991a. Distributing the gains from trade with incomplete information. *Economics and Politics* 3:21–39.

Feenstra, R. C., and T. R. Lewis. 1991b. Negotiated trade restrictions with private political pressure. *Quarterly Journal of Economics* 106:1287–307.

Findlay, R. W., and S. H. Wellisz. 1982. Endogenous tariffs, the political economy of trade restrictions, and welfare. In J. Bhagwati, ed., *Import Competition and Response*. Chicago: University of Chicago Press.

Finger, J., H. K. Hall, and D. R. Nelson. 1982. The political economy of administered protection. *American Economic Review* 72:452–66.

Grossman, G. M., and E. Helpman. 1994. Protection for sale. *American Economic Review* 84:833–50.

Harris, R. 1985. Why voluntary export restraints are "voluntary." *Canadian Journal of Economics* 18:799–809.

Hillman, A. L. 1989. *The Political Economy of Protection*. New York: Harwood Academic.

Hillman, A. L., and H. W. Ursprung. 1988. Domestic politics, foreign interests and international trade policy. *American Economic Review* 77:729–45.

Itoh, M., and Y. Ono. 1982. Tariffs, quotas and market structure. *Quarterly Journal of Economics* 97:295–305.

Johnson, H. G. 1954. Optimum tariffs and retaliation. *Review of Economic Studies* 21:142–53.

Krishna, K. 1989. Trade restrictions as facilitating practices. *Journal of International Economics* 26:251–70.

Magee, S. 1995. Endogenous protection. In D. C. Mueller, ed., *Handbook of Public Choice*. Oxford: Basil Blackwell.

Magee, S., W. A. Brock, and L. Young. 1989. *Black Hole Tariffs and Endogenous Policy Theory*. Cambridge: Cambridge University Press.

Markusen, J. R., and A. J. Venables. 1988. Trade policy with increasing returns and imperfect competition: contradictory results from competing assumptions. *Journal of International Economics* 24:299–316.

Mayer, W. 1984. Endogenous tariff formation. *American Economic Review* 74:970–85.

Mayer, W., and R. Riezman. 1987. Endogenous choice of trade policy instruments. *Journal of International Economics* 22:377–82.

Ray, E. J. 1981. The determinants of tariff and nontariff restrictions in the United States. *Journal of Political Economy* 89:105–21.

Rodriguez, C. 1974. The non-equivalence of tariffs and quotas under retaliation. *Journal of International Economics* 4:295–98.

Rosendorff, B. P. 1996. Voluntary export restraints and bargaining. *American Economic Review*, forthcoming.

Rosendorff, B. P. 1995. Tariffs, imperfect competition and the median voter. USC-Economics.

Takacs, W. E. 1978. The nonequivalence of tariffs, import quotas and voluntary export restraints. *Journal of International Economics* 8:565–73.

13 A Political-Economy Analysis of Free-Trade Areas and Customs Unions

Arvind Panagariya and Ronald Findlay

Following Viner's (1950) lead, trade theorists have generally treated trade policy as exogenous in evaluating the welfare effects of preferential trading arrangements. The general approach has been to start with a tariff-distorted equilibrium and ask whether a particular set of preferential tariff reductions between union partners is welfare-improving for each participating country, the union, and the world as a whole.[1]

The recent revival of regionalism around the world, particularly the North American Free Trade Agreement (NAFTA), has led trade theorists to take a fresh look at the theory of regional economic integration. Today the world trading system is far more complex than that represented in the stylized, Vinerian models. An important dimension of this complexity is the endogeneity of trade policies.[2] In most countries trade policies are the result of complex interactions between the government and interest groups. Sometimes governments themselves are not benign, welfare-maximizing entities and pursue objectives other than welfare maximization. This endogenous nature of trade policy, richly analyzed in a large number of contributions under the rubric of "political economy of trade policy," has important implications for the theory of regional economic integration.[3]

This chapter honors Jagdish Bhagwati by examining formally two ideas espoused by him in the area of economic integration and endogenous trade policy. These ideas, contained in Bhagwati (1993), can be summarized as follows: First, if trade policy is endogenous, reduced protection between member countries within a regional integration scheme is likely to be accompanied by increased protection against outside countries. As a corollary, a regional arrangement that appears welfare improving at first sight may turn out to be a welfare-reducing proposition. Second, between a free-trade area (FTA) and customs union (CU), the latter is likely to be less protectionist and welfare superior.

We examine these ideas within the three-good, three-country, small-union Meade (1955) model with the modification that trade policy is endogenous. We demonstrate that, as conjectured by Bhagwati (1993), the introduction of preferential trading can indeed raise protection against imports from the rest of the world. We also examine Meade's original result on welfare implications of preferential trading within our model. According to that result the introduction of preferential trading is welfare improving provided that the excess demand for the union partner's good exhibits substitutability with respect to the excess demand for the exportable. The substitutability assumption ensures that a reduction in the tariff on imports from the partner leads to an expansion of exports and hence a reduction in the anti-trade bias in the economy. In our model, since preferential trading leads to increased protection against the outside country, the substitutability assumption is no longer sufficient to guarantee trade expansion or welfare improvement.

Turning to a comparison of FTAs and CUs, suppose that the two countries are symmetric in the sense that they choose the same external tariff under a FTA. We show that in this case the common external tariff is lower and welfare higher for both countries under a CU than FTA. This result follows from the free-rider problem in lobbying under a CU not present under a FTA. In the asymmetric case with different tariffs in the two countries under a FTA, the common external tariff under a CU is lower than the higher tariff under the FTA but may or may not be lower than the lower tariff. The country with the higher tariff under the FTA is better off under a CU than under the FTA. But the same may or may not hold true for the other country. Under a CU the larger the number of members in the union the more acute the free-rider problem and the lower the common external tariff. Ceteris paribus, the larger the number of members in the union the more likely that all members enjoy a higher welfare under a CU than FTA.

Recently Grossman and Helpman (1995a), Melo, Panagariya, and Rodrik (1993) and Richardson (1993a, 1993b, 1994) have considered economic integration in models of endogenous policy formulation. Of these, Richardson (1994) is most directly relevant to our study. Richardson compares FTAs and CUs and arrives at results similar to ours. A key limitation of his model is that it allows for only two goods. Given the nature of the problem, this forces him to assume that the potential members export and import the same goods. Within this setup there is no trade between the two countries in the absence of a FTA and hence no compelling reason for economic integration. In our model there are three goods and each potential member exports to as well as imports from the other in the absence of economic integration. Therefore economic integration serves as a natural instrument for a mutual exchange of market access.

On the positive side, Richardson introduces an important new element into the analysis of FTAs not present in the previous literature. The conventional practice in the literature, such as by Meade (1955), Lipsey (1960), Berglas (1979), Riezman (1979), and Lloyd (1982), is to assume that in the post-FTA equilibrium the domestic price of a good imported from the outside country in each member country equals the border price plus the tariff levied by it. Richardson points out that though the consumer prices can differ in member countries of a FTA producer prices must be equalized by internal free trade. The rules of origin forbid the lower-tariff country from importing the outside country's goods and reexporting them to the higher-tariff country. This restriction prevents arbitrage between consumer prices in member countries. But producers in the lower-tariff country can sell *their* output in the higher-tariff country at the latter's higher price leading to arbitrage in producer prices across the union.[4] This feature leads to a lobbying equilibrium in Richardson's model under a FTA such that the lobby in potentially lower-tariff country chooses to free-ride the lobby in the other country. The outcome is a zero tariff in the former.

In this chapter, though initially we maintain the conventional assumption, for purposes of comparing FTAs and CUs, we work with both sets of assumptions. Because the conventional assumption is analytically more convenient, we derive our results first under this assumption and later point out how they change when arbitrage is allowed in producer prices. Under the conventional assumption the producer price in each country is determined by its own tariff. This feature eliminates the free-rider problem present in Richardson's model and leads to lobbying and positive tariffs in both countries under a FTA.[5]

The chapter is organized as follows: In section 13.1 we reformulate the Meade model by making trade policy endogenous. In section 13.2 we analyze the effects of preferential trading. In section 13.3 we compare FTAs and CUs. As just noted, though we maintain the conventional assumption with respect to domestic prices in the initial part of the chapter, we also deal with the case where producer prices are equalized across the union under a FTA. This task is performed in section 13.4. Concluding remarks are offered in section 13.5.

Before we begin, it may be noted that following the standard practice in the literature on economic integration, our analysis is cast in terms of tariffs. But tariffs should be viewed as representing protection resulting from various trade policy instruments such as voluntary export restraints, anti-dumping actions, and other mechanisms. We are aware that tariff increases are generally limited or ruled out by GATT bindings and GATT Article XXIV. Therefore, when our model predicts any tariff increases, they should be viewed as increases in the level of overall protection rather than tariffs per se.

13.1   The Meade Model with Endogenous Trade Policy

Let there be three countries A, B, and C and three goods x, y, and z. By assumption, each country exports one good and imports the other two. We let goods x, y, and z be export goods of A, B, and C, respectively. A and B are potential partners in a regional arrangement and C represents the rest of the world. A and B are small in relation to C such that the terms of trade are determined in C.

We outline the equilibrium in country A in detail. Equilibrium in country B can be outlined symmetrically. The role of country C is simply to absorb any excess demands and supplies from A and B at the fixed terms of trade. Each good is produced using a sector specific factor and a common factor. The factor specific to sector i ($i = x, y, z$) is labeled "sector i capital" and that common to all sectors is referred to as labor. Output, capital, and labor in sector i are denoted Q_i, K_i, and L_i, respectively. Each good is produced via a conventional constant-returns-to-scale technology,

$$Q_i = F_i(\overline{K}_i, L_i), \qquad i = x, y, z, \tag{13.1}$$

where Q stands for output and a bar over a variable is used to indicate that the variable is fixed. Goods y and z are imported, and good x is exported by A. We choose the units of goods in such a way that the world price of each good is 1. Denoting by t_i the tariff on good i, the domestic price of good i is $1 + t_i$. Because A exports good x, we have $t_x = 0$ and $t_y, t_z > 0$. Acting competitively in the goods and factor markets, firms in sector i choose L_i to maximize profits given by $(1 + t_i)F_i(\overline{K}_i, L_i) - wL_i$. The outcome is a profit function $\pi^i(1 + t_i, w)$ which is linear homogenous in its arguments. Moreover

$$\pi^i_i(1 + t_i, w) = F_i(\overline{K}_i, L_i) = Q_i, \tag{13.2}$$

$$\pi^i_w(1 + t_i, w) = -L_i, \tag{13.3}$$

where $\pi^i_i(\cdot)$ and $\pi^i_w(\cdot)$ denote partial derivatives of $\pi^i(\cdot)$ with respect to the domestic price of good i and w, respectively.

In (13.2) and (13.3), we have six equations in seven variables $F_i(\cdot)$, L_i, and w. Adding the full-employment constraint, we can obtain an exactly determined system of equations. We can then study the effects of exogenous changes in tariffs induced by the introduction of preferential trading. This is the standard Meade exercise.

Our objective is to make tariffs endogenous, however. To accomplish this in a simple way, we adopt the Findlay-Wellisz (1982) approach as simplified by Rodrik (1986) and also used by Panagariya and Rodrik (1993). Thus, we write

$$t_i = g_i(l_i), \qquad g_i(0) = 0, g_i' > 0, g_i'' < 0; i = y, z, \tag{13.4}$$

where l_i is the amount of labor employed in lobbying.

Observe that we do not allow for lobbying by factors in one import-competing industry against protection in the other import-competing industry. Nor do we allow for lobbying against protection by the owners of capital in the export sector. These assumptions can be defended partially on grounds that political process is more responsive to an industry's demands of protection for itself rather than against other industries and that the balance of political power is usually stacked against export industries. But admittedly, the assumptions are extreme, and more work on the elaboration of lobbying process as outlined, for example, in Grossman and Helpman (1994), will be fruitful.

The level of lobbying is chosen so as to maximize the return to the sector-specific factor. That is to say, lobbyists maximize $\pi^i[1 + g_i(l_i), w] - wl_i$ with respect to l_i. This yields the first-order condition

$$g_i'(l_i) \cdot \pi_i^i(1 + g_i(l_i), w) = w, \qquad i = y, z, \tag{13.5}$$

where $g_i'(l_i)$ is the derivative of $g_i(\cdot)$ with respect to l_i. Recalling that $\pi_i^i(\cdot) = F_i(\cdot) = Q_i$, the left-hand side of (13.5) can be interpreted as the revenue generated by employing an additional unit of labor in lobbying or the marginal revenue product (MRP_i) of lobbying. The right-hand side of (13.5) is the marginal cost of lobbying. Thus (13.5) says that lobbyists equate the marginal revenue and marginal cost of lobbying. Note that we assume that lobbyists take the wage rate as given. This is a standard assumption in models of lobbying.

The second-order condition associated with the lobbyists' problem requires that the marginal revenue product of labor given by the left-hand side of (13.5) be negative function of l_i. That is to say,

$$\frac{\partial(\mathrm{MRP}_i)}{\partial l_i} \equiv S_i = g_i''(l_i)\pi_i^i(\cdot) + [g_i'(l_i)]^2\pi_{ii}^i(\cdot) < 0, \qquad i = y, z. \qquad (13.6)$$

The first term on the right-hand side is negative, while the second term is positive. Therefore the right-hand side is not automatically negative. In the following, S_i will be used to denote the expression on the right-hand side of (13.6).

We can now introduce the full-employment constraint,

$$L_x + L_y + L_z + l_y + l_z = \bar{L}, \qquad (13.7)$$

where $\bar{L}$ is the total endowment of labor.

The model for country A is now fully specified. Imbedded in equations (13.2)–(13.5) and (13.7), we have eleven equations in eleven variables, L_i, F_i $(= Q_i)$, l_y, l_z, t_y, t_z, and w. We can specify country B's model analogously with the modification that it exports good y rather than x.

Before we proceed to introduce preferential trading, it is useful to make the model more compact and provide a diagrammatic representation of it. Taking advantage of (13.3), we can rewrite the full-employment condition as

$$-[\pi_w^x(1, w) + \pi_w^y(1 + g_y(l_y), w) + \pi_w^z(1 + g_z(l_z), w)] + l_y + l_z = \bar{L}. \qquad (13.7')$$

This equation, along with (13.5), can be solved for l_y, l_z, and w. Given solution values of these variables, (13.4) gives the t_i, (13.3) the L_i and (13.2) the Q_i.

Equation (13.5) gives us l_i $(i = y, z)$ as a function of the wage w. Assuming the second-order condition (13.6) holds, l_i declines as w rises. From (13.3), at constant l_i and hence a constant t_i, an increase in w lowers L_i directly. In addition, because the increase in w lowers l_i and hence t_i, it also lowers L_i indirectly. The combined demand for labor in sector i, $L_i + l_i$, is an inverse function of w.

In figure 13.1, O_yO_x represents the total endowment of labor in the economy. Measuring $L_y + l_y$ to the right from O_y, D_{L+l}^y represents the total demand (including that in lobbying) for labor in sector y. Analogously, measuring L_x to the left from O_x, D_L^x represents the demand for labor in sector x. This demand function is downward sloped for the usual reasons. Finally, $D_L^x + D_{L+l}^z$ shows the combined demand for labor in sectors x and z, $L_x + L_z + l_z$. At the intersection of D_{L+l}^y and D_{L+l}^z, the full-employment condition (13.7) is satisfied. The intersection determines equilibrium w

and the allocation of labor among the three sectors. Thus we obtain the total quantity of labor in sector i, $L_i + l_i$ $(i = y, z)$. To determine L_i and l_i separately, we use (13.5) which yields l_i given w. Given L_i and l_i and L_x, (13.2) determines the Q_i.

13.2 Preferential Trading

Let us now introduce preferential trading between A and B. In the traditional models of preferential trading, this is done by lowering intra-union tariffs exogenously. In our model, tariffs are endogenous. Therefore the essence of preferential trading must be captured through a shift in the lobbying function for good 2. Following Hillman and Moser (1995) and Grossman and Helpman (1995b), this shift can be viewed as the result of a recognition by member governments that they can enjoy political gains by exchanging market access.

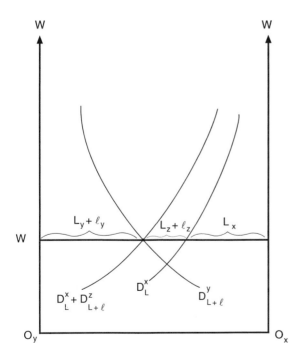

Figure 13.1
Labor market equilibrium

We will assume that the lobbying function for good 2 shifts in such a way that a given level of lobbying yields a lower level of tariff without affecting the *marginal* return on lobbying. This is accomplished most simply by replacing $g_y(l_y)$ by $-\beta_y + g_y(l_y)$ and letting β_y rise. Making this substitution into (13.5) for $i = y$, differentiating the resulting equation and evaluating it at $\beta_y = 0$, we obtain

$$S_y \, dl_y = g_y' \pi_{yy}^y \, d\beta_y + (1 - g_y' \pi_{yw}^y) \, dw. \tag{13.8}$$

Similarly, substituting for t_y from (13.4) into (13.3) with $g_y(\cdot)$ replaced by $-\beta_y + g_y(\cdot)$ and differentiating, we obtain

$$dL_y = \pi_{wy}^y(-d\beta_y + g_y' \, dl_y) + \pi_{ww}^y \, dw. \tag{13.9}$$

Given $S_y < 0$ and g_y', $\pi_{yy}^y > 0$, (13.8) implies that at a given w, preferential trading lowers l_y. Then, because $\pi_{wy}^y < 0$, (13.9) says that at a given w, preferential trading lowers L_y. In figure 13.1 preferential trading leads to a leftward shift in D_{L+l}^y. We immediately see that the wage must fall. Intuitively, at the original wage, a downward shift in the lobbying function makes lobbying in sector y less attractive and lowers l_y. The decline in l_y reduces t_y and makes sector y less profitable and lowers L_y. The reduction in L_y as well as l_y at the original wage puts a downward pressure on the wage.

The decline in wage makes lobbying in sector z more profitable. Assuming that the second-order condition in (13.6) holds, we can deduce from (13.5) that the introduction of preferential trading, by reducing the wage, raises l_z and hence t_z. Thus we have the interesting result that trade liberalization vis-à-vis the partner country is accompanied by increased protection against the rest of the world. Reduction in opportunities to lobby against one trading partner makes lobbying against the other partner more attractive. Assuming that goods 2 and 3 are close substitutes, this result captures the spirit of Bhagwati's (1993) fears regarding pernicious effects of FTAs on trade policies toward third countries. To quote him:

Imagine that the United States begins to eliminate (by outcompeting) an inefficient Mexican industry once the FTA goes into effect. Even though the most efficient producer is Taiwan, if the next efficient United States outcompetes the least efficient Mexico, that would be desirable trade creation.... But what would the Mexicans be likely to do? They would probably start AD actions against Taiwan, which would lead to reduced imports from Taiwan....

If we think of A, B, and C as Mexico, the United States, and Taiwan and of goods 2 and 3 as textile products imported from B (United States) and C (Taiwan), respectively, our result is in close conformity with this example.[6]

The effect of the introduction of preferential trading on t_y can be obtained formally by differentiating (13.4) for $i = y$ after replacing $g_y(l_y)$ by $-\beta_y + g_y(l_y)$ and using (13.8) above. We have

$$\frac{dt_y}{d\beta_y} = -\left[1 - \frac{g_y'^2 \pi_{yy}}{S_y}\right] + \frac{g_y'}{S_y}(1 - g_y'\pi_{yw}^y)\frac{dw}{d\beta_y}. \tag{13.10}$$

In (13.10) the first term is negative, while the second term (including $dw/d\beta_y$) is positive. The first term captures the effect of the increase in β_y while holding the wage constant. This effect lowers t_y by reducing the marginal revenue product directly as well as through a reduction in the output of good y. The second term captures the effect on t_y due to a change in the wage rate. Because the wage declines, profitability of lobbying rises solely on this account. The net effect depends on the relative strengths of these two effects, and it may seem that t_y may actually rise if the indirect wage effect is sufficiently strong. We demonstrate in the appendix, however, that this cannot happen; the direct effect of the rise in β_y necessarily dominates.

We next turn to the effect of preferential trading on welfare. Meade's original result is that if we have $t_y = t_z$ initially, and the excess demand for good y exhibits substitutability with the excess demand for the exportable, the introduction of preferential trading is necessarily welfare improving. Intuitively, an exogenous reduction in t_y increases the imports of that good but may increase or reduce the imports of good z. If the imports of good z rise, deleterious effects of tariffs are reduced in both goods and welfare improves necessarily. If imports of good z decline as is likely, however, the harmful effect of distortion in that sector increases. The question then is whether the loss due to this change is smaller than the gain from the rise in the imports of good y. If excess demands for goods y and x exhibit substitutability, exports of good x rise in response to a reduction in t_y. Given balanced trade, this means that there is a net expansion of imports, that is, imports of good y expand more than the decline in the imports of good z. If we now also assume that $t_y = t_z$ initially, the welfare gain due to the larger expansion of imports of good y must exceed the welfare loss due to a contraction of imports of good z. On balance, welfare improves.

In view of the results already derived, it should not be surprising that this important Meade result may not hold in the presence of endogenous trade policy. We have already seen that the introduction of preferential trading is accompanied by increased protection against third countries. Therefore there is no guarantee that substitutability between excess demands for good y and good x will be sufficient to lead to a net expansion of imports. The combined effect of a reduction in t_y and increase in t_z may well be to reduce total trade. Moreover we must take into account the effect of the introduction of preferential trading on real resources used in lobbying.

In the remainder of this section we present a formal proof of these results. We assume that preferences can be represented by a well-defined social welfare function. We can then obtain the expenditure function in the usual way. The budget constraint or, equivalently, the trade balance condition requires that expenditure and income be equal. Letting U denote utility and $E(\cdot)$ represent the expenditure function, we have

$$E(1, 1 + t_y, 1 + t_z; U) = \sum_{i=x}^{z} \pi^i(1 + t_i, w) - w \sum_{i=x}^{z} \pi_w^i(1 + t_i, w)$$

$$+ t_y(E_y - \pi_y^y) + t_z(E_z - \pi_z^z), \tag{13.11}$$

where E_i is the partial derivative of $E(\cdot)$ with respect to the domestic price of good i $(i = x, y, z)$. On the right-hand side, the first term represents profits plus wages to workers employed in lobbying, the second term wages to workers employed in production activity, and the third and fourth terms tariff revenue that is redistributed. Because good x is exported, $t_x = 0$ and the domestic price of good x is 1. Tariff rates t_y and t_z are endogenous though we keep this fact in the background.

Differentiating (13.11) totally, allowing t_y and t_z to change, we have

$$M \, dU = -w(dl_y + dl_z) + [t_y(E_{yy} - \pi_{yy}^y) + t_z E_{zy}] \, dt_y$$

$$+ [t_y E_{yz} + t_z(E_{zz} - \pi_{zz}^z)] \, dt_z - [t_y \pi_{yw}^y + t_z \pi_{zw}^z] \, dw. \tag{13.12}$$

where $M \equiv E_U - t_y E_{Uy} - t_z E_{Uz}$ is positive as long as all goods are normal in consumption. The next step is to exploit the zero-degree homogeneity of E_y and E_z in price variables. Zero-degree homogeneity of E_y in prices allows us to write

$$E_{yx} + (1 + t_y)E_{yy} + (1 + t_z)E_{yz} = 0. \tag{13.13}$$

Equation (13.13), in turn, yields

$$t_y E_{yy} + t_z E_{zy} = -\frac{1}{1 + t_y}[(t_y - t_z)E_{yz} + t_y E_{yx}].$$ (13.13')

Making use of (13.13) and an analogous expression for $t_y E_{zy} + t_z E_{zz}$, we can rewrite (13.12) as

$$M\, dU = -w(dl_y + dl_z) - (t_y \pi^y_{yw} + t_z \pi^z_{zw})\, dw$$

$$-\frac{1}{1 + t_y}[(t_y - t_z)E_{yz} + t_y E_{yx} + t_y(1 + t_y)\pi^y_{yy}]\, dt_y$$

$$-\frac{1}{1 + t_z}[(t_z - t_y)E_{zy} + t_z E_{zx} + t_z(1 + t_z)\pi^z_{zz}]\, dt_z.$$ (13.12')

Consider first the Meade result. In the absence of lobbying, $dl_y = dl_z \equiv 0$, and since t_z is exogenous, $dt_z = 0$. We also assume that tariffs on goods from B and C are equal initially, $t_y = t_z$. Taking into account these factors, (13.12') can be rewritten as

$$M\, dU = -\frac{t_y E_{yx}}{1 + t_y}\, dt_y - t_y[\pi^y_{yy}\, dt_y + (\pi^y_{yw} + \pi^z_{zw})\, dw].$$ (13.14)

With no lobbying, the full-employment constraint yields $dw = -[\pi^y_{wy}/\sum_i \pi^i_{ww}]\, dt_y$. Substituting this into (13.14) and making use of zero degree homogeneity of $\pi^y_y(\cdot)$ and $\pi^z_w(\cdot)$, we can reduce (13.14) to

$$M\, dU = -\frac{t_y}{1 + t_y}\left[E_{yx} - \frac{w\pi^y_{yw}\pi^x_{ww}}{\sum^z_{i=x}\pi^i_{ww}}\right]\, dt_y.$$ (13.14')

From (13.14'), if we lower t_y, holding t_z fixed exogenously (i.e., $dt_y < 0$) at $t_y = t_z$, we see the right-hand side is positive provided that $E_{yx} > 0$, that is, the demand for goods y and x exhibit net substitutability.[7] This is the standard Meade result.

Next, suppose that tariffs are endogenous. In this case $dt_z > 0$ and $dl_y + dl_z \neq 0$. We can no longer go from (13.12') to (13.14'). In (13.12') the first term captures the welfare effect of the change in the overall level of lobbying activity. Because w falls, l_z rises necessarily. But the decline in the profitability of lobbying in sector y (i.e., the rise in β_y) is likely to lower l_y. Thus the net effect on $l_y + l_z$ is ambiguous. The second term in (13.12') is positive, while the third one is negative under the substitutability assumption. The last term, given that dw is negative for a reduction in t_y, is also negative. Thus $t_y = t_z$ is no longer sufficient to yield an improvement in welfare under substitutability between import-competing goods and the exportable.

13.3 FTA versus Customs Union

We now assume that countries A and B have decided to eliminate trade restrictions between themselves but must choose between FTA and CU. The former allows the external tariff to be determined at the national level, while the latter requires them to be determined at the regional level. Formally, we can imagine that under a FTA, tariffs on third countries in each union member continue to be determined via the lobbying function introduced in (13.4), while under a customs union an institutional change requires the determination of a common external tariff. Note that under a FTA, we are assuming that both producer prices and consumer prices of the good imported from the outside country are different in A and B. The possibility of the producer-price arbitrage is introduced in the next section.

A key question is, How should the lobbying function be formulated in the case of a customs union? We know that if this choice is made arbitrarily, we can obtain any ranking of FTA and CU that we like. Therefore we opt for as neutral a choice as possible.[8] In the case of a customs union, we write the lobbying function for good z as

$$t_z^c = h_z(l_z^c) \equiv h_z(l_z + l_z^*), \qquad h' > 0, h'' < 0, \tag{13.15}$$

where an asterisk is used to distinguish country B's variables and superscript c is used to indicate unionwide variables under a customs union. Accordingly, t_z^c is the common external tariff and $l_z^c = l_z + l_z^*$. We assume that the regional institution is equally responsive to lobbying by agents of the two members. Who invests into lobbying is not important. What matters is how much.

Under a FTA, lobbying is done at the national level, and tariffs in the two member countries may be different. We write

$$t_z^F = g_z(l_z), \quad t_z^{F*} = g_z(l_z^*). \tag{13.4'}$$

For ease of comparison, we assume that the lobbying *functions* under a FTA are identical in the two countries.

To maintain neutrality, we assume that functions $h_z(\cdot)$ and $g_z(\cdot)$ are related with each other according to

$$h_z(l_z + l_z^*) = g_z\left(\frac{l_z + l_z^*}{2}\right),$$ (13.16a)

$$h_z'(l_z + l_z^*) < g_z'(l_z + l_z^*).$$ (13.16b)

According to (13.16a), if $l_z = l_z^* = \bar{l}_z$ so that the lobbies in each of A and B invest $\bar{l}_z$ amount of resources, the external tariff under a FTA and CU is the same. Under a FTA we have

$$t_z^F = g_z(\bar{l}_z), \quad t_z^{F*} = g_z(\bar{l}_z),$$

and under a customs union we have

$$t_z^c = h_z(\bar{l}_z + \bar{l}_z) = h_z(2\bar{l}_z) = g_z\left(\frac{2\bar{l}_z}{2}\right) = g_z(\bar{l}_z) = t_z^F, t_z^{F*}.$$

Thus lobbying functions themselves are neutral with respect to the type of regional arrangement chosen.

Another way to compare $h_z(\cdot)$ and $g_z(\cdot)$ is that under a CU, if lobbying is done by agents of a single country, say A, they will have to invest twice as much resources to obtain a given level of tariff as under a FTA. Under a CU, the tariff granted to A is also granted to B. Therefore the effort required to obtain a given tariff is twice as much. Viewed in this way, it is clear that our formulation captures the free-rider problem which is often associated with the formation of a CU. In policy discussions, it is commonly asserted that a customs union can be an instrument of weakening the interest groups seeking protection. A surrender of tariff-making power to the regional institution means less influence of interest groups within a member nation.

According to (13.16b), for a given amount of labor employed in lobbying, the *marginal* product of lobbying is higher under a FTA than under a CU. Equation (13.16a) is not sufficient to yield this condition. But the condition is plausible and is satisfied by function $g_z(\cdot) = \lambda l_z^\phi$, where λ and ϕ are constants and the value of ϕ lies between 0 and 1.

The question we wish to address now is, Can FTA and CU be ranked, and what does this ranking depend on? To answer, we must first determine equilibrium tariffs under the two regimes. Under FTA, the tariff will be determined as in the previous section. Under CU, the problem is trickier.

Protection is a private good under a FTA. But under a CU it becomes a public good subject to the free-rider problem. As we demonstrate below, this feature yields the usual outcome associated with the private provision of public goods: Only the "most desperate" buyer chooses to pay for it while the others choose to free ride.[9]

Consider the problem of the lobby in country A. Its problem is to maximize $\pi^z[1 + h_z(l_z + l_z^*), w] - wl_z$ with respect to l_z taking w as given. At the optimum, the marginal revenue product of l_z must be larger than or equal to the marginal cost of l_z. That is,

$$h_z'(l_z^c)\pi_z^z(1 + h_z(l_z^c), w) \geq w, \tag{13.17}$$

where $l_z^c = l_c + l_z^*$ is the total amount of labor employed in lobbying. An analogous condition can be written for country B's lobby. The question then is whether (13.17) and the analogous condition for B's lobby can simultaneously hold as equalities. The answer is that only by a sheer coincidence is this possible. Treating (13.17) as an equality, we can determine l_z^c as a function of w. Likewise the condition for B gives us another equation determining l_z^c as a function of w^*, the wage in B. It is unlikely that the two equations will yield the same value of l_z^c.

To explain what is going on here, assume that the wage is constant in each country. For example, we could assume that the exportable in each country (i.e., good x in A and good y in B) uses only labor. We can then represent the marginal revenue product of l_z net of the marginal cost, given by the left-hand side of (13.17) minus the right-hand side (i.e., wage), as a function of l_z^c alone. This is done in figure 13.2. By virtue of the second-order condition this curve, labeled NMRP (net MRP), is downward sloped.

Next, draw country B's net marginal revenue product curve measuring it in the same units as A's. Suppose that it lies below country A's curve, as shown by NMRP*. In this case the lobby in B will choose to free-ride the lobby in country A. The reason for this outcome is that for $l_z^* = 0$, A's best choice is $l_z = \bar{l}_z^c$, and for $l_z = \bar{l}_z^c$, B's best response is $l_z^* = 0$. Thus the solution $l_z^* = 0$ and $l_z = \bar{l}_z^c$ is a Nash equilibrium. Analogously, if NMRP* were to lie above NMRP, $l_z = 0$ and $l_z^* = \bar{l}_z^c$ would be a Nash solution. If the two curves were to coincide on the horizontal axis, the total lobbying would still be $\bar{l}_z^c$ but how it is divided between A and B would be indeterminate.

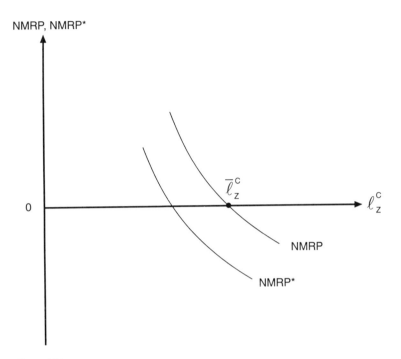

Figure 13.2
Nash equilibrium in lobbying

Observe that given $\pi_z^z(\cdot) = Q_z$, the level of output of the good imported from country C plays a key role in the determination of which lobby supplies the common external tariff. In view of (13.17), the larger the ratio of this output to the wage rate in a country, the more likely lobbying will be concentrated there. For instance, given the relative sizes of import-competing industries in the United States and Mexico, despite the lower wage in Mexico, under a customs union arrangement, one will expect the United States to be the "supplier" of the common external tariff.

For concreteness, assume that all lobbying is done in country A. To get a fix on some additional results, assume further that the exportable uses only labor. Then the wage in terms of the exportable is fixed and, hence, the same under a FTA and CU. Following Panagariya and Rodrik (1993), we now show that the level of lobbying and hence the tariff is lower under a customs union than that in A under a FTA. Letting $\bar{l}_z^c$ be the level of lobbying under a CU, we evaluate the marginal revenue product of lobbying under a FTA, given by the left-hand side of (13.5), at $\bar{l}_z^c$. Given (13.16a), $g_z(\bar{l}_z^c) > h_z(\bar{l}_z^c)$, and given (13.16b), $g_z'(\bar{l}_z^c) > h_z'(\bar{l}_z^c)$. Since (13.17) holds as an equality at $\bar{l}_z^c$ under a CU and w is the same under a CU and FTA, these inequalities imply that the marginal revenue product of lobbying under a FTA [the left-hand side of (13.5)] exceeds w at $\bar{l}_z^c$. The level of lobbying and the tariff on z in country A will be higher under a FTA than a CU.

The common external tariff can, however, be higher than the tariff in B under a FTA. We distinguish B's variables by an asterisk (*). Letting $\bar{t}_z^c$ be the common external tariff, we solve the equation $g_z(l_z^*) = \bar{t}_z^c$.[10] The solution, denoted $\tilde{l}_z^*$, gives the level of lobbying that will generate the tariff $\bar{t}_z^c$ under a FTA in B. Then, if $g_z'(\tilde{l}_z^*)\pi^{z*}(1 + g_z(\tilde{l}_z^*), w^*)$ exceeds w^*, the tariff in B under a FTA will be higher than that under a CU. A crucial factor determining the outcome is the potential output of z or, equivalently, the amount of z-specific factor, K_z^*, available. The smaller the potential output of z, the more likely the tariff under a CU will be higher than under a FTA.

An additional result that may be derived is that as the number of members in the potential regional arrangement rises, assuming that A remains the supplier of the common external tariff, the level of the external tariff declines. This is because the increase in the number of members in the union exacerbates the free-rider problem. Formally, in (13.16a) and (13.16b), $l_z + l_z^*$ and $(l_z + l_z^*)/2$ are replaced by $\sum_j l_z^j$ and $\sum_j l_z^j/m$, where j denotes a union member and m is the total number of members in the union. An implication of this result is that countries will be better off entering into a customs union with larger number of countries than with smaller number of them. But it also implies that lobbies will likely resist the enlargement of a customs union more than of a FTA.

Finally, the welfare ranking of FTA and CU is not unique except in the specific case when the tariff chosen by the two countries under a FTA is the same and the exportable uses only labor. In this case the common external tariff under a CU is lower than the FTA tariff in both countries. Moreover each country invests less resources in lobbying under CU than under a FTA. Welfare is necessarily higher under the former arrangement. In the asymmetric case, though the country that supplies the external tariff under a CU is better off under this arrangement than under a FTA, the other country may be worse off. This is because the latter may end up with higher tariffs under a CU than under a FTA. The larger the number of members, the more likely that a CU will dominate a FTA from the viewpoint of all members.

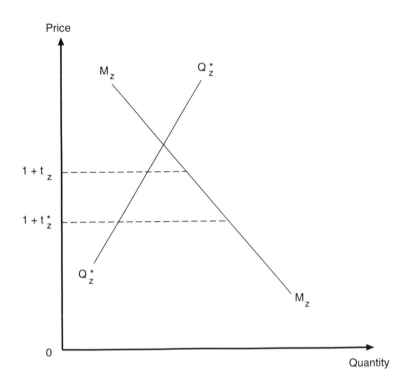

Figure 13.3
Producer-price arbitrage

13.4   The Producer-Price Arbitrage under a FTA

So far we have assumed complete segmentation of the price of z, the good imported from C, across A and B under a FTA. We now introduce the possibility of producer-price arbitrage under a FTA as in Richardson (1993b, 1994). There are three possible price configurations. We use figure 13.3, adapted from Grossmam and Helpman (1995a) whose analysis of FTAs also incorporates the producer-price arbitrage, to discuss these configurations. We take a partial equilibrium setting and begin by assuming that tariffs are exogenous. Without loss of generality, let $t_z > t_z^*$; that is, assume that the tariff on z is higher in A than B.

In case 1 shown in figure 13.3, $M_z M_z$ represents A's *import-demand* for good z while $Q_z^* Q_z^*$ represents B's *total supply* of good z. Values $1 + t_z$ and

$1 + t_z^*$ denote the border price plus tariff in A and B, respectively. As drawn, B's supply curve intersects A's import-demand curve *above* $1 + t_z$. Both the consumer and producer price in A settle at $1 + t_z$. Because imports can enter B at $1 + t_z^*$, z cannot be sold there at a price higher than $1 + t_z^*$. But given internal free trade, B's producers can sell their output in A at the higher price $1 + t_z$. B sells all of its output in A, receiving A's price $1 + t_z$. All of B's consumption comes from C at the consumer price $1 + t_z^*$. A's consumption comes from all three sources, domestic, B and C.

In case 2, not shown in figure 13.3, B's supply curve lies so far to the right that it intersects A's import-demand curve below $1 + t_z^*$. In this case all of A's imports come from B. B's producers sell a part of their output in the home market. The price settles at $1 + t_z^*$ for both producers and consumers throughout the union.

Finally, in case 3, B's supply curve intersects A's import-demand curve between $1 + t_z$ and $1 + t_z^*$. The price in A facing producers and consumers in this case is determined by the point of intersection of the two curves. Producers in B sell all of their output in A. A's imports come entirely from B and B's consumers are supplied solely by C at price $1 + t_z^*$.

To analyze the implications of producer-price arbitrage for the analysis of FTAs, we focus on case 1 only. We begin by assuming that in the absence of the producer-price arbitrage, country A chooses a higher tariff than B. If we now introduce producer-price arbitrage, it is evident that producers in B will choose to sell good z in A. If we further assume that A's demand for imports at its tariff inclusive price is larger than the total quantity B's producers want to sell at that price—the situation depicted in figure 13.3—the lobby in B will choose not to lobby at all! In this equilibrium producers in B sell nothing in their home market and hence do not need to lobby for protection there. They simply free-ride the high tariff in A. The entire quantity of good z consumed in B comes from the outside country at the world price.

The free-rider problem characterizing this equilibrium is different than in the CU equilibrium considered earlier in one fundamental respect. While country B benefits from A's lobbying, such free-riding generates no negative externality for the lobby in A. Formally, the marginal revenue product of lobbying continues to be given by equation (13.5). Therefore, ceteris paribus, the lobby in A chooses the same tariff in the presence of producer-price arbitrage as in its absence in section 13.3. What is different is that the lobby in B chooses not to lobby at all.

Turning to a welfare comparison, it is evident that country B is un-ambiguously better off in the present FTA equilibrium than in the CU equilibrium of section 13.3. This result holds because consumers in B now face world prices in all products and producers have access to A's superior terms of trade in product z. As regards country A, its equilibrium is the same as that in the absence of producer-price arbitrage. This means that the common external tariff under CU will be lower than its FTA tariff, and it will be better off under the former arrangement (see the proof in the previous section). Thus, whereas in the absence of producer-price arbitrage, it is *possible* for both A and B to be better off under a CU than a FTA, in the presence of such arbitrage, one country (B) is necessarily worse off and the other necessarily better off.

13.5 Summary of Results

In this chapter we have analyzed the welfare effects of regional integration in a model of endogenous protection. We have shown that in this setting, the introduction of preferential trading leads to an increase in protection against countries outside the preferential trading area. We have also demonstrated that the important Meade result on preferential trading breaks down when protection is endogenous. According to the Meade result, if the excess demand for the good being liberalized exhibits substitutability with respect to the exportable, the introduction of preferential trading is welfare improving. In the presence of endogenous protection, because preferential trading is accompanied by increased protection against non-partners, its effect on welfare is ambiguous.

We have also compared free-trade areas and customs unions. Here we have provided a formal treatment of the argument that a customs union is more effective than a free-trade area in diluting the power of interest groups. Under a customs union the tariff available to one country be-comes available to all countries in the union. This introduces a free-rider problem in lobbying, and all lobbying takes place in one country. The lobby chooses a lower (common) external tariff under a customs union than under a free-trade area. This means that welfare in the country where lobbying takes place is higher under a customs union than under a free-trade area. If producer-price arbitrage is ruled out, the other country may or may not be better off under a FTA than a CU. If that country chooses a lower tariff under a free-trade area than the common external tariff under the customs union, its welfare under the former arrangement is higher. If producer-price arbitrage is taken into account, since this country chooses not to lobby at all under a FTA, its welfare in the FTA equilibrium is necessarily higher than under a CU. Finally, the level of the common external tariff declines as the number of members in the union increases. Therefore the larger the number of partners in a customs union, the more likely it will improve welfare of member countries. By the same token, due to the free-rider problem, lobbies are likely to resist the enlargement of a customs union.

13.6 Appendix

We demonstrate that the effect of a rise in β_y on t_y, shown in (13.10), is negative. We first solve for $dw/d\beta_y$. The change in L_y and l_y is given by (13.8) and (13.9), respectively. The change in L_z and l_z is given by analogous equations with $d\beta_y$ set to 0. Finally, the change in L_x is $-\pi^x_{ww} dw$. Substituting these changes in labor demands into the full-employment constraint and solving, we obtain

$$\frac{dw}{d\beta_y} = \frac{1}{H}\left[\pi^y_{wy} + \frac{1}{S_y}(1 - g'_y\pi^y_{wy})g'_y\pi^y_{yy}\right], \tag{13.A1}$$

where H is defined as follows:

$$H \equiv \sum_{i=x}^{z} \pi^i_{ww} - \frac{1}{S_y}(1 - g'_y\pi^y_{wy})^2 - \frac{1}{S_z}(1 - g'_z\pi^z_{wz})^2. \tag{13.A2}$$

From equations (13.10) and (13.A1), $dt_y/d\beta_y < 0$, if and only if

$$-(S_y - g'^2_y\pi^y_{yy})H > g'_y(1 - g'_y\pi^y_{yw})\left[\pi^y_{wy} + \frac{1}{S_y}(1 - g'_y\pi^y_{wy})g'_y\pi^y_{yy}\right].$$

Taking (13.A2) into account and canceling terms with $1/S_y$ as a factor, this inequality holds true if and only if

$$-(S_y - g'^2_y\pi^y_{yy})\left[\sum_{i=x}^{z}\pi^i_{ww} - \frac{1}{S_z}(1 - g'_z\pi^z_{wz})^2\right] + (1 - g'_y\pi^y_{wy})^2$$

$$> -g'_y(1 - g'_y\pi^y_{yw})\pi^y_{wy},$$

or, equivalently, if and only if

$$-(S_y - g_y'^2 \pi_{yy}^y)\left[\sum_{i=x}^{z} \pi_{ww}^i - \frac{1}{S_z}(1 - g_z'\pi_{wz}^z)^2\right] + (1 - g_y'\pi_{wy}^y) > 0.$$

Given the signs of various partial derivatives, this inequality necessarily holds true.

Notes

We thank Gene Grossman and Poonam Gupta for many helpful comments.

1. For instance, see Meade (1955), Lipsey (1960), Berglas (1979), Riezman (1979), and Lloyd (1982).

2. Another dimension, not addressed in this chapter, is the increased interdependence of different regional arrangements. Today the world is dividing *simultaneously* into a few large trading blocs. This means that regional arrangements can no longer be analyzed in isolation as has been the case with much of the Vinerian literature. Krugman (1991) and Deardorff and Stern (1991) provide models of trading blocs that emphasize this interdependence.

3. Among key contributions to this literature are Krueger (1974), Brock and Magee (1978), Bhagwati and Srinivasan (1980), and Findlay and Wellisz (1982). Two book-length treatments of the subject are Magee, Brock, and Young (1989) and Hillman (1989). Models of regional integration with endogenous policy are discussed later in the text.

4. If the supply in the lower-tariff country is sufficiently large, arbitrage in producer prices can also lead to arbitrage in consumer prices. See Grossman and Helpman (1995a) and section 13.4 for more details.

5. Of course, we do have a free-rider problem in the CU equilibrium as does Richardson.

6. Observe that the Bhagwati result can arise through alternative mechanisms. For instance, if the government wishes to maintain a certain level of output in the industry, it will increase protection against the third country as it liberalizes trade with respect to the partner.

7. As noted earlier, the general condition in the Meade model is that the *excess* demands for the product whose tariff is reduced and the exportable exhibit substitutability. Because all goods exhibit substitutability in production in our model, the substitutability in demand ensures that excess demands exhibit substitutability.

8. We draw heavily on Rodrik and Panagariya (1993), who in turn draw on Rodrik (1986).

9. For a review of the literature on private provision of public goods, see Cornes and Sandler (1986). Also see Hillman (1989, 1991) and Ursprung (1990) in this regard.

10. Recall that the lobbying function is assumed to be the same in B as A. Therefore no asterisk is used to distinguish the lobbying function in B from that in A.

References

Berglas, E. 1979. Preferential trading: The *n* commodity case. *Journal of Political Economy* 87:315–31.

Bhagwati, Jagdish. 1993. Regionalism and multilateralism: An overview. In J. de Melo and A. Panagariya, eds., *New Dimensions in Regional Integration*. Cambridge: Cambridge University Press.

Bhagwati, Jagdish, and T. N. Srinivasan. 1980. Revenue-seeking: A generalization of the theory of tariffs. *Journal of Political Economy* 88:1069–87.

Brock, William A., and Stephen P. Magee. 1978. The economics of special interest policies: The case of the tariff. *American Economic Review* 68:246–50.

Cornes, Richard, and Todd Sandler. 1986. *The Theory of Externalities, Public Goods and Club Goods.* Cambridge: Cambridge University Press.

Deardorff, Alan, and Robert Stern. 1991. Multilateral trade negotiations and preferential trading arrangements. Mimeo.

Findlay, Ronald, and Stanislaw Wellisz. 1982. Endogenous tariffs, the political economy of trade restrictions, and welfare. In J. Bhagwati, ed., *Import Competition and Response.* Chicago: University of Chicago Press.

Grossman, Gene, and Elhanan Helpman. 1994. Protection for sale. *American Economic Review* 84:833–50.

Grossman, Gene, and Elhanan Helpman. 1995a. The politics of free trade agreements. *American Economic Review* 85, forthcoming.

Grossman, Gene, and Elhanan Helpman. 1995b. Trade wars and trade talks. *Journal of Political Economy* 103:675–708.

Hillman, Arye 1989. *The Political Economy of Protection.* Chur, Switzerland: Harwood Academic Publishers.

Hillman, Arye 1991. Protection, politics, and market structure. In E. Helpman and A. Razin, eds., *International Trade and Trade Policy.* Cambridge: MIT Press.

Hillman, Arye, and Peter Moser. 1995. Trade liberalization as politically optimal exchange of markets. In Mathew Canzoneri et al., eds., *The New Transatlantic Economy.* Cambridge: Cambridge University Press.

Krueger, Anne O. 1974. The political economy of the rent-seeking society. *American Economic Review* 64:291–303.

Krugman, Paul. 1991. Is bilateralism bad? In E. Helpman and A. Razin, eds., *International Trade and Trade Policy.* Cambridge: MIT Press.

Lipsey, Richard. 1960. The theory of customs unions: A general survey. *Economic Journal* 70:498–513.

Lloyd, Peter. 1982. 3 × 3 theory of customs unions. *Journal of International Economics* 12:41–63.

Magee, Stephen P., William A. Brock, and Leslie Young. 1989. *Black Hole Tariffs and Endogenous Policy Theory.* Cambridge: Cambridge University Press.

Meade, James E. 1955. *The Theory of Customs Unions.* Amsterdam: North-Holland.

Melo, Jaime de, and Panagariya, Arvind, eds. 1993a. *New Dimensions in Regional Integration.* Cambridge: Cambridge University Press.

Melo, Jaime de, Dani Rodrik, and Arvind Panagariya. 1993b. The new regionalism: A country perspective. In J. de Melo and A. Panagariya, eds., *New Dimensions in Regional Integration.* Cambridge: Cambridge University Press.

Panagariya, Arvind and Dani Rodrik. 1993. Political economy arguments for a uniform tariff. *International Economic Review* 34:685–704.

Richardson, Martin. 1993a. Endogenous protection and trade diversion. *Journal of International Economics* 34:309–34.

Richardson, Martin. 1993b. Tariff revenue competition in a free trade area. Mimeo. Forthcoming in *European Economic Review.*

Richardson, Martin. 1994. Why a free trade area? The tariff also rises. *Economics and Politics* 6:79–95.

Rodrik, Dani. 1986. Tariffs, subsidies and welfare with endogenous policy. *Journal of International Economics* 21:285–99.

Riezman, Raymond. 1979. A 3 × 3 model of customs unions. *Journal of International Economics* 72:820–29.

Ursprung, Heinrich. 1990. Public goods, rent dissipation, and candidate competition. *Economics and Politics* 2:115–32.

Viner, Jacob. 1950. *The Customs Union Issue.* New York: Carnegie Endowment for International Peace.

Index